DON'T MISS THIS

MISS THIS

IN THE

NEW TESTAMENT

MORE *DON'T MISS THIS* PRODUCTS
FROM EMILY BELLE FREEMAN AND DAVID BUTLER

NEW TESTAMENT

Don't Miss This 2023 Journal:
A Companion to Your Come, Follow Me *New Testament Study*

Don't Miss This Poster Set—New Testament

Don't Miss This Stickers for Scriptures—New Testament

Don't Miss This Tip-Ins for the New Testament

OLD TESTAMENT

Don't Miss This in the Old Testament:
Exploring One Verse from (Almost) Every Chapter

Don't Miss This 2022 Journal:
A Companion to Your Come, Follow Me *Old Testament Study*

Don't Miss This Poster Set—Old Testament

Don't Miss This Stickers for Scriptures—Old Testament

Don't Miss This Tip-Ins for the Old Testament

DOCTRINE AND COVENANTS

Don't Miss This in the Doctrine and Covenants:
Exploring One Verse from Each Section

Don't Miss This 2021 Journal:
A Companion to Your Come, Follow Me *Doctrine and Covenants Study*

Don't Miss This in the Doctrine and Covenants Poster Set

Don't Miss This Stickers for the Doctrine and Covenants

BOOK OF MORMON

Don't Miss This in the Book of Mormon:
Exploring One Verse from Each Chapter

Don't Miss This 2020 Journal:
A Companion to Your Come, Follow Me *Book of Mormon Study*

DON'T MISS THIS

IN THE
NEW TESTAMENT

EXPLORING ONE VERSE
FROM EACH CHAPTER

EMILY BELLE FREEMAN
and DAVID BUTLER

DESERET
BOOK

Salt Lake City, Utah

Library of Congress Cataloging-in-Publication Data

(CIP data on file)

ISBN 978-1-63993-065-4

Printed in the United States of America
Lake Book Manufacturing, Inc., Melrose Park, IL

10   9   8   7   6   5   4   3   2   1

For the woman in the produce section who never dared to open her scriptures until she started studying with this community.

For the man at the tire store who decided to come back to church in January because of what he was learning here.

For the woman who lost her husband and doesn't want to study *Come, Follow Me* alone.

For the father working the midnight shift, the one going through a really hard time, who finds hope in listening to these words on those late nights.

For our friend going through cancer treatment, for those in the military stationed far away who listen every Sunday, for the one struggling with their faith.

For every one of you we have met, and those we still hope to run into one day, this book is dedicated to you.

We love that you are our people, we love that you represent this community, we love walking through the story of Jesus with you.

All our love,
David and Emily

OUR HOPE FOR THIS BOOK

We don't know how you will use this book, but maybe it will help if we tell you how we use the book! We each leave it out near the kitchen table. We like to read one verse a day and its accompanying devotional with our families at dinnertime and then talk about the question at the bottom while we eat. It is helping us to make the *Come, Follow Me* program part of our everyday routine.

This book is not meant as a reference manual, but more of a simple help for learners of all ages to find meaning in the scriptures by focusing on context, culture, and application. On some pages you will read the story looking for context or cultural learning. On others you will meet one of the Saints that lived in the time of Jesus Christ. Sometimes we will share our own life application from a particular verse or chapter. Hopefully the combination of all of these teaching techniques will help make your study of the New Testament more meaningful this year.

We absolutely love studying with you!

DAVID AND EMILY

INTRODUCTION

Several years ago, I was fortunate enough to get the chance to go on a trip to the city of Jerusalem and surrounding areas. I could not wait to walk in the places where Jesus walked. However, soon after arriving, I was disappointed to learn from our tour guide that "Jesus's Jerusalem" had been buried under centuries of dirt. Because of the passage of time and the many changes in the city over the years, not much remained from the first century. Each place we went, the tour guide began with a phrase that sounded something like, "We don't know for sure, but this may be near the place . . ." or, "You could imagine the possibility of . . ." I wanted to step back in time, but kept feeling like I was still in the ordinary present.

On one particular day, we went to a place inside the boundaries of the old city to an old stone staircase. As the tour guide started teaching, he told us that the steps we were in front of had been uncovered by archaeologists and dated to the first century—the time of Jesus. I couldn't wait to walk on them. I wanted to run my hand across the stones or take my shoes and socks off and stand in the place He may have stood—to touch the reality of Jesus being in that place.

We might not ever know if Jesus actually walked on those particular stones, but I do know that Jesus of Nazareth really did come to this world, and while He was here, He met people in places like that one. He shared moments with them by wells, along roadsides, on dusty steps next to pools of water, and on the sands of seashores. He was Immanuel—God with us. He came and He left His mark and His impression on this world. On people.

In the New Testament we read the stories and discover the reality of Jesus walking on the earth. This is where we learn about the mortal Messiah. We see the way He walked with people, loved people, and ministered to them while He was here. This year, as we read those words, we will kneel with Him next to the woman who reached for the fringes of His robes. We will hear the tender compassion in His voice as He spoke with the leper.

We will feel the salty wind on our cheeks as He called fishermen to something more. Perhaps better than any other book of scripture, these are the pages that allow us to run our hands across the stone, to step into His footprints, and to brush up closely against the reality of Jesus in this place.

The Apostle John, one of the lucky few who lived in this world with Jesus, ends his gospel with what I have always read as a wish for more: "And there are also many other things which Jesus did," he tells us, "the which, if they should be written every one, I suppose that even the world itself could not contain the books that should be written" (John 21:25). I have always wanted those other stories—the ones that could fill all the books. I love every story that Matthew, Mark, Luke, and John tell. I crave every experience of Paul and James and Peter. But every time the book ends, I am left wanting just one more. One more story of Jesus. One more glimpse.

Our hope as you study the New Testament this year is that the reality of the mission and ministry of Jesus Christ will come alive for you. We hope that as you read and ponder every story written on these pages, they will each leave an impression on you. As you watch Him and hear Him through these ancient texts, we hope you will feel a closeness with Him, become familiar with His character, and be more able to see this same Jesus meeting you in your own ordinary steps—leaving an impression on your heart for years to come.

And maybe, when the year is through, you will have one more story to add to the book that should be written.

Yours.

MATTHEW 1:1

The book of the generation of Jesus Christ.

Matthew was a book written to convince the Jews that Jesus was the Messiah. Many say this is why it begins with a genealogy; it was a list that contained the lineage the Messiah was prophesied to come through. But there is a far more important lesson contained within this list of names, a truth realized only if you take the time to focus on some of the stories alluded to within this list. Most Jewish genealogies contain the names of the men in the family line. This one contains the names of four women: Thamar, Rachab, Ruth, and Bathsheba. Perhaps you wonder the significance of these four women.

Thamar, *Tamar*, is a woman who was mistreated, lied to, and misused. Rachab, *Rahab*, was a harlot who lived outside the faith. Ruth was also an outsider, poor, and left to fend for herself and her mother-in-law. Bathsheba was a widow who became pregnant out of wedlock. These are the grandmothers of Jesus, the women He came through. Many might be surprised that His lineage contains stories of people whose lives were filled with pain and misunderstanding and mistakes.

Every time I read this genealogy, I see it less as a line of who Jesus came through and more of a reminder of who He came for. The poor, the marginalized, the forgotten, the outsider, the maker of mistakes. His story includes the hard things, the moments most people would normally hide from—except Matthew wrote those stories in. Why? Could it have been so that we would know and understand His willingness to meet us where we are, as we are, from the very first page of the story? Was it so that we would know His heart? —EBF

Reflect and Respond
Where do you see your story represented in the story of Jesus?

Your favorite scripture in
Matthew 1

MATTHEW 2:9

Lo, the star . . . went before them.

Whenever Jenny and I travel to a new place, we always try to find a Nativity scene to buy and bring home as a souvenir. When choosing, I always try to pick one that includes the star. It's one of my favorite parts—the star that led the wise men to Jesus.

The star was the sign that gave the wise men direction on their long journey to Jesus. They had no idea where to go; they just knew to follow the star. I am so comforted by the line, "And, lo, the star, which they saw in the east, went before them, till it came and stood over where the young child was" (Matthew 2:9). The star went before them. They didn't know all the details of their journey, but they could always look up and see the star. God had laid it out before them. There was preparation for their journey. A path planned out. God was steps ahead of them, leading them.

Soon after the wise men visited Mary, Joseph, and Jesus, the family was directed in a dream to escape into Egypt. Where would they live? How long would they be there? How would they make money? When I think about this surprise change for them, I wonder if they gained courage from the wise men—a group of people who didn't know all the details of their journey but knew they were being led. The wise men had brought gifts too—gold, frankincense, and myrrh—gifts that would perhaps fund the unexpected journey. Maybe Joseph and Mary would look at the gifts of the wise men and see them as a star. Evidence that the Lord was preparing for them and was laying out the path ahead of where they would go. —DB

Reflect and Respond

When have you followed the star? When have you seen the Lord preparing the way for you?

Your favorite scripture in Matthew 2

MATTHEW 3:3

The voice of one crying in the wilderness.

Most of what we read about John the Baptist is unexpected—the wilderness, the camel's hair, the locusts and wild honey. His story is filled with details that remind us how this just wasn't the way things were done. John was not of the world; he wasn't even in the world. He was in the wilderness. It's fascinating how many people were drawn to learn from him there. John spoke of one mightier than he was, whose shoes he was not worthy to bear. One who would baptize with the Holy Ghost and with fire. "Then cometh Jesus from Galilee . . ." (Matthew 3:13).

Perhaps the same is true in our lives. Maybe change requires doing something unexpected, going to a place out of the way, listening to a voice that will lead us onto the path that will bring the greatest blessings in our lives. Sometimes finding truth requires walking away from the world, from the distraction, from whatever is making it hard to hear.

When I was a senior in high school, we moved to a place far from home. Things were different there. The change wasn't easy for us; I still remember how hard those first weeks and months were. One evening my sister and I found ourselves sitting in an unexpected testimony meeting in a living room filled up with only youth. There were no leaders there. I remember thinking how strange it was. *People back home would never show up to something like this*, I thought to myself. Then one girl stood up and shared her testimony of Jesus Christ. Her story felt vulnerable and sweet, and I knew she knew the Savior from the way she described Him. I remember thinking, *I want a testimony like hers*. That unexpected testimony in that unexpected place changed the trajectory of my relationship with Christ. —EBF

Reflect and Respond

Whose testimony has changed or influenced what you know about Jesus Christ?

Your favorite scripture in **Matthew 3**

MATTHEW 4:3

If thou be the Son of God.

After Jesus's baptism, He went into the wilderness, where He was tempted by the devil. He had heard the voice of God in the river, and now He was hearing the voice of the adversary.

He was tempted by Satan to turn stones into bread, to leap from the top of the temple in an act of spectacle to the crowd below, and to bow down and worship the devil in exchange for lands and power. Perhaps we could read these as examples of the common temptations all of us face—the temptation for pleasing the appetites, for fame, and for wealth. But in addition to these, there seems to be another temptation in the story.

The devil begins his temptations with the line, "If thou be the Son of God . . ." (Matthew 4:3).

If you really were His Son, would He leave you without bread? If you really were His child, would you be in this wilderness? Would it be so hard? Each of the temptations seems to have an underlying attack on Christ's identity. "*If you really were His . . .*" And just like he did with Jesus, the adversary does the same to each of us, causing us to question who we are and who we belong to.

Jesus's reply is beautiful. "Man shall not live by bread alone, but by every word that proceedeth out of the mouth of God" (Matthew 4:4). Not long before this experience, Jesus stood in the Jordan River and heard the words out of the mouth of God, *You are known. You are mine. You are fully loved.* The devil will try to tempt us to think we are not any of these, but God said otherwise. It is his word against His. —DB

Reflect and Respond
What has God said about who you are?

Your favorite scripture in Matthew 4

MATTHEW 5:3

Blessed are . . .

Every now and then (less often than I should have!) I used to call up my granny to give her an update on our lives. She would ask about Jenny and the kids and work and everything that was going on. After nearly every sentence of update I would give, she would always reply back in her endearing Southern drawl, "Oh, baby, you are so blessed." I think she said it to me one hundred times in every phone call.

As I look back on those conversations, I realize that she would always say how blessed I was after I told her about something good that was going on. "The kids are just happy and healthy." "Oh, baby, you are so blessed." "Work is going super good right now—I got a raise!" "Oh, baby, you are so blessed." "Life is great!" "Oh, baby, you are so blessed."

It isn't uncommon to associate the good things of life with God's blessings. We might be tempted to think that if life is going well, it is an indication of God's favor.

But what about when it's not?

This is why I love the beginning of Jesus's Sermon on the Mount. He turns what is blessed upside down. Blessed are those who mourn. Blessed are the hungry and thirsty. Blessed are those who are persecuted. Blessed are the poor. If Granny were writing it, she probably would've said blessed are the happy, the filled, the content and rich. But Jesus sees it differently. You are lucky—you are blessed—if you are without. Why would that be?

Perhaps those who are without have nowhere else to go except to Him. Perhaps it is the need that opens the door to relationship and to the kingdom. Blessed. —DB

Reflect and Respond

When have you seen an upside-down blessing in your life?

Your favorite scripture in **Matthew 5**

MATTHEW 6:9

Our Father which art in heaven.

When I overhear Jenny talking on the phone, I can usually guess who it is she is talking to. At the very least I know the category of person—stranger, good friend, neighbor, or sales call. She just has a different way of talking to each of them. You can hear it in her inflections, the tone of her voice, and the emotion she speaks with. Her mom is the easiest to pick out. I know in about two seconds if she is talking to her mom. The way she talks to her mom is elevated, and different from how she talks to anybody else. This is true about everyone she talks to—the relationship dictates the tone of the conversation.

When Jesus taught His disciples how to pray, He began by teaching them to start with "Our Father which art in heaven" (Matthew 6:9). I don't think He wanted them to use that exact phrase every time necessarily, but rather to begin prayer by establishing relationship. To set their hearts on who they were talking to. This relationship realization would dictate the rhythm of the conversation. They would go in as a child, and they would speak and listen to Him as Father.

He was not their boss or employer. He was not a judge or parole officer. He was their father. He is our father. And He is not just any father, but our Father in Heaven. He dwells in a higher and holier place. He is our King and our God. We pray with trust. We pray with revering hearts. And we pray with tender affection. We pray in love.

A child and a Father.

Our relationship will dictate the tone of the conversation. —DB

Reflect and Respond

How does it change the way you pray when you realize you are speaking to your Father?

Your favorite scripture in
Matthew 6

MATTHEW 7:13

Enter ye in at the strait gate.

There is a phenomenon that takes place in Southern Utah in which a wall of rock will break off and shift two or three feet from the face, creating two sheer walls that reach heavenward. Sometimes these are called slot canyons. One afternoon I found myself on a short hike walking between two of those sheer walls. The length was as long as a football field, and the walls towered at least forty feet above me on both sides. I walked on the soft sand and spread my arms, one hand touching the right wall, the other touching the left, as I made my way down the narrow path. When we got to the very end, I gathered the kids I was with. "Look back," I told them. "Next time someone teaches you about the strait and narrow way, I want you to picture this." There was a moment of pause, and then one of the boys whispered, dead serious, "Is church all you ever think about?" I laughed so hard. But I have never forgotten the visual of that path and those sheer, straight walls. If you look up the Greek translation for the word *strait* you will discover the Greek word *stenos*. It means "narrow," but it is probably from the base of *histemi*, which hints toward "covenant" or "establish." This added wisdom helps me understand the strait way with a deeper meaning. It is a covenant path, an established way, and few there be that find it. This is the way that leads to life.

Close your eyes and picture two sheer walls keeping you in the way as you walk down a narrow path. When you enter a slot canyon you are guaranteed to reach the destination at the end. No one gets lost. Perhaps that is the purpose of God's covenant path. You are guaranteed to reach the destination at the end. The covenant path will ensure you arrive there safely. —EBF

Reflect and Respond

What is one way to ensure you are staying on the strait way?

Your favorite scripture in
Matthew 7

MATTHEW 8:3

And Jesus put forth his hand, and touched him.

To be a leper in Jesus's day was possibly worse than death. It has been referred to as the living death. Not only were lepers' bodies aching, decayed, and diseased—literally falling apart—but because of the law, they were shunned from society. They were made to live outside of the typical neighborhoods. They were forbidden to come close to anyone— required to wear certain clothing that would mark them as lepers and to carry a bell they would ring to warn others approaching that there was a leper nearby. They were outcasts with broken bodies and broken hearts. How long since they had been given a hug? A goodnight kiss? A handshake?

When Jesus came down from the mount where He gave His sermon, a leper approached Him. This may have caused everyone around Him great alarm. A leper was approaching Jesus! What if he contaminated Him? The leper begged for Jesus to make him clean. "If thou wilt, thou canst make me clean" (Matthew 8:2). The leper didn't wonder about Jesus's ability; he wondered about His willingness. Was He willing to make him clean?

Jesus replied: "I will; be thou clean" (Matthew 8:3).

Before Matthew records those words, he tells us that Jesus "put forth his hand, and touched him" (Matthew 8:3). There are so many ways Jesus could have healed this man. He could have told him to wash in the river or spoken the healing words over him. Instead, He chose to heal this untouchable man with a tender touch. An act that would not only show He was willing but would also show His heart. —DB

Reflect and Respond
When has Jesus been tender and personal with you?

Your favorite scripture in **Matthew 8**

MATTHEW 9:36

He was moved with compassion on them.

Have you ever wished you could spend an entire day with Jesus? Sunrise to sunset. Do you wonder how His days were filled? Matthew 9 gives us a glimpse into the life of Christ. Sometimes I read this chapter with the hope of learning to be more like Him.

The day began with Him entering into a ship. When He had arrived into His own city, the people brought Him a man sick of the palsy, and Jesus healed him. Then He spoke with certain scribes about healing and forgiveness. Next He passed the receipt of custom and saw Matthew there, and invited Matthew to follow Him. He sat down next to eat with publicans and sinners along with His disciples. Their conversation was filled with who He chose to eat lunch with and the particulars of the law. While Jesus spoke to this group, Jairus came to plead for his daughter, who lay sick at the point of death. Immediately Jesus got up and walked with the worried father. As they passed down a crowded street, a woman who had been sick for twelve years reached out and touched His robe. He paused for a conversation about faith, then He continued on to the home where the daughter slept. After He raised her from the dead, two blind men followed Him, and He healed them, and then a dumb man came, and He healed him.

"And Jesus went about all the cities and villages, teaching in their synagogues, and preaching the gospel of the kingdom, and healing every sickness and every disease among the people. But when he saw the multitudes, he was moved with compassion on them" (Matthew 9:35–36). What governed His day was not a to-do list. It was compassion.

I want to be more like that. —EBF

Reflect and Respond
How could you include compassionate detours in the course of your days?

Your favorite scripture in Matthew 9

MATTHEW 10:7

The kingdom of heaven is at hand.

The chapter heading in my Bible for Matthew chapter 10 says: "Jesus instructs and empowers the Twelve Apostles and sends them forth to preach, minister, and heal." I love that it seems to have two sets of threes in that summary. The first: Jesus would instruct, empower, and send His disciples. He would teach them what to say. He would empower them with authority and holy confidence. And He would send them. Perhaps they didn't feel ready. How long had they been His disciples, after all? And what would they be sent forth to do?

The second set of three answers that question. They were sent forth to preach, to minister, and to heal. These are the words that describe Jesus of Nazareth and what He came to do. To preach, to minister, and to heal. Now Jesus was gathering others to do the same. To be His feet, His hands, and His heart everywhere they went.

The one message Matthew records that the disciples were preaching was one we heard from Jesus several chapters previous. It was, "The kingdom of heaven is at hand" (Matthew 10:7). "At hand" is a phrase that means close by or near. These disciples would go forth with these encouraging words. No matter where you are, the kingdom is close. No matter what situation you find yourself in, heaven is near. In every day and every circumstance, God is not very far away. This was probably one of the messages that encouraged these inexperienced disciples to fulfill their mission. And it would be the message they would be sent with to anyone and everyone they met. —DB

Reflect and Respond
When have you felt God and the power of heaven near?

Your favorite scripture in Matthew 10

MATTHEW 11:29

Take my yoke upon you.

My dad taught me the practice of writing references to supporting scriptures next to a verse. Sometimes the margins of my scriptures become filled up with these scripture chains. The verses that talk about Christ's yoke, His rest, and His burden of light is one of those places for me. This is a scripture meant for the weary and the heavy-laden; the verses written in my margin bring greater understanding of this.

The first supporting scripture is found in 2 Corinthians 12:9: "And he said unto me, My grace is sufficient for thee: for my strength is made perfect in weakness. Most gladly therefore will I rather glory in my infirmities, that the power of Christ may rest upon me." I learn that it doesn't matter if I am an equal match for the yoke—His strength is actually made perfect in my weakness, and His power will *rest* on me.

The second supporting scripture teaches me about burdens being made easy and light. It is Mosiah 24:15: "And now it came to pass that the burdens which were laid upon Alma and his brethren *were made light*; yea, the Lord did strengthen them that they could bear up their burdens with *ease*, and they did submit cheerfully and with patience to all the will of the Lord" (emphasis added).

The last supporting scripture is D&C 84:24 and teaches us that if we harden our hearts and will not endure His presence, we will not enter into His rest.

From these three verses in the scripture chain, we learn that our weakness does not disqualify us from being yoked to the Lord, that His power can rest upon us if we have soft hearts and spend time in His presence, and that the Lord has the power to make our burdens light and strengthen us to bear them with ease. —EBF

Reflect and Respond

Which of these three verses brings greater understanding to Matthew 11:28–30 for you? Why?

Your favorite scripture in Matthew 11

MATTHEW 12:15

He healed them all.

Whenever people ask me for scripture study advice, one of the first things I usually share with them is to use their imagination. The scriptures are often not very descriptive, which happily leaves us the job to imagine what is happening—to fill in the spaces between the verses. We can imagine what the surroundings looked like, what the facial expressions were, or when there were pauses in the conversation. Sometimes I imagine what the emotions and thoughts were of the people who were there. I think through what I may have been feeling if I had been there and seen what I saw or heard what I heard.

Of course, when we use our imaginations, we don't exactly know if that is how the story played out. We could be wrong or right about the surroundings, emotions, and intentions of the people in the story. But the one thing it does is bring personality and life to the stories. Like this one line in Matthew 12:15: "He healed them all." It tells us that great multitudes followed Jesus, and that He healed all of them. Great multitudes are a collection of a bunch of individual people. Each of them had a name and a story. Each of them had things they were worried about or excited about. Each and every one of them had a personal encounter with Jesus. He knew their names and their stories. He knew their excitement and fears.

When we read in scripture about Jesus healing great multitudes, I think it is helpful to imagine people we know—especially those we know who need healing. To imagine their faces, and then to remember that He intends to heal them all. —DB

Reflect and Respond

When have you been in a large group, but also felt like Jesus knew your name and story?

Your favorite scripture in Matthew 12

MATTHEW 13:44

For joy thereof goeth and selleth.

Parables seem to be one of Jesus's favorite ways of teaching. Often, the parables begin with the phrase, "And the kingdom of heaven is likened unto . . ." (Matthew 13:24) or something similar to that. It is a way of saying that the parable is going to give the listener or reader a general idea of what kingdom life is like—what to expect and what could be expected out of them. How the kingdom begins or grows within people. What to anticipate or to enjoy while living kingdom life.

One of the sets of parables Jesus shares is of two lucky men who discover great treasures. The first seems to stumble upon it in a field. When he discovers the treasure, he sells everything he has (in great joy!) in order to buy the field with the treasure in it. The second man is also in search of treasure, and he finds a pearl of great price. When he finds it, he also sells everything that he has in order to purchase the pearl.

This is what the kingdom of heaven is like, or perhaps what it is like when you discover it. You will recognize it as treasure. It will be so good that you would be willing to give up or sell anything in order to have it. It will thrill you more than anything else in this world. If what you see as the kingdom or gospel does not fill you with that kind of excitement, joy, or anticipation, perhaps you have not quite discovered it.

Seek for it.

When you do find it, it will fill you with joy, and everything you do afterward will be motivated by that joy. —DB

Reflect and Respond

What is so great or precious to you about the kingdom or gospel of Jesus Christ?

Your favorite scripture in **Matthew 13**

MATTHEW 14:29

He walked on water, to go to Jesus.

The story of Peter walking on water has six important steps that might be helpful to understand in our own stories of growth and becoming. Consider these:

1. Fear	see Matthew 14:26–27
2. Stretching	see Matthew 14:28
3. Success	see Matthew 14:29
4. Doubt	see Matthew 14:30
5. Saving grace	see Matthew 14:31
6. Testimony	see Matthew 14:32–33

There are several things that are surprising about this journey. First, we learn that a moment of fear and awe can produce the type of situation that enables stretching. Perhaps you have felt a lack of control in a situation that someone else has mastered, and their success gave you courage to try to conquer that fear. Second, we learn that stretching moments can lead to success and learning, but also that great doubt can follow great success. Has that ever been true in your own life? Next, we learn in drowning moments where we find ourselves soaking wet and windblown, the Savior will send His saving, healing, enabling grace immediately. It is personal experiences like these with the Savior that increase our testimony of Him.

I love to consider where Jesus was when this journey was taking place. Was He on the shore yelling instructions to Peter? Was He in the boat trying to explain what Peter should do? No. He was in the water. With Peter. Within reaching distance. Perhaps that is the greatest lesson of them all. —EBF

Reflect and Respond

Which of the six lessons do you relate to most as you consider your story right now? Why?

Your favorite scripture in
Matthew 14

MATTHEW 15:27

Yet the dogs eat of the crumbs
which fall from their masters' table.

One of my favorite psalms says, "For a day in thy courts is better than a thousand [elsewhere]. I had rather be a doorkeeper in the house of my God, than to dwell in the tents of wickedness" (Psalm 84:10).

The writer of this psalm would pick one day in the presence of God over a thousand anywhere else—even Disneyland, I suppose. And even if he had to be a doorkeeper, he would rather have that lowly job in God's house than any other position in some other place.

This is the same spirit as that of a mother we meet in Matthew 15. She was an outsider who came to Jesus for a miracle for her afflicted daughter. Jesus's response is a little strange for modern readers—He tells her that His mission is first to the house of Israel (which she was not a part of), and then in later times to others. In an analogy, He told this woman that the order of feeding people at the kitchen table goes to the children first before the dogs. It sounds culturally offensive to us today, but she was not offended. She agreed. There was an order to things. But then her reply was that the dogs get to eat the crumbs that drop from the children's table.

Jesus commended her for her great faith and desire. It seems to me as if she were saying, I will take anything. Even your crumbs. I would rather have crumbs from your table than all the delicacies on any other.

Even the small pieces of what Jesus has to offer can make a difference.

And they did for this woman and her child. —DB

Reflect and Respond

What are some of the crumbs—the small parts of the gospel—that you wouldn't trade away?

Your favorite scripture in Matthew 15

MATTHEW 16:16

Thou art the Christ.

I went into labor when I was seventeen weeks pregnant. The labor and delivery nurses told me that at that many weeks along the pregnancy wasn't viable, and I was sure to lose the baby. My doctor sent me home on bed rest and I began to pray.

The next six months were filled with saving that baby, which meant complete bed rest for me. I remember the tears, the great anxiety, the worry that it would all be for nothing, but I also remember being sustained by Christ. Those months were filled with priesthood blessings. I read the entire standard works during those months. It was the first time I had ever done that. It wasn't because I loved reading scripture, but because I was desperately seeking Him. I had been promised that my faith would determine the outcome of the pregnancy. I spent every day trying to increase my faith in Him.

When it was over, several moments were seared into my memory. Dr. Brown placing tiny Grace into my arms and telling the nurses, "Look at this baby. She is a miracle. She would not be here if it weren't for the faith of her mother." My dad telling me to write the miracles down, how I wouldn't remember the sweet details if I didn't record them. I vividly remember the ride home from the hospital, Grace safely nestled into her car seat, Greg looking over to ask if I was glad it was over. I remember a great sense of worry that I was going to forget what I knew of Jesus. Over the course of those days He had become more to me than a painting on the wall or a porcelain figure on the piano. He had become real. I knew He was the Christ, the Son of the living God. He had sustained me through the trial. I never wanted to forget. —EBF

Reflect and Respond

Which parts of your story have deepened your testimony of Jesus Christ?

Your favorite scripture in
Matthew 16

MATTHEW 17:4

It is good for us to be here.

For several Christmases, a friend of ours invited us to be a part of an opportunity to spread some much-appreciated Christmas cheer to people and families in need. On Christmas Eve we would gather at a local high school's cafeteria and sort out boxes of food and clothing. Then on Christmas morning, we would all divide up the boxes and head out to deliver them. Usually, the delivery time was right in the middle of when Christmas morning was at its peak. The places we took the boxes weren't usually close to our house, and it was sort of a hassle to pull all the kids, especially the littlest ones, from their gifts, find their coats, gloves, and boots, and pile in the car to go make our deliveries.

But without fail, when we did, we would experience something we never could have without leaving our home. I can remember one particular Christmas piling into an elevator with my sister's family, riding up to the top floor of an apartment complex, and then knocking on each of the doors with boxes in hand. The hallway was a little dingy and the elevator was sketchy. But there on the top floor, as people opened their doors to the Christmas surprise, as they listened to us sing and gave us Christmas hugs, I thought of something Peter said to Jesus. He took Peter and other disciples to a high mountain. There at the top, He showed His glory to them. In the light of that glory, Peter said to Jesus, "Lord, it is good for us to be here" (Matthew 17:4).

On the top of that apartment complex mountain, bathed in that same glory, I thought to myself the same words. "Lord, it is good for us to be here." —DB

Reflect and Respond
When have you felt to say this same expression?

Your favorite scripture in Matthew 17

MATTHEW 18:27

Then the lord of that servant was moved with compassion.

In one of Jesus's most striking parables, there was a servant of a lord who had somehow squandered his master's money. When he came in for his accounting, it was discovered that the servant owed the master 10,000 talents. It is difficult to translate ancient money into modern currency, but by some estimates, a single talent could be worth around 30,000 US dollars. And this man owed ten thousand of those! Whatever the exchange rate, the man had an astronomical, unpayable debt. It's what makes his plea so silly when he tells the master to give him time to pay it back. There would be no way he could accomplish that. It would take him 800 lifetimes to pay it back.

In consequence, all of the man's possessions would be sold and the man, his wife, and his children would be sold as well. The man collapsed and begged for mercy. When the lord saw him, he had compassion on him and he forgave his debt.

That is a remarkable level of compassion. A ten-thousand-talent level of compassion. In order to forgive the debt, the master himself would have to take on the responsibility and consequence of the money owed. The debt did not disappear. Rather, it was transferred to the lord. Forgiveness has a cost, and the lord was willing to pay it. It may have meant the master would lose his kingdom. It may have meant that he himself would be sold off as a debtor. We don't know, but we do know that whatever the cost, and however high the cost, the master was willing to pay it. All because of his compassion. —DB

Reflect and Respond

How does it feel to know you have a Lord who is compassionate and willing to forgive your debts?

Your favorite scripture in Matthew 18

MATTHEW 19:20

What lack I yet?

One day, a rich, young ruler in the community approached Jesus with a question. "What do I need to do to have eternal life?" Jesus's answer was simple: keep the commandments. "Which ones?" the young man asked. Jesus then listed several of the Ten Commandments after which the man replied, in essence, "I have kept all of these since I was a kid—what lack I yet?" What else do I need to do? Jesus's instructions were a little shocking. He told him to sell everything and give it to the poor. Everything? His house, clothes, hats, animals, jewelry, pots and pans—everything?

When the young man heard Jesus's words, he walked away sorrowfully. Jesus then turned to His disciples and said it is easier for a camel to get through the eye of a needle than for a rich person to get into the kingdom. That scenario caused one of the disciples to ask, "Who then can be saved?" (Matthew 19:25). *If that guy can't make it, I don't think any of us can!* Jesus, overhearing, said in reply, "With men this is impossible; but with God all things are possible" (Matthew 19:26).

And perhaps that was the lesson Jesus was teaching the rich young man—the boy who checked all the boxes to get into heaven. "Which one is left?" he was asking. What else do I need to do? In His clever way, I think Jesus was showing the boy that it would be impossible for him to earn his way in. That's what some rich people are used to—earning and deserving. But as rich or good as he was, it wouldn't ever be enough. He needed something more. His question was, "What lack I yet? What more do I need?" Jesus's answer seemed to be, "Me." —DB

Reflect and Respond

What are some of the areas of your life where you could use God's help?

Your favorite scripture in Matthew 19

MATTHEW 20:13

Friend, I do thee no wrong.

One of the most common phrases I hear bouncing off the walls of my house is the line, "But that's unfair!" I think it is a requirement for children to learn it. And unfortunately, the demand doesn't go away. We all want things to be fair.

That's what makes Jesus's parable of the laborers in the vineyard such a tricky one. In this parable, workers are hired at the beginning of the day to work in a vineyard. They contract out for a penny for the day. Later in the day, the foreman hires more workers who come into the vineyard to work, and he continues to do this until the last hour of the workday, when he hires one last group to come in to work, promising them he will pay them whatever is right.

At the end of the day, the workers line up for their pay and the foreman makes a scene. He pays the last-hour workers first, and he pays them a full day's wage. When he moves down the line and gets to the first workers, he pays them the same. They call foul! Unfair!

But wasn't it fair? Isn't that what they agreed upon?

But perhaps unfair is what we want. Do we want the Lord to be fair with us? Give us what we deserve? At first I thought yes, but then I decided I didn't want the Lord to be fair; I wanted Him to be merciful. If I consider myself a first-hour worker, and think to myself that I have earned everything I get, I will always live feeling cheated. But if I see myself as the last-hour worker—and recognize I was picked up late, didn't do much (although my best), and was still given a full day's wage, I will feel and live in mercy. —DB

Reflect and Respond

What are some of the ways the Lord has been unfairly generous to you?

Your favorite scripture in Matthew 20

MATTHEW 21:3

The Lord hath need of them.

I am always intrigued by the man who stood in the place where two ways met in Mark 11:4. It seems he must have been the keeper of the colt Jesus would ride into Jerusalem. The verses hint at the fact that this certain man knew someone would come for the colt and that it would be for the Lord, but all of the clarifying details are left out of the text. All we know is this: a certain man stood in a place where two ways met, ready to offer whatever the Lord needed next.

Matthew gives us a little more insight into the story. "Go into the village," Jesus told them. "Ye shall find an ass tied, and a colt with her . . . bring them unto me" (Matthew 21:2). This rendering says, "If any man say ought unto you, ye shall say, The Lord hath need of them; and straightway he will send them" (Matthew 21:3). In the margin next to this verse I have written, *Who was that man? Would I have done the same?*

Maybe you stand at a place where two ways meet today. Sometimes the place where two ways meet can be a defining moment in a life. If that is ever true of me, I hope to be prepared to offer whatever the Lord needs next. It is an interesting way to live. A consecrated way of living.

The giving of whatever is asked because the Lord is asking of it.

Maybe someday we will meet the man who stood in the place where two ways met. Maybe he will give us the details of his story, how he knew about the men who would come, the ones who would ask for the donkey, how they would be sent by the Lord, and how he would give them the colt without question, simply because the Lord needed it. —EBF

Reflect and Respond
What are you prepared to give up for the Lord today?

Your favorite scripture in Matthew 21

MATTHEW 22:40

On these two commandments
hang all the law and the prophets.

It seems to be a common problem for all of us—too much to do with not enough time. I wonder if it has always been this way. At the beginning of every new year my Instagram account is bombarded with ads for new planners and organizing methods. All the gadgets and formulas to prioritize my life. These companies and ideas exist simply because the problem does—the problem of picking and choosing the most important thing to do.

A certain lawyer came to Jesus and asked Him to prioritize. Of all the commandments in the law, which was commonly said to be 613 total, which one was the greatest? Which of them was most important? Jesus answered back with no written hesitation.

Easy. Love the Lord. Love Him with all of your heart, and all of your soul, and with all of your mind. That's number one.

And the second—it is practically the same. It is like unto the first. Love your neighbor. That's number two.

Love God. Love people. That's it.

Of every way we can spend our time, efforts, talents, money, energy, intellect, hope, passion, desire, or intentions, these two would be the greatest. The law of the Lord is simple. It is not easy to do, but it is simple. Everything else Jesus has taught or will teach falls into these two categories.

The answer really is and has always been love. —DB

Reflect and Respond

What are some ways you can show love to God and other people today?

Your favorite
scripture in
Matthew 22

MATTHEW 23:16

Woe unto you, ye blind guides.

One of my dearest friends was blind, but it didn't keep her from living life to the fullest. She traveled often, spoke at large events, and ministered to many both inside and outside of our faith community. We lived right by each other and often traveled to the same events. Because of that, I would often lead her to where she needed to go. She often referred to me as her guide dog, which she thought was hilarious.

Being a guide is not easy. There were many times I would forget to tell her a hill was approaching, or a step; once I even forgot about the wall that I walked her right into without paying attention. It also came with its own set of problems for me. I can remember leading her onto a stage in front of thousands of women and her stepping on the hem of my pants just as I stepped forward. I had to use both hands to hold my pants up and she crashed right into me, right in front of everyone. Remembering that occasion brings this scripture verse into perspective for me: "Woe unto you, ye blind guides" (Matthew 23:16).

How can you trust a guide who cannot see ahead?

This is a chapter about trusting someone to guide us. Someone who can see what is happening ahead. One who will know the dangers, obstacles, and pitfalls that might get in our way. One sent to protect us as we walk the path toward home.

"O Jerusalem, Jerusalem, thou that killest the prophets, and stonest them which are sent unto thee . . . behold, your house is left unto you desolate. For I say unto you, Ye shall not see me" (Matthew 23:37–39).

Who is your guide? Where is your guide leading you? —EBF

Reflect and Respond

How have the words of an apostle or prophet guided your life recently?

Your favorite scripture in Matthew 23

MATTHEW 24:13

He that shall endure unto the end,
the same shall be saved.

Jesus had a very tender conversation together with His disciples on the hillside of the Mount of Olives, overlooking the city of Jerusalem. It was just days before He was going to be crucified and leave them. This was still a shock to them, and they didn't fully grasp what was happening. What they did know was that He was leaving. One of them asked, "When are you coming back?" I have always loved this question, particularly because it came before He ever left. If they were wondering when He was coming back before He even left, they must have really liked each other.

Jesus proceeded to tell them what their lives would be like. How they would face prison and persecution. How people would hate them and abuse them. How their world would spin in commotion. He gave similar predictions about the disciples that would live in the time right before He would come again. Perhaps He was speaking about us. We certainly live in a time period that looks troublingly similar to the one Jesus prophesied about. There is a lot of hurt and turmoil. Often, disciples wonder how to live in such a time. Luckily, Jesus spoke to this.

He gave a piece of counsel and advice to His disciples in the past that I have always held on to in the present. It was to simply endure. "He that shall endure unto the end" will be saved (Matthew 24:13). Just don't give up. It will be hard at times. It will be frustrating during other times. The world will be in commotion, and you will be disappointed with yourself and others. But just don't give in. Stay trying all the way to the end. He is coming. —DB

Reflect and Respond

Who is someone you can encourage today to just keep trying?

Your favorite
scripture in
Matthew 24

MATTHEW 25:12

I know you not.

The three parables in chapter 25 have several things in common.

	Ten virgins	The talents	The goats
They were entrusted with something	oil	talents	people
They had to wait a long time	bridegroom tarried	after a long time	when He comes
There was a dividing factor	wise/foolish	5/2/1	sheep/goats
Knowing the Lord	"I know you not"	"I knew thee"	"When saw we thee"
	(Matthew 25:12)	(Matthew 25:24)	(Matthew 25:38)

When we combine all of these lessons together, we learn something important. First, the Lord wants us to grow and increase. In the parables it is oil, talents, and people. In our lives it might be the Spirit, the opportunity to become more, or serving people. Second, there was a period of testing. The bridegroom didn't come until midnight. The Lord traveled to a far country. We all have to wait for the Son of Man to come again. Third, there was a dividing factor. The wise brought oil, the foolish didn't. The five and two talents were doubled, the one talent wasn't. Some served the stranger and the naked, some didn't. Last, it came down to knowing the Lord. Joseph Smith teaches us that Jesus told the virgins, "Ye know me not" (JST, Matthew 25:12). The man who didn't increase his talent told the Lord, "I knew thee that thou art an hard man" (Matthew 25:24). In the last parable, the servants didn't recognize the Lord when they saw the stranger, the naked, the sick. All three parables teach important lessons: We must take what we have been entrusted with seriously. We might be required to wait. Our goal is growth, increase, and progression. Last, we must come to know the Lord. This is how we prepare to meet Him. —EBF

Reflect and Respond

How are you preparing for Him to come again?

Your favorite scripture in Matthew 25

MATTHEW 26:10

She hath wrought a good work upon me.

When Jesus was together with friends, enjoying one of His last meals of mortality, a woman came into the dining area carrying an alabaster box of ointment. Alabaster is a precious light-colored stone that was used at times to hold even more precious perfumes, oils, and ointments. When she came near Jesus, she broke open the alabaster box and began to pour the contents out on Jesus, anointing Him in a way that was fit for a king.

Perhaps it was a surprise visit and an even more surprising act, because at least one of the disciples got angry with what was happening. The oil she was pouring out was very expensive, and the disciple who was troubled by it called it a waste. "This ointment might have been sold for much, and given to the poor" (Matthew 26:9).

Jesus quickly came to the woman's defense. Perhaps in His explanation He was referring to the shadow of things to come. Just as that particular woman poured out what was most precious to her upon the Lord, so too was He about to pour out what was most precious to Him onto her. And onto the rest of everyone there.

I only wish that Matthew had recorded some of the woman's thoughts and responses to the angry disciple. I would have liked to hear what she would've said about what she did. Was it a waste? I like to think she would've replied like this: "Oh, no, it wasn't a waste. I wish I could've given more. For He has given me so much. I didn't pour out ointment; I poured out my love. And He was worth every drop." —DB

Reflect and Respond

What is one way you could pour out your love for Jesus today?

Your favorite scripture in Matthew 26

MATTHEW 27:21

Whether of the twain will ye that I release?

Some say it was some sort of tradition, or perhaps it was something new that Pilate, the Roman official, thought might please the crowds. Whatever the case was, Pilate offered the people of Jerusalem a choice of one prisoner they could release. The two options were Jesus of Nazareth and Barabbas, the criminal.

Barabbas was in prison for the riot and sedition that he had caused in the streets. He was also there for murder. Jesus was there on false charges and accusations. Pilate himself even said he could not find any wrong with Him. It seems as if Pilate was trying to sway the vote by picking someone like Barabbas as the other option. Would they want the gentle carpenter to go free, or would they like the thug Barabbas to be on the streets again?

In a horrible surprise, the crowds of people chanted and demanded that Barabbas go free. They picked the criminal. And so he was set free of all charges, and Jesus, the innocent One, was sent to the cross.

How unfair.

The guilty one should have to bear the punishment.

On that day, Barabbas went free because Jesus went to the cross.

He took his place.

As I read the story, I see myself in Barabbas. I am the guilty one. The criminal. I deserve the punishment. Not Him. But Jesus, the innocent One, went in my place. Because He went to the cross, I am set free. —DB

Reflect and Respond

How does it make you feel to know that Jesus was willing to take your place?

Your favorite scripture in
Matthew 27

MATTHEW 28:6

He is not here: for he is risen.

I grew up with an interior designer—my mom. I think she may have changed the floors or countertops or light fixtures every seven days. She is ultra-talented, has an amazing eye, and is always in high demand for her work. Along the way, I picked up a few design rules from her. Fashion is always more important than function. Put things in odd numbers, unless you are going for a square look. And if it is comfortable, it probably isn't cute.

I was well trained.

I don't know if she ever said this to me or not, but I think she would disagree with a picture of a graveyard or tomb in my house. Especially in the living room. It just doesn't go. However, there is one exception. Jesus's empty tomb. It is a picture even she would frame large above her mantel. It is beautiful to her and to me.

When Mary and others first saw the empty tomb, it was a symbol of despair and defeat. It was another hard blow. The enemy had killed the Lord and now they had stolen His body. But when some of the disciples arrived at the tomb, they were met by angels who said some of the most hopeful words ever spoken. "He is not here: for he is risen" (Matthew 28:6). The empty tomb is a symbol and sign of victory and love. Of overcoming. For if Jesus is no longer there, then death has no more power. If Jesus is no longer there, then what He had promised He actually pulled off. Which means He is more than just a street preacher or Nazareth carpenter; He is truly the saving Son of God.

If Jesus is not there, it means He came to be among us again. —DB

Reflect and Respond

Jesus is no longer in the tomb. Where have you seen or sensed Him recently?

Your favorite scripture in Matthew 28

MARK 1:17

I will make you to become fishers of men.

I wonder if when the disciples first met Jesus, they even imagined in the slightest what their lives would turn into because of it. Many of them were fishermen on the Sea of Galilee, a body of water in the little region of Judea. No one would have known their names besides the relatively few families that lived in the area. They probably never thought they were destined for any kind of greatness, expecting that they would fish and live out their lives on the banks of that sea. Their greatest potential, they may have thought, was to become great fishermen. Masters of the catch.

Then Jesus came to their shore.

He called them to follow Him. To leave behind their nets and begin to live differently. Part of His call included this promise: "I will make you to become fishers of men" (Mark 1:17). This was a different path. Not one they had been on. They were fishers of fish, but Jesus was calling them to something more.

Perhaps they looked at their dirty hands and tangled nets and wondered if they could be anything different. After all, they were only fishermen. But it was Jesus who promised that He, Himself, would make them become something different. If they followed Him, He could help them to discover a new potential. A chance to become something great.

Without Him, they would have lived simple lives as fishers of fish. With Him, they became something different. Something more.

Something extraordinary. —DB

Reflect and Respond

What do you think Jesus has in mind for you? What could He make you to become?

Your favorite scripture in
Mark 1

MARK 2:3

Borne of four.

Could you imagine if you were sitting in a friend's house, listening to Jesus speak, when all of a sudden the roof began to open up? And not just a little. Piece by piece, the roof opened up big enough for four people to lower their friend's bed (with their friend on it!) down into the middle of the house. That would be unforgettable.

But the one thing I want to remember from this story is not the roof opening up, or the bed coming down, but the four who opened the roof and then lowered the bed. Somehow, they got word that Jesus was nearby. Immediately they thought of their friend who was sick with the palsy, unable to walk. I can imagine their conversation. The four telling their friend that Jesus was near, that Jesus could help him. Perhaps the paralyzed boy refuted, *how would I even get there?* Then one of them speaks up, *we will carry you.* We don't know how it came about, but that is exactly what they did. They carried him. And when they got to the house where Jesus was, there was no way in through the door because of the crowds of people. So, they thought outside the box and lifted him onto the roof. And then, as we already read, they opened it up and lowered him down.

I love these four. Four who knew that they alone couldn't help their friend, but they knew that Jesus could. So they brought their friend to Him. This is a picture of what it means to be a missionary. Taking someone to Jesus. Carrying someone to Jesus. Realizing that there isn't just one way to come unto Him. This story reminds us that everyone comes differently. —DB

Reflect and Respond
When has someone carried you or brought you closer to Jesus?

Your favorite scripture in
Mark 2

MARK 3:13

And calleth unto him whom he would.

We don't get to read much about the choosing of the Twelve. Mark gives us a hint of the process: *He called whom He would.* Peter is mentioned first, then the sons of thunder. Simon the Canaanite. Judas, who would betray Him.

There are a few things that stand out in this account. First, I love that Jesus gave people nicknames—the Sons of Thunder, Simon who was known for his zealous nature, and we find out later that Peter was the rock. Nicknames suggest endearment. Friendship. Being known at a deeper level. Spending enough time with someone that you know something unique about them. Whenever I read these verses, I can't help but wonder what Jesus might call me. *I wonder what He might call you.*

I also find it interesting that Judas was picked as one of the Twelve from the very beginning. He experienced the same miracles, the same teaching, the same opportunities as the other eleven. He sat at the same table, and Jesus let him. He allowed it. Right up until the very last day. Perhaps it is what He does for each of us. Allows us a seat at His table. Gives us a front-row seat for His miracles, provides opportunities for learning, hopes we will become endeared to Him. And yet, He honors our agency. The power of choice. A bag of silver for a life. *What are you choosing?*

So many lessons in Mark 3:13–19. Just seven short verses, and sometimes just a few verses a day are all you need. Here is one more from just verse 13: He went up into a mountain, and He called who He would, and they came unto Him. *Would you have climbed the mountain?* —EBF

Reflect and Respond

Which is your favorite lesson from these seven verses? Why?

Your favorite scripture in Mark 3

MARK 4:40

Why are ye so fearful?

I have to admit, I read those words from Jesus for many years and thought they were sort of patronizing. "Why are you so afraid?" As if they shouldn't be!

But they should have been. They were on the Sea of Galilee when a storm popped up out of nowhere. That was somewhat common with that particular fishing lake. But this storm was something fierce. The waves beat upon the ship, covering it and filling it with water. The disciples, many of whom were fishermen and used to a storm here and there, were terrified. They thought they would die. That's how big the storm was. And Jesus? He was asleep.

Those might be the most uncomforting words in the whole New Testament. The disciples were facing one of the greatest storms of their lives, but Jesus was fast asleep. And then when they woke Him up, He looked at them, calmed the sea, looked back at them and asked, "Why are ye so fearful?" (Mark 4:40). I was not even there, and I can think of twenty logical reasons.

I wondered about this question until one night when my young son came into our bedroom in the middle of the night to wake me up. When I finally came to myself, I heard him tell me he was afraid. I then asked back, "Why are you afraid?" The same question that Jesus had asked. And I wasn't mad at him or thinking he was overreacting; I simply wanted to know. I wanted to talk through it with him. To show him he didn't need to be afraid—especially if we were there.

Perhaps that is what Jesus was teaching His disciples.

Teaching them to remember who He was, and that He was there. —DB

Reflect and Respond

What is something you are fearing right now? How does it change to know that Jesus is near?

Your favorite scripture in
Mark 4

MARK 5:34

Daughter, thy faith hath made thee whole.

I wonder if it was hard for Jairus when Jesus stopped on the side of the path to speak to the woman with the issue of blood. Did his heart pound in his chest with worry over the delay? Was he impatient watching the conversation? Did he want to tell the woman to wait until he had finished his errand first? It had been twelve years; surely she could have waited a few hours more. And yet, I read the account and there are words that stand out to me—how she *felt* she was healed, how she came *knowing* what was done in her, how it was *faith* that had healed her (see Mark 5:29–34), and I can't help but wonder if maybe the father of the girl who lay at the point of death was meant to learn something from this woman's example. Perhaps he needed a lesson on what faith looked like, because before they started walking again a message came from the house, "Thy daughter is dead: why troublest thou the Master any further?" (Mark 5:35). Jesus responds simply, "Be not afraid, only believe" (Mark 5:36).

Was it easier for Jairus to believe because of what he had just witnessed?

Can faith strengthen faith?

Two daughters. One twelve years sick, the other twelve years old. One unclean by illness, the other unclean by death. Both made whole by faith. Because of Him.

Perhaps you don't have an issue of blood, but I wonder what issue you might have? Is there someone with a similar story who might strengthen your faith? Give you strength? Help you to believe in Him?

Trust faith to strengthen faith. —EBF

Reflect and Respond
Who might strengthen your faith today?

Your favorite
scripture in
Mark 5

MARK 6:56

. . . that they might touch . . . the border of his garment . . .

We often hear people talk about the power of one righteous person and the influence they can have. Then people tell the stories of Alma, or Esther, or David and we become intimidated. We think perhaps it is only well-known remarkable souls that are difference makers. The famous ones. Because you never hear about a no-name person who made a great difference in the lives of a lot of people.

Unless you start looking carefully.

Then you will find those stories everywhere in scripture. A verse here and a verse there. Mark 6 has one of those verses, "And whithersoever he entered, into villages, or cities, or country, they laid the sick in the streets, and besought him that they might touch if it were but the border of his garment: and as many as touched him were made whole" (Mark 6:56).

It hints of a story I know and love. A story of someone who had been sick for twelve years. A woman who had done all and still grew worse. A woman lying in the street. A woman who reached out to touch His robe and was healed. How did all of those people know to carry their loved ones who were sick into the streets? *All of the villages and all of the cities and the countries.* Could it possibly have been because of one woman's story of her personal experience with Jesus Christ? A woman who was healed because she touched His robe. A woman whose name we don't even know? I like to think so.

Your story? Your personal experience with Jesus Christ? Your healing? You might be surprised to know that sharing that story could inspire someone else for good. A village even. Maybe a whole country. —EBF

Reflect and Respond

How could you share your witness of what Jesus has done for you?

Your favorite scripture in Mark 6

MARK 7:34

And looking up to heaven, he sighed.

So many things are automated these days. Last week, I went to McDonald's and ordered all my food on a kiosk and then picked it up from a designated area without ever talking to a single McDonald's employee. Groceries can be ordered and delivered through an app without any person-to-person contact too. ATMs give you cash in a transaction between just you and a robot. And don't get me started on voice-automated customer support telephone services. I am over them. They never understand what I say. I get caught in an endless automated menu loop. "Talk to a representative!"

It is sad to lose the personal touch. It is why I love the little details Mark includes in a little-known story. As you read the Gospels, it feels like Jesus is healing people left and right. It almost feels automated. But on one particular day, a man who couldn't hear and also had a speech impediment came to Jesus for help. "And he took him aside from the multitude" (Mark 7:33). That is so sweet to me. He took him to be one on one. And once they were aside from the group, Jesus touched his ears and then looked up into heaven and sighed before saying, "Be opened."

There are several reasons why someone might sigh. It might be fatigue, frustration, confusion, contemplation, a time for gathering strength or compassion. I have my guess what the reason was, but the thing I love about it being included is the expression of emotion it conveys. This wasn't an automated experience. Jesus took him aside and He felt something when they were together—something that made Him sigh. —DB

Reflect and Respond

When have you felt like Jesus has taken you aside, one on one, and felt the emotions you were feeling?

Your favorite scripture in Mark 7

MARK 8:14

Neither had they in the ship
with them more than one loaf.

A miracle can't bring faith to someone whose heart is set on unbelief. Perhaps this is the lesson Jesus was trying to teach after the miracle of the seven loaves multiplied. He fed four thousand that day. Seven loaves turned into seven baskets overflowing, and that was after everyone had been filled. But somehow the seven baskets were forgotten. What they currently had in the ship was one loaf. We don't know what happened. We aren't sure who forgot the baskets. What we do know is that the disciples were extremely worried about the lack of bread.

There was a choice in that moment. Unbelief or faith in Him.

It's true, there was only one loaf in the boat.

But that boat also included one other thing. Jesus.

That seems to be the lesson underlying the miracle here. The logistics of the miracle were far less important than the reality of Him. The Bread of Life was far more important than the bread left over. The miracle was Him.

Do you understand?

Do you see?

Do you remember?

These are the three questions He asked the disciples on that afternoon. Beware of unbelief. When you remember the five loaves among five thousand and the twelve baskets overflowing, when you consider the seven loaves among the four thousand and the seven baskets overflowing, it's not about the one loaf.

See Him. Remember Him. —EBF

Reflect and Respond

How have you learned to see and remember Him?

Your favorite
scripture in
Mark 8

MARK 9:27

Jesus took him by the hand.

Once our family was walking through an area that was packed full of people. So much was going on. People were coming and going and moving from every direction, street performers were gathering crowds, and it was a lively, bustling scene. As we started into the thick of the people, my little girl moved in closer to my side and instinctively grabbed my hand. I watched my two little boys do the same thing to their mom. No one suggested it—it just came naturally. Then we walked through the unfamiliar crowd together.

I am not sure when we learn it, but even little kids know that when you are nervous, or scared, or even when you want to show affection, you hold someone's hand. It is a symbol and signal of security and safety. As a kid, I held my parents' hands. As a parent, I hold my kids'. I actually like it when they reach for my hand. It is a simple reminder that they are still mine and that they still need me.

My heart breaks every time I read the story of the desperate father who brought his hurting son to Jesus. His pleas for help echo some of my own. "If you can do anything . . ." "have compassion on us . . ." "help us . . ." "help me" (Mark 9:22). I see a father in the story reaching as a son. Grasping for any kind of help. And then Jesus casts out the trouble in the hurting boy. In doing so, He also cast out the trouble in the father. And then Mark says that "Jesus took him by the hand" (Mark 9:27). Like you would do if someone were scared. Like you would do in times of worry or distress. Like you would do when you wanted to show tender affection. —DB

Reflect and Respond

When have you felt God reach out and hold your hand?

Your favorite scripture in Mark 9

MARK 10:21

Then Jesus beholding him loved him.

The New Testament gives us the unique opportunity to learn about the character of Christ. We are able to watch Him respond to real-life situations and circumstances. If we choose, we can learn from the personal encounters and apply His teachings to our own lives. From the four Gospels we learn of Christ's forgiveness, grace, tenderness, compassion, and love, among other attributes.

The story of the rich young ruler found in Mark 10 contains a compelling lesson on Christ's love. There is one defining moment in the story that illustrates this love. Before the counsel was given to give to the poor, before the invitation to take up the cross, before the young man was invited to follow Him, there is one sentence that stands out. "Then Jesus beholding him loved him" (Mark 10:21). He loved him.

He didn't wait to see how the young man would respond to determine how He felt; He loved him already. What if we were to learn something from this encounter? Could we be better at viewing someone through the lens of Christ?

Could we lead with love?

We don't know what happened to this rich young ruler. We know that on that day he went away grieved because he had many possessions (see Mark 10:22). He walked away knowing that what Jesus asked seemed too hard for him to accept just then. But he also walked away knowing he was loved. I like to think that maybe one day that would draw him back. The same as it did for Nicodemus, who also walked away but then returned. Love is powerful like that. —EBF

Reflect and Respond

How could you share the love of Christ with someone today?

Your favorite scripture in Mark 10

MARK 11:9

Hosanna; Blessed is he
that cometh in the name of the Lord.

It must have been quite the spectacle to see Jesus riding into Jerusalem during the Passover preparation days. The city would have been more crowded than usual because of the upcoming festival. As Jesus rode in, all of the city was moved. Some with wonder and others with adoration.

As He began His descent into the holy city, people began to gather. They started to line the streets. Many of them laid out pieces of their clothing in His path—a royal, welcoming gesture. Others cut down palm branches to wave as He passed by, shouting the sacred cry, "Hosanna! Hosanna!"

Hosanna is a one-word prayer. It is a word that could be translated from Hebrew as "save us now" or simply just "help!" Sometimes my most powerful prayers are only one or two words.

Help.

Sorry.

Please.

Thank you.

As Jesus came into Jerusalem, the people seemed to be welcoming Him not only into their city, but into their homes, lives, and hearts. Each of them with a need for saving.

And each of them calling out for help to the One who could. —DB

Reflect and Respond

What one-word prayer is on your heart these days?

Your favorite
scripture in
Mark 11

MARK 12:42-43

And there came a certain poor widow...
and he called unto him his disciples.

When I was serving as a bishop, I had such a tender place in my heart for those who were serving in our ward as Primary teachers. Every time I thought about them, my heart surged with gratitude. I loved them dearly. I still do. Part of the reason, I am sure, is that I had a house full of little Primary-aged kids, so I had a particular soft spot for the teachers who were teaching my own. But I genuinely adored and admired everyone who was giving their time so freely to minister to the little ones of our neighborhood. It was not an easy job to teach and look after these young kids. And often, many of the teachers probably felt overlooked and unseen. This happens with all of us. Moms, dads, crossing guards, nurses, counselors. Often the efforts we put forth to help are not noticed by others, but they are noticed by God.

During one of His last days, Jesus was in the temple courts with His disciples. He noticed a certain poor widow coming into the treasury to pay her offerings. The temple would have been crowded with people. There would have been hustle and bustle and noise echoing off the stone walls. She easily could've been overlooked. She was only putting in two mites after all. But Jesus saw her. And He saw her offering and her heart. He called over His disciples to see her and to teach them a lesson about sacrifice. Perhaps He needed to call them over because they didn't notice her. But He did.

We might be overlooked by everyone else—even some of His disciples—but we are seen and looked over by Him. —DB

Reflect and Respond
When have you felt seen and looked over by God?

Your favorite scripture in Mark 12

MARK 13:14

The abomination of desolation.

Have you ever wondered about the abomination of desolation spoken of in end-times prophecy? The one spoken of by Daniel the prophet? The best place to learn more about it is actually in the book of Daniel. In chapter 11 of Daniel, we read of the conflicts and events that will lead up to the Second Coming. In this chapter we read of two kings whose hearts are full of mischief. One of the kings would be against the holy covenant, and his goal would be to pollute the sanctuary of strength and take away the daily sacrifice. In place of the sacrifice would be "the abomination that maketh desolate" (Daniel 11:31).

History helps us to understand what is being told here. In 167 BC, Syrian forces were determined to suppress Jewish religious practices. They entered the sanctuary of strength, or the temple, intent on stopping the work that was taking place there. They stopped the daily burnt offerings and set up an idol in place of those offerings. During this time some of the Jews turned against the covenant, but others stood strong. Mark tells us that if we ever see this happen, the profaning of the holy place, we will see affliction such as we have never seen since the beginning (see Mark 13:19).

We don't know exactly what this will look like in our day, but what we do know is the importance of keeping sacred the holy covenant, respecting the holy temple, and standing strong in holy places. —EBF

Reflect and Respond
How do you keep holy covenants sacred?

Your favorite scripture in
Mark 13

MARK 14:8

She hath done what she could.

Many years ago, I stood in a dusty courtyard and watched five men carving alabaster boxes out of stone. The process requires a gentle hand because alabaster is so fragile. When the work was done, the men would hold the small box up to the light. Alabaster is translucent, and as they held up the box, the light would fill the empty cavity inside. After I had watched them carve the boxes for a while, I went inside to purchase a small box of my own. I bought a tiny, round box with a lid, small enough to fit in the palm of my hand. It is a soft rose color, and sometimes I take it out and hold it up to the light. I keep a vial of spikenard in my box. It reminds me of the story found in the book of Mark, of the woman who brought what was most precious to her and offered it to the Lord.

Some complained as they watched her spill the precious ointment on the Savior's head; they felt it was a waste. But Jesus felt she had wrought a good work, explaining that she had "done what she could" (Mark 14:8). Almost as if it didn't matter *what* she had done—what was important was that she had done something.

Sometimes we wonder if we have done enough, if our offering is worth anything, if what we have to give pales in comparison to what someone else is doing. What is "precious" to one person might not be "precious" to someone else. Perhaps what makes an offering "precious" is the sacrifice, the giving of what one can. That will look different for each of us. But He will see the good work we have wrought. He will know. The process will allow our heart to become translucent, and we will be filled with the light that comes from Him. —EBF

Reflect and Respond

What is your precious offering?

Your favorite scripture in Mark 14

MARK 15:21

Simon . . . who passed by.

Do you wonder what Simon was doing in Jerusalem on that day? What brought him into the city? Why was he there with his two boys?

Somehow, he ended up in the same place as Jesus. After the scourging where the soldiers smote and spit upon Him, after the crown of thorns, in the moment they led Him out to crucify Him, Simon, the father of Alexander and Rufus, happened to be passing by (see Mark 15:21). The scriptures tell us the soldiers compelled one Simon to bear the cross and that he bore the burden to Golgotha.

He didn't plan to be part of history; he was just passing by.

Later that afternoon, after they parted the garments of Jesus, hung the superscription of His accusation over His head, and placed the two thieves on His right hand and on His left, another group passed by. "And they that passed by railed on him, wagging their heads . . . mocking . . . and they . . . reviled him" (Mark 15:24–32). This group, too, made history.

I don't think it is coincidence that on the day of the Crucifixion, two types passed by—Simon, a man who would help bear the burden, and a crowd of onlookers, who railed and mocked and reviled. I believe those two vignettes were included to help us recognize an important truth.

Interestingly, those two types still make up our world today. Some take up the cross and covenant to bear burdens and mourn with those that mourn and comfort those that stand in need of comfort, and others still mock and revile.

Which type are you? —EBF

Reflect and Respond
What do you think it means to take up the cross?

Your favorite
scripture in
Mark 15

MARK 16:20

And they went forth.

Each of the four Gospels ends differently. Matthew invites the reader to go forth to teach and baptize people from all nations. Luke gives a reminder of the joy that comes from continually worshipping Him. John reminds us that the story isn't over, that there are not enough books in the world to contain everything Jesus did or would do, and we are invited to watch the story continue to unfold. Mark wrote this: "And they went forth, and preached every where, the Lord working with them, and confirming the word with signs following" (Mark 16:20). It is as if Mark wanted us to help continue the story, to be witnesses knowing that He would continue to confirm our testimony. We are so familiar with a story that ends with the words "the end," but this one doesn't. The Gospels each end with an invitation to continue the journey, to keep the word alive, to spread the gospel. I love that the story doesn't end, but instead continues even to this day. I wonder, if you were to look back over the last year of your life, could you think of personal experiences or intimate encounters in which the Lord has worked with you in your own story, confirming the truth of Mark's word that He would be with us?

For many years as a seminary teacher, I would ask the students in my class to keep a journal of the times when they saw the hand of their Lord in their life. In the beginning it was hard. They would ask if they could choose something from the past year. From summer. From the last couple of weeks. But by the end of the year, they had learned to recognize Him everywhere. If we want to know if the Lord is working with us, all we have to do is look for the signs. —EBF

Reflect and Respond

Where have you seen the Lord working in your story recently?

Your favorite
scripture in
Mark 16

LUKE 1:38

Behold the handmaid of the Lord.

LUKE

I love weddings. I love the gathering of longtime friends, the banquet tables of the very best finger foods, and, of course, the dancing. Weddings are everything happy packed into one fantastical evening. One of my most favorite parts is the bride and groom running out to their car through a line of sparklers and cheers. I am smiling just thinking of it.

Sometimes, and perhaps oddly, when I read Luke 1, I think about the wedding Mary may have been looking forward to. She was engaged to be married to Joseph the carpenter. Perhaps she dreamed of what their wedding and eventual life would look like together—to live and raise a family in their hometown of Nazareth. But all of that changed when the angel Gabriel came with his announcement that she would be the mother of the "Son of the Highest." Her whole life would now be different. It wouldn't look like anything she may have thought. No wedding. No feast. No celebration. There was the potential of punishment, the whole town gossiping behind her back, and the possibility of never being married or taken care of. She would eventually give birth in a cave, escape as a refugee into Egypt, and one day find herself at the foot of a cross.

This is the life she would live if she said yes to the angel. My heart surges when I read her words. "Behold the handmaid of the Lord" (Luke 1:38). In other words—I will do whatever He asks. I am His. And she did. Her whole life. And yes, she experienced the heartbreak and sorrow of that choice, but she also lived the thrill, the wonder, and the sparkle of it too. —DB

Reflect and Respond

What do you think your life might look like if you give it over into the Lord's hands?

Your favorite scripture in
Luke 1

LUKE 2:15

The shepherds said one to another,
Let us now go even unto Bethlehem.

From the very moment scripture whispers the idea of Jesus being born through Mary, a profound lesson is taught. Mary could have carried that baby entirely by herself. Delivered Him too. It had been done before by single mothers who were left to face the unfairness of life alone. But God gave Mary Joseph. He sent someone so she wouldn't travel alone. On the night of the birth, Joseph and Mary found an innkeeper who directed them to a small cave. Immediately after the baby was born, shepherds arrived: "Let *us* now go" (Luke 2:15; emphasis added). Soon after, wise men would follow.

I don't think I've ever noticed it before, how the message at the root of the Christmas story is that nobody comes alone. Beginning with Mary. *It's still true today.*

My neighbor stopped by one day. She'd been praying for her sister for years, pleading that somehow she would find her way back to church. To Him. Then a new gal started working at her sister's place of work. After a couple of days, she told my friend's sister she wanted to be friends. "You won't believe this," my neighbor said with a twinkle in her eye, "but she invited her to church last weekend. *Our Church.* And my sister took her girls and went! Do you believe that? She went!" Then with eyes sparkling she told me of her instant response: "Thank you, Jesus, for sending someone."

Someone is lonely today. Carrying the weight of the world. Wondering if anyone will remember them. Jesus will know. Ask Him if He might help you to see where you are needed. He will answer. It's what He does. Sends someone. —EBF

Reflect and Respond

When has the Lord sent someone to you?

Your favorite scripture in
Luke 2

LUKE 3:12

What shall we do?

Three questions followed the promise given by the Baptist about empty valleys filled, uncrossable summits brought low, crooked things being made straight, and rough ways made smooth (see Luke 3:5).

"What shall we do . . . ?" The people asked, and the Baptist answered, "He that hath two coats, let him impart to him that hath none."

"What shall we do?" the publicans wondered. "Exact no more than that which is appointed you."

"What shall we do?" the soldiers demanded. "Do violence to no man . . . be content" (Luke 3:10–14).

Each was given an answer according to his station in life, his circumstance, the particulars of his own condition. The accepting of the invitation would not come easy. Give half, take less, be content. But the promise, it seems, would make it worth it.

I consider my own life—the empty places, the rough patches, what seems uncrossable. In those moments I often pray the same prayer, *"What should I do?"* I find it interesting that their reaction to the answers was a mix of expectation and musing (see Luke 3:15). I wonder how often that is my reaction as well. It was there within the expectation and the musing that John lifted their thoughts higher: "One mightier than I cometh, the latchet of whose shoes I am not worthy to unloose" (Luke 3:16). One mightier than I, the One who can make straight that which is crooked, fill that which is empty, and smooth out that which is rough. John invites us to discover Him by walking a disciple's path. —EBF

Reflect and Respond

Spend some time in prayer today and ask the question found in Luke 3, "What shall we do?"

Your favorite scripture in
Luke 3

LUKE 4:29

And led him unto the brow of the hill . . .
that they might cast him down headlong.

I have stood on a hill overlooking the Nazarene valley. A place that some scholars think Jesus might have stood when the people of Nazareth led Jesus to the brow of the hill, hoping they might cast Him down. He walked away.

My thoughts were filled with a whole city of people who wouldn't believe because Jesus had actually come out of their country. When they asked why He wouldn't perform His miracles there, He spoke of the many widows and lepers who filled Israel at the time of Elijah and Elisha and yet the two who experienced healing were a widow from Sarepta (Zarephath) and Naaman the Syrian. People who were removed enough from the culture and climate that their hearts would be open to believe. People whose situation was so dire, belief was the only option left.

Perhaps that is the way of miracles.

Maybe each of us stands at the brow of the hill. We can list all of the reasons why what we are longing for won't happen. It's not hard to let belief crash headlong over the cliff. But Jesus walked away from the place of doubt and disillusionment. He walked into a life of miracles. First a synagogue where He rebuked a devil and then to a home where He rebuked a fever. As the sun set over that new city that evening, "all they that had any sick with divers diseases brought them unto him; and he laid his hands on every one of them, and healed them. . . . And the people sought him, and came unto him, and stayed him, that he should not depart from them" (Luke 4:40, 42).

One group filled with belief-dashers; the other group filled up with seekers of miracles. I want to be found in the second. —EBF

Reflect and Respond

How could you walk away from a place of doubt and into a place of belief?

Your favorite scripture in
Luke 4

LUKE 5:4

Launch out into the deep.

It was after a long night of fishing. Peter and his fellow fishermen had not caught a single fish. Zero. They were probably exhausted, frustrated, and ready to get home. They were washing and hanging up their nets when Jesus came with a request. He wanted to borrow their boat to use as a sort of platform for teaching a small crowd of people. "Thrust out a little" was all He asked (Luke 5:3). Just a small favor. A little inconvenient for tired fishermen. But Peter agreed.

Soon after the sermon, Jesus turned again to Peter and asked him to "launch out into the deep, and let down your nets" (Luke 5:4). This was more than just pushing the boat out a little. This would require rowing, and dragging the nets, and then a repeat of washing and hanging them to dry. Besides, the fish weren't biting that day, and Peter was beyond tired. Despite all the arguments Peter may have had in his head, he replied back to the Lord, "Nevertheless at thy word I will let down the net" (Luke 5:5). And so, he did.

To his surprise, the nets started to wrap up whole schools of fish. There were so many that the nets started to break. He called his friends and their boats over for help and the fish filled all of the boats, causing them to begin to sink.

None of this would have happened if Peter hadn't put his boat out a little from the land. None of this would have happened if he hadn't launched out into the deep—committing himself to the Lord in a deeper, more significant way.

None of this would have happened unless Peter set aside his arguments and replied, "nevertheless," not my way, but yours. —DB

Reflect and Respond

In what ways is Jesus asking you to launch out into the deep, to become more committed?

Your favorite scripture in **Luke 5**

LUKE 6:48

And digged deep, and laid the foundation.

The temporary wall that had been put up around the construction site was there for safety, but the clear plastic allowed visitors to watch the work taking place within. Giant earthmovers pulled dirt and debris away from the foundation so that it might be examined and strengthened. I watched, fascinated at the work taking place, intrigued that a foundation could be strengthened this many years after a building was complete.

Speaking of our own spiritual foundations, President Russell M. Nelson counseled, "It is now time that we each implement extraordinary measures—perhaps measures we have never taken before—to strengthen our *personal spiritual* foundations. Unprecedented times call for unprecedented measures . . . these *are* the latter days. If you and I are to withstand the forthcoming perils and pressures, it is imperative that we each have a *firm* spiritual foundation built upon the rock of our Redeemer, Jesus Christ" ("The Temple and Your Spiritual Foundation," *Liahona*, November 2021).

In Luke we are given a few hints for building a foundation: dig deep and make sure it is founded upon a rock. I consider the moving of earth and debris, and what that might look like in my life right now. The digging deep. It is a process that takes effort and time. Perhaps I should set aside more time for digging deep. Next, I consider the rock. My thoughts turn to Jesus Christ. Am I founded upon Him? Is my life founded upon Him? Is there anything that I am participating in that would shift my focus from Him? Maybe you feel like you built your foundation years ago, but this temple reconstruction project has given me reason for pause. *Is it worth digging deep to reexamine my foundation and make it stronger now?* —EBF

Reflect and Respond

How might you dig deep in order to strengthen your spiritual foundation?

Your favorite scripture in Luke 6

LUKE 7:44

Seest thou this woman?

Is it possible the woman we read about who would wash the Savior's feet with her tears had just previously been at the place where Jesus taught the sermon to those who were weary and heavy-laden, the sermon given to those seeking rest? Perhaps that is why she came, even though she was a sinner. Maybe she was longing for that rest.

When she walked into the room weeping, when she washed His feet with her tears, the Pharisee who had invited Jesus in simply saw a sinner. Jesus recognized a woman who loved much. Sins could be forgiven. But what of loving little? Can that be overcome?

Have you ever wondered what loving much might look like? Jesus describes for us exactly what He saw: A woman who noticed the feet of Jesus had not been washed when He entered the home, a sign of hospitality neglected. We discover Jesus had not been welcomed in with the kiss of a friend, but this woman made up for it by kissing His feet. The gift of anointing had not been extended by the host, but this woman had given up her most costly possession as a gift for Him. With one story, Jesus defines the difference between loving much and loving little, and we learn which is of greatest importance in His eyes—the welcoming in, the service of love, the offering of our finest.

I can't help but wonder what He sees when He looks at me . . .

I may not be perfect, but sins can be forgiven. It seems what is of greater importance is the quality of my love, and learning to become the manner of woman she was. I want to pattern my life after hers. I know what it is to be weary and heavy-laden. In those moments, may I be led to love first. —EBF

Reflect and Respond
How could you love much today?

Your favorite
scripture in
Luke 7

LUKE 8:30

What is thy name?

When Jesus saw the man out of the city, the one who had devils, with no clothes, the one who lived among the tombs with chains bound around his wrists and ankles, His first response might surprise you. Jesus looked past the chains and the nakedness and the devils and asked one question: "What is your name?" (see Luke 8:30). He wanted to know who this man really was. It is a powerful lesson that becomes even more powerful when you watch how the conversation proceeds. The man answers, "Legion," which conveys the idea of 6,000 armed and strong warriors of evil, but Jesus saw something more. So He removed the devils, and clothed the man, and then He healed his heart. It shouldn't surprise us that the man wanted to remain at the feet of Jesus forever. He knew there would be safety there. But Jesus suggested something different: "Return to thine own house, and shew how great things God hath done unto thee" (Luke 8:39). It seems this became the man's life work; it is what would guarantee his safety and his happiness. In a time afterward Jesus stopped by to visit again. At His return many were there waiting to receive Jesus, because of the great work this man had done.

A twelve-step meeting I attended with a friend brought this story to life for me. The facilitator leading the discussion described his life before Christ. It was a life filled with exhaustion trying to outrun the addiction that chased him every minute of every hour of every day. Then he found Christ, and after that nothing was ever the same. Now he spends many evenings facilitating twelve-step meetings, teaching the great things of Jesus Christ, helping people find who they really are through Him. It is what keeps him safe. It is where he finds happiness and healing. —EBF

Reflect and Respond

How might you help someone find healing by giving a reminder of who Christ sees in them?

Your favorite scripture in
Luke 8

LUKE 9:62

And looking back.

I love to mow the lawn. My husband, Greg, keeps trying to talk me into hiring the boys across the street, but I can't give it up. It is my favorite thinking place. It is often where I pray. There is something about the straight lines and the repetition that is good for a soul.

I like to mow the front yard in diagonal lines. It is a little tricky to get it right, so I have a method I use. There is a certain line on the sidewalk I start from, and a particular post on the back fence that I focus on as I mow that first strip. If I take my eyes off that back fence post even for a second, it can throw off the straight line. It is this concept that helped me to understand the lesson being taught at the very end of Luke 9. I'm always worried about the Lord telling the man not to bury his father, not to bid his family farewell. Sometimes I get so worried I forget the point of the lesson. It's contained in two words, "follow me" (Luke 9:59).

Keep your eye on the fence post.

Don't get distracted by the going on of life.

Remember Peter straightway left his nets and followed Him.

The underlying lesson becomes clear when you read that last verse, "And Jesus said unto him, No man, having put his hand to the plough, and looking back, is fit for the kingdom of God" (Luke 9:62). He's talking figuratively.

A farmer would know that to make a furrow you must pick a point in front of you and go toward it, the same way I know to pick a point on the back fence post. The same is true about the kingdom of God. You can't look back.

Focus on Him. —EBF

Reflect and Respond

What are you doing to keep your focus on Him?

Your favorite scripture in
Luke 9

LUKE 10:33

Came where he was.

When I read the story of the man who was stripped and wounded and left half dead, I often focus on the lesson of what the Samaritan did to offer relief. But there is an important lesson that takes place before the Samaritan begins to bind up the wounds, or pour the oil, or carry the man to the inn.

The lesson is found as we watch the response of each passerby.

The thieves left him "half dead" (Luke 10:30).

The priest "passed by on the other side" (Luke 10:31).

The Levite "came and looked on him, and passed by on the other side" (Luke 10:32).

The Samaritan "came where he was . . . and went to him" (Luke 10:33–34).

It is what I know to be true about the Savior. He met people where they were, as they were. He walked into the leper colonies, into the back rooms of dying daughters, into stormy seas and forgotten wells. He sat down for lunch, He walked the path with those who mourned, He showed up in moments of weeping. It is what He was best at. Meeting people where they were as they were, but He didn't intend to leave them there. He came to lift them up.

When He extends the invitation at the end of this parable, perhaps this is what He was talking about. "Go, and do thou likewise" (Luke 10:37).

Meet people where they are, as they are.

Lift hearts, heal wounds, bear burdens. Lift them up.

When He comes again, He will repay us (see Luke 10:35). But until then, our job is to take care the way He would if He were here. —EBF

Reflect and Respond

Who needs you to meet them where they are? How might you be on His errand there?

Your favorite scripture in Luke 10

LUKE 11:13

If ye then . . . know how to give good gifts . . .
how much more shall your heavenly Father. . . ?

Christmas morning takes a long time at my house. I am part of the problem. I want things to go slowly. One reason is I don't want the magic to end, but the main reason is I want to watch each of the kids open their gifts one at a time. I like to see their anticipation as they tear open the paper. Their fingers and hands shaking. I love watching their initial reaction when they see the gift—working through what it might be at first glance—and then the thrilling realization. I have had my share of fails on Christmas morning, but for the most part, I am a pretty good gift giver.

I live for it.

This giving experience must not be unique to me, though, because Jesus used the analogy of dads giving gifts when He was teaching His disciples to pray. He asks them if a child asks for bread, do dads give stones? Or if they ask for fish, do they get a snake? And if a child wanted an egg, is there any dad out there who would give a scorpion? (see Luke 11:11–12). Of course not. Good dads don't give things that harm their children.

"If ye then, being evil, know how to give good gifts unto your children: how much more shall your heavenly Father give . . . ?" (Luke 11:13). It's a beautiful question. It's an even more beautiful realization. To know that God is the giver of all good gifts. That His intentions are good. That when you ask, seek, and knock, He will give, show, and open to something good.

Perhaps it is worth remembering that God doesn't give stones, snakes, or scorpions. He is the Father of every good gift. —DB

Reflect and Respond

When have you received a good gift from your Good Father?

Your favorite
scripture in
Luke 11

LUKE 12:32

It is your Father's good pleasure to give you the kingdom.

We just talked about how gift-giving is my love language. I genuinely get excited to choose gifts for people. And not just any gifts—I like to think through them and give something meaningful. Or sometimes it is just something spontaneous so someone knows I was thinking of them. I suppose I like receiving gifts as much as the next guy, but giving is my jam.

Jenny, on the other hand, does not like receiving gifts. I think she has resisted every single one of the gifts I have ever gotten for her. When I pressed her about it once, she said she feels undeserving of the gifts. That I was being too nice to her. I said the same thing to someone once, and they replied, "Then you might have a hard time with grace."

It is true. Sometimes we receive grace the way we receive gifts. We feel like we are undeserving of something so kind. But by very definition, grace is not something we deserve or earn. It is, in fact, a gift. And gifts are more about the goodness of the giver than the goodness of the receiver. Jesus taught His disciples this same lesson. Perhaps when He told them how carefully and tenderly the Father would watch over them and care for them in their ministry, they felt the same kind of undeservedness or unworthiness. So, Jesus taught them something about Him—and how the gifts were more about the giver than the receiver.

"Fear not, little flock; for it is your Father's good pleasure to give you the kingdom" (Luke 12:32).

It is His good pleasure. It is what He wants.

It is what He is excitedly working toward. —DB

Reflect and Respond

What do you think is in God's good pleasure to do for you right now in your life?

Your favorite scripture in Luke 12

LUKE 13:12

Woman, thou art loosed from thine infirmity.

One day, while Jesus was teaching in one of the synagogues, there was a woman who was in attendance with a severe problem. She was bent over in what seems to be agony, because she couldn't even lift herself up fully. I wonder when I read stories like this what her life must have been like. Whatever her condition was, she had been battling it for at least eighteen years.

There at the synagogue that Sabbath day, Jesus saw her and called her over to Him. When she had come to Him, He spoke these words, "Woman, thou art loosed from thine infirmity" (Luke 13:12). Just like that. You are loosed from this. You are set free. What once was your burden is now no longer.

I don't think I've waited for something for eighteen years. But this woman had. I have not battled something so crippling that it has left me bent over. But many have and many do. Perhaps this story can give great hope to those who are waiting and battling. I don't think that woman knew that her healing was coming on that particular day. But it did. And I don't know when or how, but one day each of us will be seen by Jesus and called over to be near Him. He will know our infirmity and how long we have carried it. And with His healing words He will set us free.

Before this Sabbath at the synagogue, the woman may have referred to herself as someone bound. From that day forward, perhaps she referred to herself as the one Jesus set free. —DB

Reflect and Respond

What do you think it felt like to be loosed from eighteen years of heartache?

Your favorite scripture in
Luke 13

LUKE 14:22

There is room.

Dinner parties are one of my favorite events to host. There is something magical about watching a table come together—the dishes, the goblets, the silverware. If it is an important dinner, there are centerpieces and maybe even names beautifully penned and standing at each place setting. The smell of food cooking in the oven, sparkling sodas, the music turned low. There is that moment, just before the first guest walks in, when you look around the room, everything in its place, and you sense the anticipation of a beautiful evening to come.

I always imagine a night like this when I begin reading about the parable of the great supper. It helps me to understand why the master of the house was so angry when everyone canceled at the last minute. There is much to learn from his response. He didn't blow out the candles, throw out the meal, and climb into bed upset. Instead, he told his servant to go out into the streets and bring in the poor and the maimed and the halt and the blind (see Luke 14:21).

It is an act of radical generosity that doesn't stop there. When the servant returns and says there is still room, the master sends him into the highways and hedges. He asks him to invite the people who never get an invite. *You will have to tell them I want them to come*, he explains to the servant. "Compel them to come in" (Luke 14:23). He just wanted his home to be full.

I want to be a hostess like that. I want to extend an open invitation to everyone. Room at my table. I want my invitation to be, "There is a place for you, you belong here, there is room." It is the invitation of the Savior. Radical generosity. I want a heart like His. —EBF

Reflect and Respond
Who could you invite in?

Your favorite
scripture in
Luke 14

LUKE 15:9

Rejoice with me.

On the wall of my front entry hangs one of my favorite earthly treasures. It is a framed page from an old Geneva Bible from the sixteenth century. The chapter on the page is Luke 15—arguably, according to me, the greatest chapter in all of scripture. In my opinion, it shows the character and heart of God better than most other places in scripture.

It is a chapter of three stories. Jesus was having a meal with some people of not-so-good reputation when the Pharisees questioned Him. Why do you eat with these people and treat them so well? They are sinners! Jesus's response was a story about a lost and found sheep, a lost and found coin, and a lost and found set of boys.

In each of these stories, something was lost, then it was found, and when it was found, there was a party. In each of the stories, someone acts over-the-top about the thing that was lost. My favorite is the father in the parable of the two lost boys. The younger one demands his inheritance early from his father. The boy runs off and wastes all of it in riotous living. Soon, the boy is living in a pigsty sharing slop with the swine. It is in this place that he realizes that being a servant in his father's house would be better than the life he currently had. So, he returned home.

And when he returned home, while he was still far off, the father came running to meet him. There wasn't a lecture or a demand or an apology; there were instead hugs and kisses and a call for celebration, "Let us eat, and be merry: for this my son . . . was lost, and is found" (Luke 15:23–24). All while the boy still stunk like pig.

A little over-the-top. But that is what God is like. —DB

Reflect and Respond

How do you think these stories of lost and found demonstrate God's love for us?

Your favorite
scripture in
Luke 15

LUKE 16:10

He that is faithful in that which is least
is faithful also in much.

One of the strangest parables of Jesus is also one of my favorites. Several Bible scholars disagree on what Jesus was trying to teach with this particular parable, which makes me even more intrigued by it. It is a story of a business owner who employs a steward or representative to do business on his behalf. The steward was not good with the management of the owner's money, and soon he was approached and asked about it. The business owner mercifully gives the steward a chance to fix the problem—which he does in a really unconventional way. Thinking to himself that he might be fired, he goes to each of the people who owed his master money and gives them an incredible deal to settle their debts. They all agree, thinking the steward and his master are amazingly good and kind. The man was probably thinking he could get work with some of these others he was now in good graces with.

When he returns to the business owner, who has discovered what the steward has done, the business owner commends him for his efforts. "Well done! How clever of you!"

It is such a strange conclusion. At first it seems like he is honored for his dishonesty. But perhaps he is honored for his wisdom and effort. For thinking outside of the box and giving it his all. Now, if he would just do this in a more responsible way, it would be a win-win.

Sometimes when I read this parable, I wonder if perhaps He was teaching His disciples to act similarly. Just like the steward was good in his line of work, the disciples should seek to be good in theirs as well—the work of salvation. Be clever. Put forth effort. Think outside the box. —DB

Reflect and Respond

What are some ways you could put a newly invigorated or different kind of effort into the work God is having you do right now?

Your favorite
scripture in
Luke 16

LUKE 17:16

Giving him thanks.

I keep a small print of a painting of the ten lepers in my scriptures in Luke 17. The picture portrays the healed lepers, running with pure exuberance at their good fortune. Inexpressible joy is written on their faces as, in unbridled celebration, they rush to be declared clean by the priests and to show family and friends the miracle that has changed their lives.

In the painting, one man, a Samaritan, stands at the back of the group. The scriptures tell us that rather than running off, this man turned back "and fell down on his face at [Jesus's] feet, giving him thanks" (Luke 17:16).

He is clearly in awe of what has occurred, obviously reflecting on the fact that he has miraculously been made whole. He looks back to where the Savior must be standing.

The Savior must have watched them turn to go: "He may have followed them with His eyes, as, but a few steps on their road of faith, health overtook them. But the grateful Samaritan with voice of loud thanksgiving, hastened back to his healer . . . and in humblest reverence fell on his face at the feet of Him to Whom he gave thanks. This Samaritan had received more than new bodily life and health: he had found spiritual healing. It was one thing to apply to Jesus for healing, but it was far different to turn back and to fall down at His feet in lowly worship and thanksgiving.

"That made a man a disciple" (Alfred Edersheim, *The Life and Times of Jesus the Messiah*, Vol. II, 329–30).

The leper who returned reminds me of the importance gratitude plays in both worship and discipleship. —EBF

Reflect and Respond
What part does gratitude play in the making of a disciple?

Your favorite scripture in
Luke 17

LUKE 18:16

For of such is the kingdom of God.

My boy, Jack, and I went to Malawi on a humanitarian service and building trip one summer. While we were there, we followed our pastor friend, weaving through the streets of a little village until he led us to a small wooden door. Behind that door was the orphanage he ran—with forty-one little orphans squeezing out a place on the floor. We spent some time with them singing and dancing. First, a song from America: "Twinkle, Twinkle, Little Star." Then they would take a turn teaching us one from Malawi. We went back and forth, losing track of time, and nearly missing our flight because of it.

I loved everything about that time in the orphanage, but there was one particular moment I won't forget. There was a little one with hands stretched up, not quite tall enough to be seen above the top of the little sea of beautiful black hair. She was buried and seemingly forgotten. But one of the girls on our trip, Em J, saw her, and walked over to scoop her up, and secure her on her hip. Immediately, and almost instinctively, the little girl leaned into Em J and nestled her head right into her chest. She had been crying, but now her tears had stopped.

Later that night, my friend Jordan said something about the moment. She had seen it too. She said, "When I saw that orphan lean into Em J, I actually saw me. Or at least what I want to be me, with Jesus. Forgotten in the crowd. Reaching for help. And then being scooped up secure in His arms. To stop worrying so much and just settle in. To lean in and be loved."

For such is the kingdom of God. —DB

Reflect and Respond
What does it look like to you to lean in and be loved by Jesus?

Your favorite scripture in
Luke 18

LUKE 19:3

He sought to see Jesus who he was.

Here is what we know about Zacchaeus—nobody liked him, he was short, he was rich. Those are the details we are given when we begin the story of the man who climbed a tree in Jericho. It seems like such an odd thing for a wealthy man to do; grown men don't usually climb trees.

But this one did.

Somehow all of Jericho knew Jesus was coming, because it sounds like everyone came out to see. Everyone including Zacchaeus, who wanted to see who Jesus was, but couldn't because there were too many people, and he was too short. In a moment of spontaneity, Zacchaeus ran ahead of where Jesus was walking and climbed a sycamore tree to see Him.

Two thoughts cause me to pause here in the story. First, what is the press in my life that prevents me from seeing the Lord? Second, to what lengths am I willing to go to see Jesus? One significant lesson that I learn from these thoughts is that *a desired outcome* combined with *an action of faith* often leads to a miracle. Either of those by itself might not lead to the result we are hoping for, but together they are powerful. It was desire and an action of faith that caused Zacchaeus to climb the tree. That is where Jesus found him.

"When Jesus came to the place, he looked up, and saw him" (Luke 18:5). I can't help but wonder what made Him look up. He told Zacchaeus to come down; Jesus wanted to visit his house. The man nobody liked. I love that Jesus called him by name.

This story teaches the power of choice, desire, and the action of faith. It reminds us how those three things can lead to a relationship with Him. —EBF

Reflect and Respond

What is your current desire? What is your action of faith? Where is your sycamore tree?

Your favorite scripture in Luke 19

LUKE 20:24

Whose image and superscription hath it?

Jesus spent much of the last days of His ministry teaching in the temple courts. A lot of the recorded teaching came when people approached Him with questions. Some of them were sincere, but most of the ones written down were not. One of those insincere questions came from a pair of spies who were sent to trap Jesus in His words. They asked Him about the tribute tax. This was a tricky question because many Jews struggled with the idea of paying homage to Caesar—considering it a form of idol worship. Would Jesus endorse that kind of thing? On the other hand, if Jesus opposed the Roman law, He would be guilty of treason or rebellion.

His answer was both clever and instructive. He asked them to get out one of the Roman coins and to see whose image was on it. When they answered back that it was Caesar, He told them to "render therefore unto Caesar the things which be Caesar's, and unto God the things which be God's" (Luke 20:25).

I love that Jesus had the people look at the image on the coin to decide who it belonged to. The word *image* takes us back to the beginning chapters of Genesis, where we learn that Adam and Eve were called and commissioned to be image bearers of God. They were created in His image. Not only would they and their posterity be claimed and recognized as His, but they would also promise and strive to live out their lives as He would.

When people saw them, they would think of Him.

Whose image and name do you bear? —DB

Reflect and Respond

Who are some people you know that remind you of the goodness of God?

Your favorite scripture in
Luke 20

LUKE 21:28

And when these things begin . . . look up, and lift up your heads;
for your redemption draweth nigh.

I might be in the minority, but I am one of those who cannot wait for the Second Coming. It feels like Christmas to me. It makes me so excited to think about it. I think I wish on every birthday candle for it to come quickly. I have heard others express the exact opposite. They are worried or scared or intimidated by it. Perhaps some of that comes from the chapters of scripture that some of us refer to as the signs of the times.

Some of the signs of the times, or the signs that the Second Coming is near, are not very pleasant. We read about pestilence and war and rumors of war. There are signs of nation rising against nation, earthquakes in diverse places, and the love of many waxing cold. I can see why someone might be overwhelmed by things like this.

But Jesus's advice to His disciples is the opposite of overwhelmed. He told them that when you see these things, "see that ye be not troubled" (Matthew 24:6). Later in that same conversation with His disciples, Jesus gave them a parable about these signs. He compared them to the leaves on a fig tree. When you see leaves starting to bud on a fig tree, you know that summer is near. So, when you see these signs, you know that His coming is near also.

It is a good thing. Just like summer is. Jesus seems to be teaching that when you see these signs—even the unpleasant ones—let it be a reminder that He, Himself, is on the way. Let those signs spark hope and anticipation in you. These signs might be interpreted that everything is out of control, but it isn't. Jesus is coming.

And He is coming to make everything right. —DB

Reflect and Respond

What is something you are looking forward to about the
Second Coming?

Your favorite
scripture in
Luke 21

LUKE 22:45

And when he rose up from prayer,
... he found them sleeping.

Throughout a majority if not all of the Gospel accounts, we see Jesus very composed. He always seems to be in control of the situation He is in, no matter what is happening. The day they dragged the adulterous woman into the temple courts in what must have been a commotion, Jesus calmly wrote into the sand. When there was an uproar in the synagogue in Nazareth, Jesus just silently slipped through the crowd. Every trick question and insult thrown at Him was replied to calmly and cleverly. He seems to always be composed—except for turning over the tables in the temple and there in the Garden of Gethsemane.

It breaks my heart to read of Him collapsing to the ground. I am pained to read His desperate appeal to the Father. A prayer that sounds like pleading. The agony and great drops of blood from His pores are just crushing to consider. I thank God for the angel that came to strengthen Him in some of His hardest hours.

As Jesus was writhing in pain and agony and trouble of spirit, just a stone's throw away were three of His closest disciples, sleeping. I used to be angry with them. How could they sleep at a time like this! Your friend and your Master is in desperate need and you are having a nap!? And then one day, I saw the scene differently. I saw it as a picture of the gospel. Jesus in agony, and the disciples in peace.

Because of what He suffered, each of us can find that same peace.

We can sleep calmly at night because of the agony He endured.

It is a picture of the gospel. —DB

Reflect and Respond

What peace and reassurance have come into your life because of what Jesus endured for you?

Your favorite
scripture in
Luke 22

LUKE 23:42

Remember me.

My good friend and I used to study scripture together almost every day before she died. We always had a topic of study of some sort or another. In the year before she died, we tried to find every example in scripture of Jesus meeting someone where they were, as they were, and lifting them from there.

We talked about the woman at her well and Peter in the water. We studied the lame man at his pool, the blind man with his parents, and the daughter of Jairus in her bedroom. There was the shamed woman in the temple courtyard, the leper in his colony, and the man in the Gadarenes. We kept track of all the stories we could think of. We reminded each other how this was the pattern of Jesus, the message of His life. *He meets us where we are.*

The week before Easter I found one more. I remember how the discovery felt so tender. I told my friend, Kris, this would be her favorite so far. She wondered if there could be a favorite. "Remember the criminal?" I ask her, "Jesus met him on his cross." I will never forget her gasp or the conversation that followed. We talked about how, in the very last moments of His mortality, in the midst of His own excruciating pain, Jesus was still living out His mission of meeting people where they were, as they were.

Even on the cross.

I love the criminal's plea in that moment, "Remember me when thou comest into thy kingdom," and the answer Jesus immediately gave, "To day shalt thou be with me in paradise" (Luke 23:42–43).

Even in the very end, His was a mission of lifting. —EBF

Reflect and Respond

What is your favorite story of Jesus meeting someone where they are?

Your favorite scripture in
Luke 23

LUKE 24:32

Did not our heart burn within us . . . ?

There come times in all of our lives when things get turned upside down. We all experience disappointment and unexpected turns of events. One of the most difficult parts of walking through these kinds of thorny paths is feeling like you are walking it alone.

That is likely how many of the disciples felt in the days after the Crucifixion. Things were going great and then all of a sudden, He was taken and killed, and it was over. And then, the tomb was empty, and the confusion became foggier. What next?

During these days, two of the disciples were walking along the road to a town called Emmaus. As they were walking and talking, Jesus came and began to walk with them. They spoke with Him and recounted the events of their last several days. He spoke back to them of the prophecies in the scriptures. When they got to the town, they invited Him to stay. He did, and while there He broke bread and blessed it. All at once, the disciples knew it was Him, and then He was gone.

As they looked back over the hours they had spent together, one of them recalled, "Did not our heart burn" while He was with us (Luke 24:32)? Perhaps initially they felt alone, forgotten, and abandoned by Him, but as they looked back, they realized that He was there all along. Sometimes in the moment of tragedy it is hard to recognize His presence, and like the disciples on the road to Emmaus, we may need to look back and remember. And perhaps in doing so, we also will realize He was there walking alongside all along. —DB

Reflect and Respond
When you look back, what times do you see when He was there?

Your favorite scripture in
Luke 24

JOHN 1:39

Come and see.

John 1 captures what seems to be the first time many of the well-known disciples first met Jesus. It is fun to watch it unfold. It starts with John the Baptist introducing two of his friends to Jesus. "Behold the Lamb of God!" (John 1:36). They began to follow Him, and Jesus asked them what they were looking for. They replied that they wanted to know where He lived and perhaps what His story was, and why John was so thrilled about Him. His response was simple: "Come and see" (John 1:39). And so they did. And they stayed all day.

Soon after, one of them went and found his brother, Simon Peter, and told him they had found the Messiah. Shortly after Peter, Philip came. After Philip, Nathanael. Each person who met Jesus next went and found someone else. When Philip first told Nathanael about Jesus, Nathanael was skeptical. Jesus was from Nazareth, a small and insignificant town in the area. How could the Messiah come from a place like Nazareth? But Philip was wise, and he simply replied, "Come and see" (John 1:46). Just come and see for yourself.

And so, he did—and like everyone else who came and saw, he stayed all day. Each of the disciples were changed by their encounter with Jesus. Their lives would alter dramatically and they would experience miracles and wonders because of it. But each of their journeys started the same. They heard about the possibility, and then were invited: "Come and see" (John 1:39). —DB

Reflect and Respond
What might you experience if you "come and see" Jesus for yourself?

Your favorite scripture in
John 1

JOHN 2:4, JST

What wilt thou have me to do for thee?

At first pass, it might feel like a simple miracle. A whispered plea from a mother to a son. Waterpots in backrooms. Servants the only witnesses. Yet it was significant enough that this small miracle turned disciples into believers. Why?

It started with a plea for what they didn't have, wine, a necessity at every wedding feast. Joseph Smith translates the Savior's response, "What wilt thou have me to do for thee?" (John 2:4, footnote *a*). The understanding of the text makes me wonder how many times He has asked me the same thing, *what would you have me do for you?* I find it noteworthy that He used what was already in the home for the miracle. Six waterpots. Water. A ladle to draw with. It was just a few moments, a few people, a few pots in the back workroom. What came from those few moments was the finest of wine.

Some scholars suggest that the waterpots were possibly used for purification, the cleaning of feet when one would enter the house. I love this idea. That which seemed an afterthought, an ordinary necessity, average and overlooked, became the means for the very finest wine of the evening. It was the beginning of miracles, the very first one. From this first miracle we learn several important truths—Christ can change whatever He touches. He can turn what is often overlooked into something exquisite. He often saves the best for last.

I think of my own life. I wonder, what do I need Him to do for me right now? And what do I have that He can work with? It might feel ordinary; I might feel average and overlooked. But it seems that this is where He does His best work. The beginning of miracles in a life. Creating something exquisite. His finest. —EBF

Reflect and Respond

What would you have Him do for you right now?

Your favorite scripture in
John 2

JOHN 3:16

For God so loved the world.

Nicodemus was one of the Pharisees—a ruler of the Jews. It did not take long for him and other members of the ruling classes to take notice of what Jesus was doing. It was different than what they were used to and unexpected. Many of the Pharisees began to feel threatened by His message and His miracles. Perhaps this is why Nicodemus came to see Jesus under the cover of night. Perhaps He saw and sensed something good about Him and wanted to learn more without his fellow Pharisees discovering his interest. Nicodemus knew that God was with Jesus of Nazareth, but there were some things he still could not figure out.

Together they talked of scripture. Nicodemus asked his questions, and Jesus replied with answers. Jesus read his heart and knew of his wondering. He taught Nicodemus about entering the kingdom of heaven and the workings of the Holy Spirit. You can almost sense a spiritual tug-of-war happening in Nicodemus's heart. So much intrigue. And so many questions. But what about tradition and culture and what he had always believed?

In their conversation, Jesus said to Nicodemus one truth that was perhaps brighter than the rest. "For God so loved the world, that he gave his only begotten Son, that whosoever believeth in him should not perish, but have everlasting life" (John 3:16). Nicodemus would perhaps leave with more questions than he came with, but he would also leave certain about one thing. God loved the world. And God loved Nicodemus. It's why He sent His Son. And anyone—including him—could believe and have everlasting life. —DB

Reflect and Respond

How does it make you feel to know that God sent His Son because of His love for you?

Your favorite scripture in
John 3

JOHN 4:4

And he must needs go through Samaria.

I imagine that the day was warm and the sun was at its peak. As Jesus sat by the well, a woman from Samaria approached, and He asked her for a drink. She immediately wondered if this man had misunderstood who she was. How many of us experience feelings such as hers? Sometimes when we consider having a relationship with the Savior, we may feel we are inadequate; we might wonder if the Savior recognizes us for who we really are. But herein lies an important lesson—Jesus considered this moment with the Samaritan woman of utmost importance because she was of great worth in His eyes. Before He began teaching her, He made her feel valuable. As they talked, Jesus revealed His insight into her life and the problems that she dealt with day to day, and she soon realized that He did in fact know who she was. He gently prodded until she finally allowed room for Him in her heart. Then, what began as an ordinary task suddenly became life-changing.

The same can be true in our own lives. He knows us. Just as He knew every detail of this woman's life, He knows every detail of ours. And just as He taught her with the simple analogies that were a part of her daily work, He will teach us in ways that we can understand. "She had come—like so many of us, who find the pearl in the field which we occupy in the business of everyday life—on humble, ordinary duty and work" (Alfred Edersheim, *The Life and Times of Jesus the Messiah*, Vol. I, 408). And it was here that she was taught.

Likewise, some of our greatest learning moments may come as we go about our ordinary daily tasks. We must learn to watch for these moments, for these "pearls in the field" of our everyday lives. It is often in the ordinary that His greatest lessons are taught. —EBF

Reflect and Respond

Where have you experienced one of His lessons in the ordinary moments of your life?

Your favorite scripture in John 4

JOHN 5:6

And knew that he had been now
a long time in that case.

I love the scripture stories that use words like "straightway" or "immediately." Patience is not my gift. It seems I have a lot to learn about a hidden lesson taught at the five porches of Bethesda.

Perhaps you remember the story of the man who lay by the pool of Bethesda waiting for the waters to stir until the one day when Jesus came and told him to take up his bed and walk, "and immediately the man was made whole" (John 5:9). Maybe what you remember about the story is just that, how he was immediately made whole.

But there is another lesson here.

This certain man had been afflicted with this infirmity for thirty-eight years. That's half a lifetime for most people. He spent his days surrounded by a multitude of impotent folk *waiting* for the water to be stirred. That's thirty-eight years of waiting. Every single day. Scriptures tell us, "When Jesus saw him lie, and knew that he had been now a long time in that case, he saith unto him, Wilt thou be made whole?" (John 5:6).

Jesus knew.

It had been a long time, and He still let him wait. All those years.

I have often wondered if there is a doctrine of waiting. Lessons that can only be learned through patience. Important growth that takes place over time. You might find it interesting to note that *Bethesda* can be translated from Greek as "the house of kindness." *Kindness* and *waiting* are not two words I would put in the same sentence in this situation, and yet this story does. Perhaps He is trying to stretch our understanding. Maybe wholeness takes time. —EBF

Reflect and Respond

What have you learned in the waiting?

Your favorite
scripture in
John 5

JOHN 6:9

But what are they among so many?

There was a day in Jesus's ministry when a crowd had gathered to hear Him teach, but they did not have anything to eat. Jesus turned to His disciples and asked if they had any food to give them. Andrew said that all they had were five barley loaves and two fishes, "but what are they among so many?" (John 6:9). It was all they had, but it wasn't enough. There were more than 5,000 people there.

Still, Jesus asked for the five loaves and two fishes. He blessed them and gave them to His disciples to then give to the crowds. When everyone was filled, the disciples gathered all the leftover fragments and the leftovers alone filled twelve baskets.

Sometimes we look at who we are and what we have to offer, and it isn't much. Five loaves' and two fishes' amount. We wonder—what am I among so many?

But Jesus still calls for what we have.

He blesses it, multiplies it, and leaves us astonished.

Then, He gives us the leftovers. —DB

Reflect and Respond

What five loaves and two fishes do you have to put into the Lord's hands?

Your favorite scripture in
John 6

JOHN 7:29

I am from him, and he hath sent me.

I have been a teacher of scripture for many years, and one of the most common questions people have when reading scripture is who is speaking—particularly when it says "Lord" or "God." They want to know if it is the Father or the Son. This is not a surprising question. It is difficult to know, especially since They share some of the same titles. Even Jesus's disciples wondered similar questions. It was Philip who asked Jesus to "shew us the Father" (John 14:8). To Philip, and repeatedly to others throughout His ministry, Jesus taught clearly that it was the Father who sent Him, and everything He was doing was a reflection of who the Father was.

Elder Jeffrey R. Holland once taught, "It is the grand truth that in all that Jesus came to say and do, including and especially in His atoning suffering and sacrifice, He was showing us who and what God our Eternal Father is like, how completely devoted He is to His children in every age and nation. In word and in deed Jesus was trying to reveal and make personal to us the true nature of His Father, our Father in Heaven" ("The Grandeur of God," *Ensign*, November 2003).

Jesus was teaching the Father's will and truth. Jesus was showing us who the Father was and what His heart is like. Like Jesus said to Philip, "He that hath seen me hath seen the Father" (John 14:9). He was from Him, and He came and lived and died because the Father sent Him to.

We might be confused about who is actually speaking or who the scriptures are speaking about while we read, but because of the life, ministry, and sacrifice of Jesus, we never have to be confused about either of Their devotion, love, and unyielding loyalty to us. —DB

Reflect and Respond
List some of the attributes that you know about both the Son and the Father.

Your favorite scripture in
John 7

JOHN 8:8

Again he stooped down.

When I go speak at the prison, I always take a story out of the scriptures with me. There is nothing I have to share that is more important than Him. It was true on the day I showed up to speak in the women's section of the Pocatello prison.

I took the story of the woman in John 8 who did not want to be where she was. Often when I tell this story I ask people to close their eyes. There is an important lesson that plays out if you watch what Jesus does instead of just listening to what He teaches. You will remember the woman caught in adultery. The one who had been set in the midst of the crowd of men. The woman who surely did not want to be in that place at that time.

The lesson I love most is found in phrases like this:

"Jesus stooped down." . . . "He lifted up himself."

"Again he stooped down." . . . "When Jesus had lifted up himself" (see John 8:6–10).

Why so much moving from down to up? Stooping and lifting? Is there a lesson here? I think so. So did the woman in the prison that afternoon. After reading the verses, I had the women open their eyes again and I asked them what they had learned. A woman sitting right in the middle of the group raised her hand, her eyes glistening with the hint of unshed tears. "He met her on her level," she said quietly. "He stooped to where she was. That is where the lifting began."

It is a beautiful lesson for all of us, no matter where we are.

He will meet us where we are. —EBF

Reflect and Respond
When has this been true in your life?

Your favorite
scripture in
John 8

JOHN 9:25

One thing I know, that, whereas I was blind, now I see.

One thing the enemies and opponents of Jesus could not explain away were His miracles. But they sure tried. Usually, they claimed He was doing His miracles by the power of the devil. But why would the devil give power to someone to undo some of the work he, himself, had caused? It just wouldn't make sense. But the opposing side was relentless. If Jesus was indeed performing miracles by the power of God, then He must be from God. And if He were from God, then they would have to follow Him and change their ways. This is why the miracles were so threatening to them.

On one particular occasion, Jesus healed a man who had been blind from his birth. He was well known, and many of the people of the city knew that he had been blind. Imagine their surprise when they saw him walking around, seeing! The Pharisees had a fit. They could not accept it. They stirred the crowds with their reheated arguments. They brought the man's parents in to interrogate and threaten them. But when they asked their questions, the parents replied, "He is of age; ask him" (John 9:21). The Pharisees went and found the man who was once blind and continued the interrogation. When they railed on the character of Jesus, the man simply replied, in essence, "*You are missing the point. I don't know if He is a sinner or a prophet or whatever else you may think. What I know is that I was blind, and now I see. And it was He who made it happen*" (see John 9:25). Sometimes we don't know the details, but we experience the outcomes—and that's all that matters.

He is all that matters. —DB

Reflect and Respond

Even though you don't know everything about Jesus, what is one thing you have seen Him change in your life?

Your favorite scripture in
John 9

JOHN 10:11

I am the good shepherd.

To fully understand the parable of the good shepherd, it is important for us to understand sheepherders of that time. "In the East the flocks are at night driven into a large fold, and charge of them is given to an under-shepherd . . . when the shepherd comes in the morning, 'the doorkeeper' or 'guardian' opens to him. Having thus gained access to His flock . . . the Shepherd knows and calls them, each by his name, and leads them out. Then the Eastern shepherd places himself at the head of his flock, and goes before them, guiding them, making sure of their following simply by his voice, which they know" (Alfred Edersheim, *The Life and Times of Jesus the Messiah*, Vol. II, 189–90). Christ said of Himself, "I am the good shepherd: the good shepherd giveth his life for the sheep" (John 10:11). As the Good Shepherd, He has promised to lead us, protect us, heal us, defend us, and comfort us.

If you are weary or footsore, lost in solitude, or climbing among stony places, remember this: there is One who has set aside everything to seek for us. "Is this not the very work of the 'Good Shepherd,' and may we not, each of us, thus draw from it precious comfort? It is not [difficult to imagine] how in folly and ignorance the sheep strayed further and further, and at last was lost in solitude and among stony places; how the shepherd followed and found it, weary and footsore; and then with tender care lifted it on His shoulder, and carried it home" (Edersheim, 256).

He is the Good Shepherd. He will find us, carry us, keep us in His tender care. —EBF

Reflect and Respond
How has Christ been a shepherd for you?

Your favorite
scripture in
John 10

JOHN 11:22

I know.

When we talk about Mary and Martha, we often refer to a story that took place in their home one evening around dinnertime. Because there are only a few details to work with in that story, we sometimes assign Mary as more believing than Martha. John chapter 11 gives us a little bit of insight into Martha's faith.

It had been four days since Lazarus died. Many people had come to comfort Martha and Mary. Then someone said Jesus was coming. "Then Martha, as soon as she heard that Jesus was coming, went and met him: but Mary sat still in the house" (John 11:20). In this story, it is Martha who leads with faith. It is important to remember that. On this day, Martha chose the good part and Mary would follow.

When the Savior finally comes, we catch a glimpse of Martha's faith.

"I know, that even now, whatsoever thou wilt ask of God, God will give it thee" (John 11:22).

"I know that he shall rise again in the resurrection at the last day" (John 11:24).

"I believe that thou art the Christ, the Son of God" (John 11:27).

It is Martha who leads with faith. In a time of great distress and sadness, she turned to faith in Christ and in the principles she had been taught. She clung to what she knew. It was that belief that would allow her to witness the glory of God, the miracle (see John 11:40).

Perhaps the same is true in our own life. Consider your own story right now. How might you cling to what you know? How might you lead with faith? —EBF

Reflect and Respond
What do you believe? What do you know?

Your favorite scripture in
John 11

JOHN 12:21

Sir, we would see Jesus.

The final week of Christ's life began with a triumphal entry into Jerusalem. Just before that happened, there was a certain group of Greeks that came up to worship in Jerusalem. They came to Philip and said, "Sir, we would see Jesus" (John 12:21). Somehow they had heard of this man, they were drawn to Him, and now they wanted to know more.

They weren't the only ones. Just after His triumphal entry into Jerusalem, "all the city was moved, saying, Who is this?" (Matthew 21:10). Again, they were drawn to Him, wanting to know more. "And the multitude said, This is Jesus" (Matthew 21:11).

We might read these accounts and wonder why His ministry had to come to a close when it seemed like things were just picking up. People wanted to see Jesus, they wondered who He was. They were drawn to Him.

But the Father had a greater plan in mind.

Just a few verses later, in that same chapter, Jesus explains, "And I, if I be lifted up from the earth, will draw all men unto me" (John 12:32). All men. Not just the ones from Greece, not only those found in the crowd in Jerusalem. All men. From every generation of time. Across the entire world. God's plans were bigger.

Today those two questions are still being asked. Those who want to see Jesus, those who wonder who He is.

The ministry of a disciple is to respond—this is Jesus.

Let me teach you what I know of Him.

Hopefully through our actions and our testimony they will be drawn to Him. —EBF

....

Reflect and Respond
Who is Jesus to you? Why are you drawn to Him?

Your favorite
scripture in
John 12

JOHN 13:6

Lord, dost thou wash my feet?

Have you ever noticed that in the last hours of Jesus's life He still did what He had spent His life doing? He served. Maybe what got Him through His hardest hours at the end was turning outward toward others. He forgave the centurions, He lifted the man next to Him on the cross, and He left His disciples with an act of love that they would always remember.

It was after supper, when Jesus set aside His garment and took a towel, then He poured water into a basin and began to wash the feet of His disciples. When He got to Peter, the disciple asked, "Lord, dost thou wash my feet?" (John 13:6). Peter was worried about the Savior stooping to serve him, about letting Him wash away the filth, of allowing Him to enter his mess. Perhaps there are moments we all feel this way. But Jesus responded that if Peter was not washed, he would have no part with Him. Immediately we see the exuberance of Peter, because next he asked Jesus to wash his feet, his hands, and his head. He didn't just want a little part; he wanted everything. Jesus responded, "He that is washed . . . is clean every whit" (John 13:10).

This story hints toward the importance of ordinances, but it also causes me to ask one question every time I read it: *what does it mean to have a part with Jesus?* There are so many ways we might answer that, but a hint is given in verse 14. "If I then, your Lord and Master, have washed your feet; ye also ought to wash one another's feet. For I have given you an example, that ye should do as I have done to you" (John 13:14–15). If His part is to serve, our part must be to do the same. To become the servant. It is how we walk after Him. —EBF

Reflect and Respond
How might you turn outward today?

Your favorite scripture in
John 13

JOHN 14:27

Peace I leave with you, my peace I give unto you.

I had a conversation with a woman once whose life was in total disarray. It was almost exhausting to listen to her tell her story. I felt like I was living it. Everything that you could imagine going wrong went wrong, was going wrong, and, if the pattern continued, would probably go wrong in the future. I felt helpless. There honestly seemed like nothing I could do except listen. But I yearned to do something more!

Once it seemed like we got to the end of the trouble, I asked her what seemed to me a silly question. It was all I could think to ask. "Well, how are you feeling in all of this?"

Her answer was one I don't want to forget. She said, "I have peace." Immediately I wondered how that could be. I could see no evidence of peace in her life. Financially, socially, and mentally it seemed like there was nothing happening that I would call peace. The problems were still ongoing. There wasn't a solution that anyone could see. Her relationships and pending future were anything but settled. And yet, she said she had peace.

Then I remembered the words Jesus spoke to His disciples just hours before their world turned upside down. "Peace I leave with you, my peace I give unto you." *My* peace. "Not as the world giveth, give I unto you" (John 14:27). The world might give the kind of peace that solves everything. The kind that takes away any of the problems that we are facing. But He gives a different kind. One that seems to come from the inside out. An inner contentment and strength to face whatever it is we might be facing. Perhaps that is the promised peace she was experiencing. —DB

Reflect and Respond
When have you experienced this same kind of inner peace?

Your favorite scripture in **John 14**

JOHN 15:25

They hated me without a cause.

One of the last discourses Jesus gave was on love and hate. In those last conversations, He pointed out what might lead someone to either greater love or hate. This is how He described those who were against Him and His disciples.

1. "They know not him that sent me" (John 15:21).
2. "They hated me without a cause" (v. 25).
3. "He that hateth me hateth my Father also" (v. 23).

On the other hand, Jesus taught the principle of love.

1. "Greater love hath no man than this, that a man lay down his life for his friends" (v. 13)
2. "Ye are my friends, if ye do whatsoever I command you" (v. 14).
3. "Love one another, as I have loved you" (v. 12).

It must have been frustrating for someone who loved so well—who healed infirmities, who lifted hearts, who forgave sin—to be hated. He was in the business of love. It was the work of His life. And yet, His life would end because of hate.

Even now we live in a world where people choose to love or hate the Lord.

Let me be found on the side of love. Let me know Him. Let me love His Father. Let me serve the way He did. Let me follow His commandment.

Let me love the way He loved. —EBF

Reflect and Respond

What is one way you could love like Christ today?

Your favorite scripture in John 15

JOHN 16:7

It is expedient for you that I go away.

Perhaps Jesus knew what He was about to tell His Apostles in the upper room would be tough to believe, because He started with the phrase, "Nevertheless I tell you the truth" (John 16:7). When I read that I think, *Well of course you are going to tell the truth. When have you lied?* I am not sure if that is what He meant, but it seems to me as if He were warning them that what He was about to say might be a little unbelievable, so He promised first it was true. A kind of, "You are going to have to trust me" type of line.

On the very day before Jesus left His disciples, He said to them, "It is expedient for you that I go away" (John 16:7). It is needful for me to leave. Important. Good for you. "For if I go not away, the Comforter will not come unto you; but if I depart, I will send him unto you" (John 16:7). I don't know about you, but if I got the choice to have Jesus by my side or the Comforter in my heart, I would think to pick Jesus by my side ten out of ten times. But Jesus saw it differently. He not only thought it was a good idea but even said it was expedient for Him to do. I am not sure why Jesus had to leave in order for the Comforter to come, but it seems as if the experience of living with the Holy Spirit in their hearts would be so valuable, Jesus would even be willing to leave them in order for them to have it.

That is hard to believe. But this would not be the first time I will or would need to trust that Jesus knows what is best, what is expedient for me. —DB

Reflect and Respond

Why do you think living with the Comforter in your heart would be more needful than Jesus by your side?

Your favorite scripture in John 16

JOHN 17:3

That they might know thee.

I remember memorizing Moses 1:39 in seminary: "For behold, this is my work and my glory—to bring to pass the immortality and eternal life of man." I also remember my first thought when I began memorizing that scripture. *Eternal life feels so far away. Why would the Father's work be about something that seems so out of reach?*

Then I stumbled on this verse in John 17: "And this is life eternal, that they might know thee the only true God, and Jesus Christ, whom thou hast sent" (John 17:3). Was that true? Could eternal life have something to do with coming to know Heavenly Father and Jesus Christ? If it were true, then could I experience the blessing of His work now, today, and every day that my pursuit was to know the Father and the Son a little better? I decided to try it out.

That new understanding became the work of my life. At sixteen years old, I determined to spend a little time every day coming to know the only true God and Jesus Christ. It is still my focus today.

Consider this . . . if His work is to bring to pass us knowing Him better, then we should see signs of that everywhere. And if our work is also trying to know Him better, then He should see signs of that everywhere as well.

It is the building up of a relationship.

I can't think of a greater work. —EBF

Reflect and Respond

What are some things you do to help you know the Father and the Son a little better?

Your favorite scripture in
John 17

JOHN 18:35

What hast thou done?

On the night before Jesus was crucified, He was led into the hall of judgment. This is where He had a conversation with Pilate. "Art thou the King of the Jews?" (John 18:33). Jesus asked if Pilate was asking for himself or if someone else had told him that was true. Pilate responded by reminding Jesus that he was not a Jew, but the accusation was from the chief priests. Then he asked Jesus a question that haunts me every time I read it. "What hast thou done?" (v. 35).

Sometimes people talk about their life flashing before their eyes in moments like this. I wonder if that might have happened for Jesus. Looking back over the past three years, what had He done? The changing of water to wine, the healing of the nobleman's son, casting out unclean spirits, healing of lepers. He had taught a higher law, healed a centurion's servant, brought to life a widow's son, and raised a twelve-year-old daughter from her deathbed. He gave sight to the blind, lame men walked, thousands were fed. He encouraged Peter to walk on water, sent missionaries out to share the good news, raised Lazarus from the dead. He left every place He went better than He found it. He was the peacegiver, bestower of grace, author of forgiveness. His was a life of compassion and tenderness.

"To this end was I born, and for this cause came I into the world" (John 18:37). Pilate found in Him no fault at all.

Even still, the Jews wanted Him gone. "Away with him, crucify him" (John 19:15). Why? What has He done? —EBF

Reflect and Respond

What is your favorite story from the ministry of Jesus Christ?

Your favorite scripture in
John 18

JOHN 19:30

It is finished.

According to my count and others, there are seven statements that are recorded from Jesus on the cross. Each one of them could be a sermon on its own. Each one of them reveals something about the heart and character of Jesus.

Consider what we learn when Jesus promised paradise to a pair of thieves. Who could turn a crucifixion hill into a promise of paradise? Only He. Or what about when He called for forgiveness to the very soldiers who were nailing His hands and wrists to the cross. What mercy! Or what about the tender feelings He had for His mother? How He put her into the care of another? Who would think of someone else's feelings when they were suffering so intensely? Jesus. Of all the statements made from the cross, my favorite is His last. His final statement before giving up the ghost. From the cross Jesus cried out these three words: "It is finished" (John 19:30).

That scene on Calvary must be one of the ugliest and most heartbreaking moments this world has ever known. It was dark and dreadful. Yet, so many people view that moment and the symbol of the cross as something of victory. Only Jesus could take something so ugly and turn it into something beautiful. It was the greatest manifestation of love the world has ever known. When we look to Jesus on the cross, we see what we are worth in His eyes. That He is for us. We see what He was willing to do for us. The extent He was willing to go and the price He was willing to pay to set us free. It is finished. Death is finished. Sin is finished. The devil has power and claims over you no longer. You are free. —DB

Reflect and Respond

How will you live your life knowing that Jesus set you free with such a great act of love?

Your favorite scripture in
John 19

JOHN 20:14

And knew not that it was Jesus.

Have there ever been times in your life when you have questioned where Jesus is? Perhaps you felt forgotten. Maybe abandoned by Him. Mary Magdalene had a similar experience. It was a time of great sadness. She stood at the tomb weeping. I wonder if, in her moment of greatest despair, she went to the only place she knew to find Him. But things did not get better when she arrived there; instead they grew worse. She stooped down to look into the tomb, and Jesus wasn't there. *We all have empty tombs.*

She must have felt so alone. Abandoned. The scriptures said she wept (see John 20:13). When she turned around again, Jesus was standing there, but she did not recognize Him. How often has that been true in your story? We have been promised Jesus will be in our midst, but sometimes we don't recognize Him there. What Mary knew was that Jesus had been crucified, His body placed in a tomb, and now He was missing. That was her level of understanding. But then, everything changed.

He spoke her name, and she turned herself (see John 20:16). She turned to Christ. Then her understanding increased, she learned something about Jesus that she hadn't known before. He had risen. He lived. Her testimony of who He was increased. Sometimes the same will be true for us. We will learn everything we can of Christ, and then one day a trial will come. It will stretch us. It might cause us to wonder if we have been abandoned. There may be important truths about Jesus that we have not uncovered yet. Perhaps we will weep. But there will be a moment of recognition as He lifts our belief to a higher degree. We will turn ourselves and see Him standing there. Greater understanding will come. —EBF

Reflect and Respond

Reflect on a time when your understanding of Jesus Christ increased. What did you learn?

Your favorite scripture in John 20

JOHN 21:1

After these things Jesus shewed himself again.

When I read the book of John cover to cover, it feels like John chapter 20 is the conclusion chapter. It ends with the story of Mary at the tomb, and Thomas finally seeing the Lord, and then these final words: "But these are written, that ye might believe that Jesus is the Christ . . . and that believing ye might have life through his name" (John 20:31). The end. Amen.

But then the story continues with one more chapter. And that additional chapter starts with some of my most favorite words. "Jesus shewed himself again" (John 21:1). That is something that disciples in every age of time can expect. That Jesus will show Himself again. That He will return. That He will keep coming back. He is not done with us.

On this particular day that He came back, He performed similar miracles for the disciples to those of the days when they had first met Him. Nets broke with fish and ships started to sink again. They had gone back to fishing, but it was almost as if the Lord were telling them the miracles weren't finished. There was still more to come. Peter was called to be a shepherd—something new for a fisherman.

And then the book seems to end again. "And there are also many other things which Jesus did, the which, if they should be written . . . I suppose that even the world itself could not contain the books" (John 21:25). I suppose it ends the same way it started. With a promise that there is more. Jesus will show Himself again. And those books—I think they might be the ones we will write. —DB

Reflect and Respond

If you were to record a story of Jesus in your life, which one would you write?

Your favorite scripture in John 21

ACTS 1:3

By many infallible proofs.

"Prove it!" I think that phrase filled up most of my recesses in fourth grade. Who was fastest? Smartest? Tallest? Some things could be proved. A foot race. A math problem. There was a method for sorting things out.

After Jesus died and went to heaven again, the Apostles were charged with running the Church. After the betrayal of Judas, there was a vacancy that had to be filled. They decided to choose a man who had known Jesus beginning from the baptism of John. One who had been in company with Jesus and the Twelve *all the time* (see Acts 1:21). One who would become a witness of the Resurrection.

At the very beginning of the first chapter of Acts, Luke describes a group of people who had seen Christ alive during the forty days before His ascension to heaven, how they had "many infallible proofs" that He had been there (Acts 1:3).

This is a chapter about the making of a witness. Someone who knows Jesus because they have been in company with Him. One who has received infallible proof that He is the Redeemer of the world. You and I could become a witness like that. How are you keeping company with Jesus? What does that look like in your life? As you consider your days, your weeks, your months, where are the infallible proofs that He has been present in your life?

The test for who would become His witness on that occasion had to do with the heart, because the Lord knows the hearts of men (see Acts 1:24). I hope, when my heart is laid bare, that it will witness of my belief in Him. —EBF

Reflect and Respond
What is one infallible proof of Jesus Christ in your life?

Your favorite scripture in
Acts 1

ACTS 2:37

What shall we do?

About fifty days after the Resurrection of Jesus, on the feast day called Pentecost, the disciples were all gathered together as Jesus had instructed them to do. Suddenly a sound came from heaven, and it filled the house where they all were, whipping through like a wildfire. Each of the disciples there was filled with the Holy Ghost and began to speak and prophesy—many of them in other languages. Because of the feast, there were people gathered from all around the world in Jerusalem at the time, and all of them were able to hear the gospel preached in their own language.

This was quite a sight, considering the ones who were speaking new languages were from the back country of Galilee. How could these kinds of folks be so smart? Perhaps they were drunk, some thought. But Peter stood boldly and told them what they were experiencing was a manifestation of heaven from Jesus of Nazareth, who was now the resurrected King.

As Peter preached, the same Holy Spirit that had filled the disciples began to prick the hearts of those who were listening. The wisest among those who were touched by the Spirit asked Peter the right question. "What shall we do?" (Acts 2:37). They felt something, and now they felt to do something about it. Such is the case with the ministry of the Spirit. When He testifies, fills, or pricks our hearts, there is always something to be done about it. There is something or someone He is leading us to. —DB

Reflect and Respond

What has the Holy Spirit led and prompted you to do recently?

Your favorite scripture in Acts 2

ACTS 3:8

And he leaping up stood.

When I was very little, I was a dancer. I remember the pink leotard, the huge mirror along the back wall, the leaping. In every class we practiced leaping. I can remember the music, fastening your eyes on the far side of the room, leaving the ground, the moment of flight, and the two steps in between before you were leaping again. I would watch in the mirror to see how long I could stay in the air.

It is the leaping that endears me to this story in Acts 3. The man who had been lame from birth, who was laid daily at the gate Beautiful. Up until the day that Peter came. I love how Peter fastens his eyes upon him, how he reaches out with a covenant hand, how he lifts him. Immediately the man received strength (see Acts 3:2–7). There are so many lessons in just these few verses, but my favorite part of the story is found in verse 8: "And he leaping up stood, and walked, and entered with them into the temple, walking, and leaping, and praising God." I love the leaping.

This man, who was given a most wondrous gift, responded with great enthusiasm. Not just walking, leaping. I love his heart. There will be times in our lives when someone will fasten their eyes on us, a covenant person, and they will lift us, they will make our life just a little better than it was before. I hope we will respond to their ministering with great enthusiasm. And then, after we have realized their good gift in our life, maybe we will remember the last verse of this story, "And . . . the lame man which was healed *held* Peter and John" (Acts 3:11; emphasis added). There is something to be learned by how we respond to the ministers in our own life. —EBF

Reflect and Respond
Who has ministered to you lately? How did you respond?

Your favorite scripture in
Acts 3

ACTS 4:13

They took knowledge of them, that they had been with Jesus.

Peter and the other disciples continued to amaze the people of Jerusalem and surrounding cities. I suppose that when Jesus was dead and buried, the opponents to His way thought it was all over. But it didn't stop. It moved forward through the ministry of His chosen servants.

Perhaps if you were starting a movement, you might be tempted to pick people that were educated, wealthy, or had great influence. But Jesus chose fishermen and tax collectors. The regular folks. Those kinds of people were His starting lineup. And as people heard them preach and teach, they were amazed that someone so uneducated could speak and move people in the way that they could. Perhaps that is why Jesus chose them. They were the kind of people who had no other choice except to rely on heaven's help.

I love one particular description of Peter and John from some of the Jerusalem leaders and rulers. After hearing their rich testimony, the leadership "saw the boldness of Peter and John, and perceived that they were unlearned and ignorant men," and it caused them to marvel. They couldn't believe what they were seeing and hearing. I think their next line was an observation, but I like to think of it as an explanation. "They took knowledge of them, that they had been with Jesus" (Acts 4:13). That was not just a fact of the matter; it was the very reason for what they were able to do. They were regular people—but they were with Jesus.

If people I meet are going to make an observation about me, I would hope based on what they hear and see they would make the same one—there is someone who has been with Jesus. —DB

Reflect and Respond

Who is someone you know that you would say has "been with Jesus"?

Your favorite scripture in
Acts 4

ACTS 5:2

And kept back part.

Most people don't love the story of Ananias and Sapphira. They sold a piece of land meant to be given to the Lord, but at the last minute after it was sold, they decided to keep back a part and only gave a certain amount to the Apostles. We don't have the full particulars here—the story feels extreme with the small details that we have—but we know their choice ended up costing their lives.

In the margin of my scriptures, I have this four-word phrase linked to another verse found in Acts 20, where Paul says, "Ye know, from the first day that I came . . . after what manner I have been with you at all seasons, serving the Lord with all humility of mind, and with many tears . . . and how I kept back nothing" (Acts 20:18–20). In later verses he talks about how that mindset allowed him to finish his course with joy (see v. 24).

I consider the outcome of both of these approaches to life—to keep back a part, to keep back nothing—and I realize that only one led to joy. It makes me want to reevaluate how I live my life. What would it look like to keep back nothing? In my relationships, in my work, as I approach what I am passionate about, with God. Would my life become fuller if I kept back nothing? If I lived all in?

I think it might.

I want to approach the seasons ahead with this story in mind. I want to serve all in, love all in, embrace life all in. Perhaps it will lead to many tears on some days, but Paul reminds us how it will also lead to great joy. Maybe, when we keep back a part, something within us dies. Something that might have flourished and grown if we had kept back nothing. —EBF

Reflect and Respond

Where can you be all in today?

Your favorite scripture in
Acts 5

ACTS 6:7

And the word of God increased;
and the number of the disciples multiplied.

It is fascinating that Christianity ever made it out of the first and second centuries. There was so much stacked up against them. Persecution, numbers, cultural differences, and the Roman Empire. It is a movement that, according to observation alone, should have died out like so many others had before and after it. And yet it not only endured; it increased and multiplied.

At the beginning of Acts 6, the Twelve Apostles were overwhelmed at the tasks that lay in front of them. More and more people were coming unto Christ. The ministry, the preaching, and the decisions were too many for such a small group to handle. Under the inspiration of heaven, they decided to call assistants to help carry out the work of the kingdom together with them. They asked for men of "honest report, full of the Holy Ghost and wisdom" (Acts 6:3).

This is when we first meet people whose names you may recognize, such as Stephen and Philip. They came before the Apostles and the Apostles laid hands on their heads, and off they went. And wherever they went, "the word of God increased; and the number of the disciples multiplied" (Acts 6:7).

Sometimes I look at the world, or even just my own community, and I see a lot of work to be done. There is a lot of hurting and injustice. There is a lot of tragedy and hopelessness. There is a lot of need for Jesus—the very word of God. It is encouraging to know that I can do something about it. That when I move and speak and act in His name, the word of God is increased. That's how it's always increased—through the ministry of His disciples. Thank the Lord they are multiplying. —DB

Reflect and Respond

What can you do today to increase the word of God—the power of Jesus—in your sphere of influence?

Your favorite scripture in Acts 6

ACTS 7:54

They were cut to the heart.

When Stephen stood to testify, it was to a crowd who was not willing to listen. He spoke of Moses, of a God who heard the cries of Israel and delivered them, and of the Just One, whom they had betrayed and murdered (see Acts 7:52). The scriptures say that when the people heard his words, they were cut to the heart, but Stephen was full of the Holy Ghost. There were two separate reactions to the teachings that came from the Lord. One cut, one filled.

Perhaps there will be times in our own lives when we will have the choice to respond to counsel from the Lord. Maybe that counsel will be hard for us to accept. This story reminds us that we have a choice in how we respond—it can either cut into our heart or it can fill us with the Holy Ghost. In this story those words made the crowd so mad that they stoned Stephen, God's mouthpiece. Saul witnessed the event. Saul, who would take Stephen's place, even though he did not realize it in that moment.

When I read this story, I am reminded of the power the Spirit has to change a soul. To redirect a life. That a man who stood as a witness of the stoning of a mouthpiece of God would one day give his own life as a witness of the Lord. That it is never too late for a heart to be filled up with God.

There may come a time in your life when words will cut deep. Perhaps you might remember this story. Perspective often changes if we allow the light of the Lord to penetrate our path. Open your soul to be filled with the Spirit.

Become a witness of Him. —EBF

Reflect and Respond

What is one way you could allow the Spirit to fill your soul today?

Your favorite scripture in **Acts 7**

ACTS 8:30

And Philip ran.

I once wrote a children's book that highlighted different heroes from the Bible. One of the people I included was Philip. When I was talking with my friend, the artist of the book, I asked him if he could draw Philip wearing Nikes. Even though Philip probably wore sandals (although we don't know for sure!), I wanted to show him in running shoes because of my favorite part of his story.

Philip was doing the work and ministry God had called him to do. The city he was called to initially was Samaria. He had his ups and downs there, but for the most part, "there was great joy in that city" (Acts 8:8). It seemed like a great place to be doing the Lord's work. Even an encounter with a sorcerer named Simon turned out to be faith-promoting. One day, while Philip was preaching, an angel came to him with a new assignment. "Arise, and go toward the south . . . unto Gaza, which is desert" (Acts 8:26). This may have been a little disappointing. He was having such great success in Samaria. Maybe he didn't want to go to Gaza. It was desert, after all. But immediately after the angel said, "Arise, and go," the scriptures say that Philip "arose and went" (v. 27). That was his personality. When the Lord asked, he went.

In fact, the best part of the story is that when he got there, he saw a royal chariot from Ethiopia with a servant riding in it. Probably not the type of people who would want to hear his message. But the Spirit said, "Go near," and "Philip ran" (Acts 8:29–30). I love this man. Whenever or wherever God asked him to go, he did. And often, he ran.

I want to be a runner for God. —DB

Reflect and Respond

What is a way you could be a runner for God at this season of your life?

Your favorite scripture in
Acts 8

ACTS 9:17

Brother Saul, the Lord, even Jesus . . . hath sent me.

After Paul had spent three days in darkness, waiting, Ananias showed up. I can't imagine the emotion on both sides of the door that day. On one side, Paul, who had threatened the Saints; on the other side, Ananias, one of the Saints. Paul, defenseless, must have feared the retribution that awaited him on the other side of the door. Surely Ananias feared for his life.

It was the Lord who told Ananias to go. Truthfully, it made Ananias nervous. "Lord," he said, "I have heard by many of this man, how much evil he hath done" (Acts 9:13). The Lord wasn't swayed by his worry. "Go thy way," He told Ananias, "for he is a chosen vessel unto me" (v. 15). Ananias must have questioned what the Lord meant by "chosen," but he went. It is the first word out of the mouth of Ananias that I love the most about this story. There were so many things he could have said, so many things he could have called Saul in that moment. But the word he chose to begin their conversation was *brother*. "Brother Saul, the Lord, even Jesus . . . hath sent me" (v. 17). He called him brother.

Sometimes great sermons are taught with one word.

I wonder, who has been an Ananias for you? Who has seen you at your worst, heard hard things about you, knows the things you wish no one knew about you, and loves you regardless? In a like manner, who needs you to be an Ananias for them right now? To see them as the Lord would see them, as a chosen vessel, as who they can become? How might living with a heart like Ananias change the world? —EBF

Reflect and Respond

Who is your Ananias?

Your favorite scripture in Acts 9

ACTS 10:19

While Peter thought on the vision, the Spirit said . . .
Behold, three men seek thee.

When Peter and the other disciples began their ministry, they concentrated solely on teaching the gospel of Christ to members and descendants of the house of Israel. They understood this as their assignment. However, God had the intention to send them into all the world. For He was "no respecter of persons: but in every nation he that feareth him, and worketh righteousness, is accepted with him . . . he is Lord of all" (Acts 10:34–36).

Because this was so different than what Peter was expecting or understood, the Lord came to him in a vision that was repeated three times. It was a vision that would open his mind and understanding and convince him of the Lord's intentions. At the same time Peter was having his visions, a man named Cornelius was on his way to Peter's house. He also had had a vision. A vision that told him in the ninth hour of the day to go to the city of Joppa and find Peter. Cornelius was a man of faith, but he was not a member of the house of Israel.

At the very moment Peter was contemplating on his visions, a knock came at the door. It was Cornelius. When they met, they exchanged stories of their visions and messages. It became clear to both of them what the Lord was trying to do. Cornelius was baptized in the name of Jesus and the work and ministry began to go into all the world.

I love to watch how the Lord orchestrated this whole thing. The timing, the people, and the messages all lined up exactly as they should to help bring this about. Some might call this coincidence. I call it God. —DB

Reflect and Respond

When have you seen God orchestrating something that others might call a coincidence?

Your favorite scripture in
Acts 10

ACTS 11:12

Nothing doubting.

At the top of the margin in Acts 11, I wrote "principles of revelation." There are several steps in the process of revelation that are taught here, and I often turn to these verses for help in understanding how revelation works. Here are some of my favorite lessons:

1. Pray – The scriptures teach that most often revelation begins with prayer (Acts 11:5).
2. Visions – Revelations can come through visions, dreams, angels, or the whispering of the Holy Ghost (v. 5).
3. Ponder – This is an important step in receiving revelation. Peter tells us, "I considered" (v. 6).
4. Listen for promptings – Hearing the voice of the Lord through the Spirit is a common way people receive promptings (v. 7).
5. Ask questions that could lead to further insight (v. 8).
6. Watch for repetitive promptings; be alert to what is happening around you. Sometimes the Lord will teach us through repetition (v. 10).
7. Watch for the Lord's orchestration of events (v. 11).
8. Follow promptings without doubting (v. 12).
9. Once revelation has come, remember the first promptings to see the fullness of revelation working in your life (v. 16).
10. Believe that revelation will come and come again (v. 17). —EBF

Reflect and Respond

Which of these steps are familiar to you? Which would you like to study more?

Your favorite scripture in
Acts 11

ACTS 12:11

Now I know of a surety, that the Lord hath sent his angel.

During the time when Herod the king was persecuting the Christians, he had James arrested and put in prison with an execution order. You can imagine how much prayer was offered on behalf of James. He was a beloved friend and disciple. His family and fellow believers would have prayed intently and intensely for a miraculous release. Unfortunately, he was killed with the sword.

Soon after, Herod had Peter arrested and put in prison with an execution order. Again, you can imagine how much prayer was offered on Peter's behalf. He was a beloved friend and disciple. His family and fellow believers would have prayed intently and intensely for a miraculous release. And on the night before his execution, an angel of the Lord came to Peter's cell, opened the doors, and broke off his chains and set him free.

Sometimes I wonder what James's family thought when they saw Peter set free. Did the Lord not love James as much as He loved Peter? Was Peter more faithful? Of course not. In this story we learn that no matter who you are, sometimes in life you get the sword, and sometimes you get the angel. God is a God of miracles. He can do anything, anytime, anywhere. And sometimes He does. But other times, He has reasons for withholding those miracles. Either way, one thing is certain: even if we get the sword, God still has the intention and ability to turn that experience into an angel. He can still perform His miracles, albeit different from the one we were hoping or praying for. In the end, all will be made right. —DB

Reflect and Respond

When have you gotten the sword? When have you gotten the angel? When has God turned a sword into an angel?

Your favorite scripture in Acts 12

ACTS 13:34

I will give you the sure mercies of David.

One of the last studies my good friend and I began before she passed away was a study on mercy. It was through this study process that I discovered the translation for the Greek word for mercy, *eleos*: "especially active compassion" (Strong's Concordance). Ever since that study, I am inclined to pause and consider the word *mercy* when I come across it in scripture. In Acts 13, Paul teaches about the "sure mercies of David." I wondered what that phrase meant. I turned to the book of Psalms, because that is where David recorded much of his testimony. My study led me to Psalm 23, "Surely goodness and mercy shall follow me all the days of my life: and I will dwell in the house of the Lord for ever" (Psalm 23:6). Then I began searching the word *mercy* in all of Psalms. It appears almost 150 times. In fact, there is one psalm in which the word is repeated twenty-six times (Psalm 136) and another where the word is repeated eleven times.

A careful reading of these two psalms filled with mercy taught me a little more about the sure mercies of David. In Psalm 136 we learn that mercy, or especially active compassion, can be manifest in goodness, great wonders, wisdom, light, deliverance, rescue, strength and guidance, miracles, redemption, protection, promise, and sustenance. "His mercy endureth for ever" (Psalm 136:26). In Psalm 119 we learn that it is through His words and teachings that we receive mercy, that we can pray for His merciful kindness, that His tenderness is expressed through mercy. "Great are thy tender mercies, O Lord" (Psalm 119:156). Maybe today you might spend some time looking for the word *mercy* in the book of Psalms to learn more about the sure mercies of David. —EBF

Reflect and Respond

What have you come to understand about mercy through the teachings of David?

Your favorite scripture in
Acts 13

ACTS 14:20

He rose up, and came into the city.

One of my favorite stories is one about the Prophet Joseph Smith. It starts tragically. Joseph and his wife Emma were up all night taking turns with their sick baby. Joseph had just given the baby to Emma and was lying down for a short rest when the door to their home was broken open and a mob of angry men came busting in. They grabbed Joseph from his bed and dragged him out the door, down the stone steps, and onto the lawn, where they beat him, stripped him, attempted to poison him, and then covered his body with hot, acidic tar and feathers. When he came to and was taken back into his home, Emma fainted at the sight of him. She and other friends worked through the night scraping and cleaning the tar off his body and mending his wounds. The next morning, a group of people gathered to that same lawn, and Joseph stood battered and bruised on the same stone steps and preached a sermon. A sermon on forgiveness—perhaps with members of the mob in attendance.

It is no wonder that the Apostle Paul was one of Joseph's heroes. He too was persecuted intensely for the cause of Christ. On one particular day, Paul and his companion were preaching when an angry mob from nearby cities came and stoned Paul until they thought he was dead. They dragged his body outside the walls of the city and left him. However, as his friends and "disciples stood round about him, he rose up, and came into the city" and continued his preaching as he had been doing the day before (Acts 14:20).

Perhaps Joseph learned this kind of dedication from Paul. I'm not sure where Paul learned it from, but I'd be confident in saying they both learned it from Jesus. —DB

Reflect and Respond

What gives you strength to rise again?

Your favorite scripture in
Acts 14

ACTS 15:26

Men that have hazarded their lives
for the name of our Lord Jesus Christ.

Barnabas is described in this chapter as a man that hazarded his life for the name of our Lord Jesus Christ (see Acts 15:26). What if that was your job description? Emily Freeman: Hazards her life for the name of our Lord Jesus Christ. I love the idea of that. To hazard could also mean to surrender or to commit, but *hazard* makes the job description sound so exciting and maybe a little bit reckless.

Barnabas was a man who did that. I wanted to find an example of how he hazarded his life, and one showed up in Acts 9. After the Lord appeared to Saul on the way to Jerusalem and he entered the city blind, the scriptures tell us Paul tried to join himself to the disciples, but they were afraid of him (see v. 26). It does seem plausible, right? I mean, he had letters in hand threatening the Saints. He had witnessed Stephen being stoned to death. You and I would probably have been frightened of him as well. Not Barnabas. "Barnabas took him, and brought him to the apostles, and declared unto them how he had seen the Lord in the way, and that he had spoken to him, and how he had preached boldly at Damascus in the name of Jesus" (v. 27). Barnabas took up the cause of Paul, he stood as a witness for him, he became an advocate at a time when Paul had no one. Barnabas went to bat for someone who could have been a hazard to the work, because he believed in Paul.

The name *Barnabas* can also mean "son of encouragement." Don't you love that it describes exactly who Barnabas was? Maybe that's what it means to hazard your life for the name of Jesus Christ. Encouraging, advocating, ministering, committing. Perhaps this is what a life well lived looks like. A life well loved. —EBF

Reflect and Respond

How might you hazard your life for Christ today?

Your favorite
scripture in
Acts 15

ACTS 16:25

And at midnight Paul and Silas prayed, and sang
praises unto God: and the prisoners heard.

When I was called as a bishop, a friend of mine gave me some advice that I have never forgotten. He told me there would be people who would face things they could not overcome on their own, and they would come to me for help, and I wouldn't know what to say or do. He told me that I wouldn't be able to solve all the problems. In fact, it wasn't my job, either. Your job, he said, is to breathe hope. In places of confusion or no answers, there can always be hope. We might not know the way out right now, but there is light at the end of this particular tunnel. People need to know that. People need someone to breathe in hope.

I think about this when I read about Paul and Silas sitting in their prison cell. They had cast a devil out of a girl, and in response, the people of the city had them stripped and beaten and then thrown into prison. There, in their cell, at midnight, the two of them did what they knew best to do. They prayed and they praised. And as they did, the other prisoners heard. There was no solution, but they leaned into hope.

Suddenly the ground shook and the prison doors all fell open. The prison guard woke up and saw what had happened and thought everyone had escaped. Because he thought he would be executed for not guarding the prisoners, he thought about ending his own life. But Paul yelled out to him to stop and then encouraged him. Perhaps they didn't know what they would do about the problem or the prison or everyone else's reaction in the morning, but for the meantime, Paul breathed hope. —DB

Reflect and Respond
When has someone breathed hope into your situation or story?

Your favorite
scripture in
Acts 16

ACTS 17:27

He be not far from every one of us.

When Paul arrived in Athens, he discovered the entire city was given to idolatry. It became his mission to dispute its validity. He taught in the synagogue and also in the markets daily. Other philosophers called him a babbler, but that didn't stop Paul. As he taught, people claimed his doctrine was strange; they felt like it was some new thing. Paul called them all superstitious (see Acts 17:16–22).

If you study Paul, you learn right away that he was bold and sometimes brash. He didn't hold back. That is true in this story as well. In his teaching he came across an altar with the inscription, "TO THE UNKNOWN GOD." Then he proceeded to teach the people about this God.

He began by reminding them that God made the world and all of the things in it. His domain was the heaven and the earth, so it wasn't likely He would limit Himself to be in a temple made with hands. He was everywhere. He also did not need His image to be crafted by man, because He was alive. Then Paul taught an important doctrine: "Seek the Lord, if haply they might feel after him, and find him, though he be not far from every one of us: For in him we live, and move, and have our being; . . . For we are also his off-spring. . . . We ought not to think that the Godhead is like unto gold, or silver, or stone, graven by art and man's device" (Acts 17:27–29).

Paul testified of a living God. One we might feel after and find. One that was never far from any of us, no matter where we are. It was bold doctrine, but some clave unto him and believed because of his boldness (see Acts 17:34). —EBF

Reflect and Respond

How could you boldly testify of the truth that God is not far from any of us?

Your favorite scripture in
Acts 17

ACTS 18:5

Paul was pressed in the spirit.

Growing up, the most common phrases I heard to desribe the influence of the Holy Ghost were a "still, small voice" and a "burning in the bosom." I had no idea what a bosom was when I was younger, so that one was memorable, but not helpful. The other stuck with me, and I thought about it often. I anticipated and listened and watched for direction to come from God in a still, small way. There have been many times when I have felt led and been able to recognize what I thought was God's voice in this way.

There is another phrase from this chapter of scripture that has also been really helpful to me more recently. I like that it is a chapter about Paul. I admire the way he listens to the Lord. I feel like he is a great mentor in trying to understand the ways of the Spirit.

There is not much explanation in the phrase, but Paul had gone to a new city and found people to stay with. He stayed with them because they were of the same occupation. They related to each other, I suppose. It was comfortable. Sometimes that is a way I understand God speaking to me—when it feels comfortable. Then when Silas and Timothy came from Macedonia, the record says Paul was "pressed in the spirit" (Acts 18:5).

I am intrigued by that word, *pressed*. As if the Spirit were leaning a little heavy on him. Trying to press Himself into Paul's mind and heart. Settling, but with intention. Not pushing, but pressing. Not forcefully, but also perhaps not comfortably. A press. Since reading this chapter and having that particular phrase press on my own mind, I have watched for this kind of communication from the Spirit. —DB

Reflect and Respond

When have you felt pressed in the Spirit?

Your favorite scripture in
Acts 18

ACTS 19:15

And Paul I know.

I love to watch for verses that describe Paul's character. We know he was bold and fearless. He held nothing back (see Acts 20:20). He was an avid and active disciple of Jesus Christ.

As we study the ministry of Christ, we often come across stories of demons or evil spirits who knew who Jesus was. They knew that they would have to obey His command because His strength overpowered them. In Acts 19, we read a similar account. There was a man who had an evil spirit. The Jews brought in exorcists to call the name of Jesus over them, to try to rid them of the spirits. So, they came and spoke over the man, "We adjure you by Jesus whom Paul preacheth" (Acts 19:13). There were eight men there all trying to heal the man. The evil spirit replied, "Jesus I know, and Paul I know; but who are ye?" (Acts 19:15). It seems Paul had become enough of a threat that his name was well known in connection with Jesus, particularly with the adversary.

Does the adversary view you as a threat?

How strong is your connection with Jesus? A favorite line in the history of Joseph Smith reads, "It seems as though the adversary was aware, at a very early period of my life, that I was destined to prove a disturber and an annoyer of his kingdom" (JS—H 1:20). It reminds me how the great war in heaven spilled over onto this earth, how we fight every single day for the cause of Christ. Our boldness and convictions, our willingness to hold nothing back becomes our strength as an annoyer and disturber of evil and wickedness. We are on the Lord's team, the side of righteousness, we are His warriors. May we be avid and active witnesses of Christ. —EBF

Reflect and Respond
What makes you a disturber and annoyer of Satan's kingdom?

Your favorite scripture in
Acts 19

ACTS 20:20

I kept back nothing.

There were days serving as a full-time missionary that were not my favorite. I think I have forgotten most of them, but I clearly remember enough to know that my two years in Korea had both ups and downs. I remember one day sitting on the floor of a house I didn't know, with people I didn't know, and food I didn't know, listening to a conversation in a language I didn't know. I had the realization that I was a long way from home and a long way from comfortable. I was straining so hard to understand any word I could. I strained even harder not to cry in front of everyone there.

It was on a day like this that I stumbled upon this verse from Paul during one of his many missionary journeys. It was on a day when he was saying his goodbyes—perhaps never again to see some of the people he had served among for the rest of his life. He told them how hard he had tried. How he had served with as much humility as he could, with tears that wet his pillow at night, battling through temptations and all the persecution he had endured. And then my favorite line: "I kept back nothing" (Acts 20:20). No matter how he did it, the one thing he could say with confidence is that he gave it his all. When I read those words, I wanted to be able to say the same. I wanted to end my time as a missionary being able to repeat Paul's words.

I wanted to give and give without reservation. I wanted to get up when I failed. I wanted to say sorry when I made a mistake. I wanted to try better after days that weren't. It would not be done flawlessly, but I would hold nothing back. —DB

Reflect and Respond

What else would you add to the list of what it looks like to hold nothing back?

Your favorite scripture in Acts 20

ACTS 21:40

He spake unto them in the Hebrew tongue.

Paul journeyed into Jerusalem and met an unfriendly crowd. The people warned him it was going to happen, but still he persisted. On one occasion he was teaching in the temple, and it "stirred up all the people . . . all the city was moved . . . all Jerusalem was in an uproar" (Acts 21:27, 30, 31). The multitude tried to kill Paul.

The chief captain responded to the uproar. Paul was bound in chains, and the captain demanded to know who he was and what he had done (see Acts 21:33). Paul had been beaten so badly that he had to be carried by the soldiers into the castle. Paul asked if it would be possible for them to converse before he went into the barracks. The chief captain wondered if Paul could speak Greek. It is interesting to note that some Bible scholars think Paul was fluent in Hebrew, Aramaic, and Greek, and possibly some Latin. Paul responded that he was a Jew, and all he wanted to do was talk to the people.

The chief captain let him speak.

Then "Paul stood on the stairs, and beckoned with the hand unto the people. And when there was made a great silence, he spake unto them in the Hebrew tongue" (Acts 21:40). Paul was a master teacher. Like Christ, he knew how to meet people where they were. We see it through his example of speaking to the Jews in a language they could understand. Consider the people you teach. How have you tried to meet them where they are and speak to them in a language that they will understand? Maybe it's a Primary class, maybe it's a group of teens, maybe it is a room full of women. The Spirit can help us know how to connect in a way that will open hearts. —EBF

Reflect and Respond
How might this example change the way you teach in the future?

Your favorite scripture in
Acts 21

ACTS 22:10

And I said, What shall I do, Lord?

During one of his return trips to Jerusalem, Paul was given the chance to speak to a gathering of people. Perhaps he did this often, but on that occasion he retold his conversion story to all that were gathered there. He told them about how much he had persecuted the Christians, how he had stood consenting at the death of Stephen, and how he had been on his way to Damascus with warrants of arrest for anyone who was a believer in Jesus.

It was on that road to Damascus that he first met the Lord. He appeared to Paul in a bright light and asked him, "Why do you persecute me?" (see Acts 22:7). When Paul asked who the voice belonged to, the Lord answered telling him it was He, Jesus of Nazareth, whom Paul persecuted.

Paul was fortunate. He was on a path away from the Lord when he was stopped and given a chance to choose another way. He sort of had Judgment Day come early, and he stood to answer to the Lord for his choices. This is an experience everyone can have. On any given night, any one of us can kneel down at our bedsides and ask the Lord if there is anything we are doing in our lives that offends Him. Like Paul, He will be quick to point out to us where we are amiss. He cares too much to be silent.

We have a chance to answer those impressions we get in the same way Paul did. President Benson said of his response to the Lord, "A man can ask no more important question in his life than that which Paul asked: '. . . Lord, what wilt thou have me to do?'" ("Listen to a Prophet's Voice," in Conference Report, October 1972). This question made all the difference for Paul. It can make all the difference for us. —DB

Reflect and Respond

Perhaps tonight you can ask the Lord that same question—what will you have me to do?

Your favorite scripture in
Acts 22

ACTS 23:11

The Lord stood by him.

Paul's life was not easy. His days were made up of tribulation, adversity, and trial. It didn't matter where he went, he was persecuted for believing in the cause of Christ. On one particular occasion, it seems as if the whole world were out to get him, and that they would succeed. He was taken by force and brought to the castle. Then certain of the Jews came together and decided that they would not eat or drink until Paul was killed. It seemed there was no way out.

Paul must have been so discouraged.

The night following that incident, while Paul was still locked in the castle, "the Lord stood by him, and said, Be of good cheer, Paul: for as thou hast testified of me in Jerusalem, so must thou bear witness also at Rome" (Acts 23:11). In that moment of great distress, the Lord gave Paul a promise—*your work is not finished yet.* I wonder if the words brought peace. But the words the Lord spoke are not my favorite part of this story. My favorite part is five words: "*the Lord stood by him*" (v. 11).

I don't know your story right now. Perhaps you feel the whole world is conspiring against you. Maybe you feel discouraged or disappointed. It could be that everything suggests you have failed. The Lord will stand by you through this. In the darkest of nights, in the bleakest of situations, He will come, He will bring strength and promise, He will stand by. It is a beautiful promise, and this story is a confirming witness of His character in the midst of our trials. —EBF

Reflect and Respond

When have you felt the Lord standing by?

Your favorite scripture in
Acts 23

ACTS 24:14

So worship I the God of my fathers,
believing all things which are written.

For most of my children, I was able to have my grandfather present for their baby blessings and baptisms. At each of these events, we always took several pictures. The one picture I always wanted to get was one of my kid, me, my dad, and my grandfather all together. Four generations of faith.

One of the lines that Paul uses to defend himself is one about his own faith. He claimed to be a man who worships the God of his fathers. Fathers who believed in the words of the holy scriptures and taught them to their children and their children's children. I also am a man who worships the God of my fathers and mothers. I consider my faith one of my greatest inheritances.

One Easter morning I was thinking about my belief in the Resurrection. I started to think back as far as I could to see if I could remember where and when I first started believing and hoping in such a day. My answer was easy—my parents taught me. It is one of the gifts they gave to me. I wondered what they would say if I asked them where they learned about the Resurrection. I imagined they would also say their parents. And I bet I could repeat this, and it would become a pattern for generations.

The beginnings of faith and belief seem to be something that can be passed on to others and then received—often from parent to child. It has always been easy for me to believe in the God of promise and miracles from scripture because I was taught and shown how to believe at such a young age. —DB

Reflect and Respond

Who passed on their faith and beliefs to you?

Your favorite
scripture in
Acts 24

ACTS 25:26

That, after examination . . . I might have somewhat to write.

In my teenage years I read a book about a man who was on trial for his belief in Jesus Christ. I cannot remember the name of the book, but the story left such an impression on me that it caused me to wonder, *if I were put on trial for being a Christian, would there be enough evidence to convict me?*

It is an interesting question to ask yourself.

Towards the end of Paul's life, he continued to be questioned. On one occasion, King Agrippa and Festus did the interviewing. Festus told King Agrippa he could find no fault in the man that was worth the penalty of death. Festus asked King Agrippa to interview Paul, hoping he might find something to convict him with, "Wherefore I have brought him forth before you, and specially before thee, O King Agrippa, that, after examination had, I might have somewhat to write. For it seemeth to me unreasonable to send a prisoner, and not withal to signify the crimes laid against him" (Acts 25:26–27).

It seems King Agrippa and Festus were not concerned with Paul's religious beliefs. But the Jews were. They were willing to kill him for those beliefs. It would have been hard to remain true in those circumstances, but Paul never faltered. He remained a firm believer in Christ until the day he died.

Again I ask myself, *if I were put on trial for being a member of The Church of Jesus Christ of Latter-day Saints, would there be enough evidence to convict me?*

I hope so. —EBF

Reflect and Respond

How does your living reflect your testimony? Can people find evidence of your beliefs there?

Your favorite scripture in
Acts 25

ACTS 26:28

Almost thou persuadest me to be a Christian.

Paul, not surprisingly, was arrested and found himself standing before the powerful and influential King Agrippa. As he often seemed to do, Paul recounted his conversion story and the day he first met the Lord on the road to Damascus. He told the king that no matter how much persecution and hate he received, he knew for himself that he had seen a vision and was going to be obedient to what he saw and felt.

After sharing his witness and story with the king, Agrippa said to Paul, "Almost thou persuadest me to be a Christian" (Acts 26:28). Every time I read this, I wonder what part of the story was so persuasive to the king. Was it his description of Jesus? Was it his story of change? Was it the way he stayed so faithful to the vision despite the great persecution he had experienced because of it? What almost persuaded the king to be a Christian? And what was holding him back?

Almost being a Christian means that you almost have hope in second chances. It means you almost believe in seeing deceased loved ones again. It means you almost live every day in the love and grace of the Holy One of Israel. Paul responded to the king, "I would to God, that not only thou, but also all that hear me this day, were both almost, and altogether such as I am" (Acts 26:29). The king was almost persuaded, but Paul's wish was that he become altogether, fully devoted to the Lord. The same way the Lord was already fully devoted to him. —DB

Reflect and Respond

In what ways are you altogether a follower of Jesus Christ?

Your favorite scripture in
Acts 26

ACTS 27:25

I believe God.

When Paul set off for Rome, he knew the journey would be a mistake. It was too late in the season for travel. But no one on the ship wanted to listen to a prisoner. So they set off, even though Paul had counseled otherwise. Before long, a huge storm set in. The weather was so bad they could not steer the ship. They were so worried about the waves dashing in the ship that they had to tie the boat together with rope. Their navigation got confused because they could not see the sun or the stars. Finally, Paul stood again in the midst of them. "Sirs," he began, "you should have listened to me" (see Acts 27:21). It is one of the best told-you-so moments recorded in scripture. Then he proceeds to make them a promise that no man's life will be lost during the journey, although they would lose the ship. They must have wondered how he knew what was going to happen. He responded, "There stood by me this night the angel of God, whose I am, and whom I serve, saying, Fear not. . . . I believe God" (Acts 27:23–25). Then Paul proceeded to tell them what they would have to do to remain safe. This time they listened.

First, they cast out four anchors. Next, they cast off all of the lifeboats and anything else weighing down the ship. Now they were committed. Last, they took bread and gave thanks.

Then, they waited.

When it was finally day, they lifted up the anchors and committed themselves unto the sea . . . and it turned out just as Paul had said it would. The ship was dashed upon a small island, but not one life was lost. There is great safety that comes when we listen to God's servants and believe in Him. —EBF

Reflect and Respond

How has your life been protected because you listened to a servant of God?

Your favorite scripture in
Acts 27

ACTS 28:3

There came a viper out of the heat.

While traveling by sea to Rome, Paul and his shipmates were shipwrecked on an island. The "barbarous" inhabitants of the island greeted them kindly and built a fire for them to warm themselves by (see Acts 28:2). When the fire was getting low, Paul grabbed a bundle of sticks to add to the fire. When he did, a viper came out of the sticks because of the heat and bit Paul's hand, refusing to let go. When the superstitious islanders saw the snake hanging from Paul's hand, they assumed the worst about him. They figured he certainly must be a murderer, who despite escaping the storm, was now receiving vengeance for his crimes. Paul, still standing by the fire, shook the snake off his hand and into the fire. He was not injured or affected by the bite or venom. When the islanders saw his miraculous escape from the snake, they changed their minds about him and assumed that Paul must be a god.

Every time I read this story, I chuckle at how quickly the islanders changed their mind about Paul and what was happening. In doing so, I kind of chuckle at myself. So many of us make assumptions about others and ourselves based on things that happen. If something bad happens we think there must be a reason God is punishing us. We assume His disfavor or anger toward us. If things go well, we assume we are His favorites and there is nothing we would ever need to change.

But what if just like in this story, snakes just bite people sometimes because they are snakes? Nothing good, nothing bad. Just a snake. And we can shake it off as something snakes do. —DB

Reflect and Respond

What is something you can just shake off right now?

Your favorite scripture in
Acts 28

ROMANS 1:16

I am not ashamed of the gospel of Christ.

When I went to high school, my closest group of friends were boys. We did every-thing together. When high school was over, we went to college together. Obviously, I lived in a girls' dorm, but I spent all my time at the boys' Penrose Hall. We all served missions at the same time as well. One to Japan, one to Germany, others to California, Australia, and Brazil. Between the five of us, we reached that many countries of the world and we shared our faith in the places where we were. I still remember the letters we shared back and forth during those mission years. Five friends in different places, but all doing the work of the Lord.

I love thinking about the next group of friends that left Penrose Hall the year after we did, and the one after that . . . even still today, college kids are leaving campuses be-hind to go and teach of Christ. "I thank my God through Jesus Christ for you all, that your faith is spoken of throughout the whole world" (Romans 1:8). Each of my friends brought home a piece of the world with them when they returned, but I also like to think how they left a piece of themselves there. Faith sprinkled throughout the world.

The epistles of the New Testament are going to talk a lot about missions and con-versions and faith thriving throughout the world. Perhaps these pages will cause you to reflect on your own mission, or that of a son or daughter or friend. Paul says, "So, as much as in me is, I am ready to preach the gospel. . . . For I am not ashamed of the gospel of Christ" (Romans 1:15–16). What a wonderful opportunity we have as mem-bers of this Church to enter the world, to take our faith there, to stand as a witness of Jesus Christ. —EBF

Reflect and Respond

Which parts of the world have you left a piece of your faith in?

Your favorite scripture in **Romans 1**

ROMANS 2:4

The goodness of God leadeth thee to repentance.

I have one particular friend—a newer one, actually—who has quickly won me over. He is competent, compassionate, super well connected, and highly successful. He is honestly one of the most talented people I have ever met. He has no reason or benefit to be friends with me. And yet, he is. And not only is he a friend; he is a super good friend. I could call him right this second and he would drop all that he was doing to talk or help me out in any way I needed. I am on an "anything, anytime" level with him. His goodness is fascinating.

I have realized that because of that goodness, I find myself just as willing to give whatever I can to him anytime, anywhere. And not just him, but all of my other friends and potential friends as well. He has inspired me to be the same kind of person to others around me. Liberal in my help, advice, and compassion.

That is what I hear Paul saying to the Saints in Rome in this particular verse. There are many ways that we could be compelled to repent and follow the Lord. Someone could threaten us with punishment and scare us into obedience. Someone could promise us mansions on high if we live our lives the way we should. But neither of these seem to be as effective as the way Paul is presenting. It is the "goodness of God" that leads to repentance (Romans 2:4). It is when we consider how liberal He has been with His compassion, forgiveness, and grace that our hearts are softened and turn to Him. When we consider how good He is, it leads us to want to listen to Him, be with Him, and walk in His ways. —DB

Reflect and Respond

Have you ever been treated so well by someone it caused you to change the way you treat others?

Your favorite scripture in **Romans 2**

ROMANS 3:23

All have sinned, and come short.

I have learned to watch football. It hasn't come easily for me; it's like a whole new language. My kids have found the process of me becoming a football fan hilarious. Like the time I asked in the family text, "Where are the Broncos located again?" Or the day Garett was drafted, and they took what seemed like a million pictures of us with a man I had never met before and I asked Greg who he was, and he said, "John Elway," to which I replied, "I don't know what that man does." At the first NFL game I ever attended, my good friend texted to ask the score. "I don't even know where the scoreboard is," I told him. One thing I do know is what it means to come short of a first down and how absolutely imperative it is to the game to get one.

Romans 3 talks about salvation, grace, and faith. Sometimes it is in a language we don't understand. There are words like *propitiation*, *righteousness*, *forbearance*, and *justification* that might leave us confused. There is one part that does make sense, though. Just like in a football game, there are times we are all going to come short (see Romans 3:23). God knew that would happen, even for the righteous. So, He created a plan. In the book of Romans, it says this: "Whom God hath set forth to be a propitiation through faith in his blood, to declare his righteousness for the remission of sins that are past, through the forbearance of God" (Romans 3:25). With time and study, this verse might read like this: *God prepared Jesus to bring mercy through faith in His atoning sacrifice, to make up for your coming short because of past sins.* It is a beautiful promise. And it's ok if we don't understand it all now. With time and practice, we will. —EBF

Reflect and Respond

What is one thing you believe about grace as it relates to coming short?

Your favorite scripture in **Romans 3**

ROMANS 4:21

What he had promised, he was able also to perform.

When I think about the story of Abraham, I am amazed every time. But I am probably not as amazed as he was. He actually lived his own story. One day, God came and found Abraham, and when He found him, He promised Abraham ridiculously amazing promises. Impossible promises. One of those was that Abraham would inherit a promised land. This particular promised land was occupied at the time the promise came. Yet it was still promised. Another promise, and perhaps the most well-known, was that Abraham would have a child with his wife Sarah, who was old and well beyond the years of child-bearing. Again, impossible.

Abraham and Sarah were not only promised a single child, but also promised a family and posterity that would number the stars of the heavens. That posterity, they were promised, would not only fill the world, but they would be the means of blessing all of the nations and families of the world with great blessings.

This is a story that Paul recounted to the Roman Saints as a way to teach them about the character and nature of God—the same God who was still offering impossible promises to them. We might look at what God has promised to us—the things we can become and overcome, and think, "Impossible." But consider the story of Abraham, Paul said. Abraham knew that the God who promised such impossible things was also able to perform them. So, he trusted Him. That same God who fulfilled impossible promises with Abraham is the God who will fulfill impossible promises for us. He who promised is also able to perform. —DB

Reflect and Respond

What are some of the promises that seem impossible to you?
Consider how He is able to fulfill them in your life.

Your favorite scripture in Romans 4

ROMANS 5:20

Where sin abounded,
grace did much more abound.

There was a time in my life when I attended several twelve-step meetings with a friend. We would go once a week. I don't know if you have ever been to one, but there is a beautiful feeling that welcomes you right when you walk in the door. For many months I wondered what that feeling was. It felt a little like love, but it wasn't love. Also hope, but it wasn't hope. I wondered about it for a long time, until one afternoon when I read this scripture: "But where sin abounded, grace did much more abound" (Romans 5:20). I immediately realized the tangible feeling I felt in that twelve-step meeting was grace abounding. Sometimes I substitute the word *sin* in my scriptures to read *weakness*, because grace applies to weakness too. *Where weakness abounded, grace did much more abound.*

That has been true in my story.

You might also replace the word *sin* with *tribulation. Where tribulation abounded, grace did much more abound.* That has also been true for me. At the beginning of this chapter, Paul teaches us how we grow in tribulation. He teaches,

"Tribulation worketh patience;

and patience, experience;

and experience, hope:

and [through] hope . . . the love of God is shed abroad in our hearts . . .

For when we were yet without strength . . . Christ died for us" (Romans 5:3–8).

I love this example of how grace works, helping us to both *overcome* and *become* through Christ. Whether it is sin, weakness, or tribulation, grace will abound and give us enabling strength. —EBF

Reflect and Respond

When has grace abounded in your life?

Your favorite
scripture in
Romans 5

ROMANS 6:23

The wages of sin is death; but the gift of God is
eternal life through Jesus Christ our Lord.

My oldest boys have both recently gotten part-time jobs and are now learning all of the things that come with that. Schedules, time off, having to say no to friends because of their work commitments, and above all, paychecks. They both worked at the same place for a while, and when their paychecks would come, my older son would compare his check with his younger brother's and claim he was scammed every time. "Why does he keep getting more than me?" For some reason, it took a little bit for him to understand that the more you work, the more you get paid. That's how wages and paychecks operate.

I love the analogy of paychecks that Paul assigns to sin. Death, he said, is the wages of sin. The more we sin in our lives, the more we bring death into them. Our relationships with God and others slowly die, our potentials die, and our spirits die. It is not God that we need to be afraid of, it is the effects of sin. They naturally breed death. The more we sin, the more death we experience. It's how it works.

God, on the other hand, offers us life. He offers us renewed hope and vibrancy. He offers us the chance to be more alive toward Him, others, and the world and possibilities around us. Sin brings death, but God brings life. The difference is that the life He offers does not come as wages, but as a gift. We don't earn it; it is given. It is a gift that is offered through the work of Jesus Christ. Our job is to receive the gift. We won't deserve it like we do with wages, but that is the very definition of a gift. Paychecks we earn. Gifts are given. —DB

Reflect and Respond

When have you seen sin breed death into situations and God breed life into others?

Your favorite
scripture in
Romans 6

ROMANS 7:6

We should serve in newness of spirit,
and not in the oldness of the letter.

Have you heard the phrase "letter of the law" versus the "spirit of the law" and wondered what it meant? Paul introduces the idea here by saying "that we should serve in newness of spirit, and not in the oldness of the letter" (Romans 7:6). Paul refers to the oldness of the letter, speaking of the law of Moses, and the newness of spirit, referencing the Sermon on the Mount. The higher law. The letter of the law was given to help the carnal man overcome sin. The spirit of the law was given to help us embrace the holy within and become something more. It helps us become like Him.

It worked like this: The letter of the law forbade killing; the new law forbade getting angry with a brother. The old law forbade adultery; the new law embodied a higher standard—purity of the mind and heart. The old law taught to love your neighbor and hate your enemy; the new law taught you must love your enemy.

The old law kept the carnal man in check; the new law was an invitation to become something more through Christ.

This idea of a higher law and its ability to help you become was hinted at in the very beginning verses of the Sermon on the Mount, "And seeing the multitudes, he went up into a mountain; and when he was set, his disciples came unto him" (Matthew 5:1). Living the new law requires us to leave behind the multitude, to choose to ascend higher toward Christ through a way of living that will lift us.

The spirit of the law helps us to become. —EBF

Reflect and Respond

What is one way you try to live the spirit of the law?

Your favorite
scripture in
Romans 7

ROMANS 8:31

If God be for us,
who can be against us?

I feel like God is often blamed for a lot of the unfair or wrong that happens in the world. When we observe or experience these hard things we are often quick to say He is indifferent or unwilling to help. He is pegged as our enemy or sometimes as someone who is just champing at the bit to catch us in sin or punish us for our choices. Like He is out to get us.

Romans 8 pushes back hard against this kind of misunderstanding. It is a chapter that reestablishes God as someone who is for us. A God who is on our side. Sin and temptation and the adversary are our enemies, not God. Our struggle is not with God; we overcome *with* God. In other words, we do not struggle *against* Him; we struggle against our problems in companionship *with* Him. In that struggle, we come out as conquerors "through him that loved us" (Romans 8:37). That is the outcome He is hoping and fighting for. Because He fights for us. With Him by our side, nothing else could ever prevail.

"For I am persuaded," Paul said, "that neither death, nor life, nor angels, nor principalities, nor powers, nor things present, nor things to come, nor height, nor depth, nor any other creature, shall be able to separate us from the love of God, which is in Christ Jesus" (Romans 8:38–39).

Was there anything missing from that list? If there is, you can add it. Because there is nothing that can overcome us or cause God to stop being for us. —DB

Reflect and Respond
When have you seen evidence of a God who is for you?

Your favorite
scripture in
Romans 8

ROMANS 9:21

Hath not the potter power over the clay.

When I read about the Lord as a potter, I am reminded that each of us is a creation of His hand. I assume that it is His ultimate hope that each of His masterpieces will return home. But the plan also includes agency, and Paul teaches the importance of understanding vessels of honor and vessels of dishonor. The lesson is best understood as we watch how God responds.

To vessels of dishonor, God responds with wrath to make His power known, but He also endures with much long-suffering the course these vessels pursue (see Romans 9:22). For the vessels of honor, He makes known the riches of His glory and mercy (see v. 23).

The Lord endures and is patient, He blesses and extends mercy, and He watches to see what will happen. We are reminded that it is in His discretion to "call them my people, which were not my people; and her beloved, which was not beloved" (Romans 9:25). There is an opportunity for those who are not His people to be called the "children of the living God" (v. 26). Isaiah promised a remnant would be saved, and that the Lord would "finish the work" (v. 28). Isaiah reminds us the Lord of Sabaoth would help us attain to righteousness (see v. 29).

The word *Sabaoth* (Hebrew for "hosts") hints toward a God of angel armies. I love the thought of a God who will fight for His masterpieces, the work of His own hand, no matter what the vessels look like. He will give us all the chance to attain righteousness, but He won't force us. He wants to call us all part of His beloved family because we have chosen to be there. —EBF

Reflect and Respond

How does it make you feel to know you are the creation of His hand?

Your favorite scripture in **Romans 9**

ROMANS 10:15

How beautiful are the feet of them that preach the gospel
of peace, and bring glad tidings of good things!

This is a scripture from the book of Isaiah, the Old Testament prophet. It is a scripture that you can find quoted several other places in other books of scripture as well. It seems to be a favorite among many people—including me. It just doesn't get old.

I went to my grandmother's ninetieth birthday party. Most of the people there I knew well—cousins, aunts and uncles, and longtime friends. However, there was one nice lady I met for the first time. I had never seen her before, but since she was invited to the ninetieth birthday party, I figured she must have had some connection with Grandma. It was not long into our conversation that the connection became apparent. It was something she seemed delighted and anxious to share. She had lived close to my grandparents for decades. They were a part of the same ward, but this particular lady had not been to church or active in her faith for many years. "Until your grandma showed up on my porch. She took me back to church." She continued talking fondly about my grandparents and what they both meant to her. She had a sparkle in her teary eyes the whole time she talked about them. "They are the reason I am a woman of faith today." For all intents and purposes, she could've been quoting Isaiah just the same way Paul did.

For how beautiful are the feet of Pat and Allan Butler, who preached the gospel of peace to a neighbor and friend, and brought glad tidings of good things to a front porch.

Each of us has someone we can assign that verse to. I wish I could hear every one of the stories you would share. They would never get old. —DB

Reflect and Respond

Who has the beautiful feet that brought you the glad tidings of good things?

Your favorite
scripture in
Romans 10

ROMANS 11:4

I have reserved to myself seven thousand men.

God will not give up. A remnant will be saved. This is the message of Romans chapter 11. God has reserved a remnant who will be ready and waiting when He returns. "I have reserved to myself seven thousand men, who have not bowed the knee to the image of Baal. Even so then at this present time also there is a remnant" (Romans 11:4–5).

This scripture reminds me of a conference talk I heard when I was nineteen years old. I was sitting in my dorm kitchen at BYU watching a small TV that had antennas. Marvin J. Ashton stood up to speak and gave a talk that was for me a call to action. In his talk he quoted a statement from President Benson: "For nearly six thousand years, God has held you in reserve to make your appearance in the final days before the Second Coming. Every previous gospel dispensation has drifted into apostasy, but ours will not. . . . God has saved for the final inning some of his strongest children, who will help bear off the kingdom triumphantly. And that is where you come in, for you are the generation that must be prepared to meet your God. . . . Make no mistake about it—you are a marked generation. There has never been more expected of the faithful in such a short period of time as there is of us. . . . Each day we personally make many decisions that show where our support will go. The final outcome is certain—the forces of righteousness will finally win. What remains to be seen is where each of us personally, now and in the future, will stand in this fight—and how tall we will stand. Will we be true to our last-days, foreordained mission?" ("Stalwart and Brave We Stand," *Ensign*, November 1989).

I want to be one who God has reserved for these last days. I want to be part of the remnant. —EBF

Reflect and Respond
How are you helping to "bear off the kingdom triumphantly"?

Your favorite scripture in Romans 11

ROMANS 12:13

Given to hospitality.

When I visited South Carolina, I was insistent on finding some sort of souvenir with a pineapple on it. I love pineapples. I know I am not the only one, but I think I love them more than most. The majority of people love them because they are delicious and they remind them of tropical places where they grow. And that is true about me too. I could eat pineapple on the beaches of Hawaii for all the rest of my days and have no complaints.

However, I also love them because of their symbolism. Pineapples have been a symbol of hospitality in the Southern states for many years. You will often find pineapple decor on people's porches and homes in this area of the country. The roots of this tradition go back to colonial days when it was difficult to get pineapples. They grew in other places and were expensive to ship. So, if you had a pineapple on the table for one of your invited guests, it was a sign of great honor and respect to them. People even used to rent pineapples for the evening in order to show high hospitality to guests coming over. I wish I owned a pineapple rental business.

Paul seems to give a list to the Roman Saints, encouraging them and teaching them the ways of Christian living. One of the things he says is to be "given to hospitality" (Romans 12:13). It reminds me of this pineapple principle—to live a code of conduct. One where you show great honor and respect to other people. A way of living that makes others feel special and welcome when they come into your home or life. Perhaps Paul would even suggest everyone either rent or buy a pineapple for when people come over. —DB

Reflect and Respond
Who do you know who is "given to hospitality"?

Your favorite scripture in
Romans 12

ROMANS 13:12

The armour of light.

It is time to wake up (see Romans 13:11).

That is Paul's call to the Saints of his time. *The end is closer than we believe.* I wonder if someone needs to teach that now. Sometimes I feel that we are in a time of great warfare. A spiritual battle is raging. Each of us can consider our own circles of influence and see the losses we have sustained. It is nearing the end, and sometimes my soul wants to cry, *wake up!*

Paul is not going to face the battle alone. Instead he invites people into the fight: "The night is far spent, the day is at hand: let us therefore cast off the works of darkness, and let us put on the armour of light" (Romans 13:12).

What is this armor of light?

My thoughts are drawn to the book of Ephesians, to the whole armor of God—loins girt about with truth, the breastplate of righteousness, feet shod with the gospel, the shield of faith, the helmet of salvation, and the sword of the spirit. I picture what that might look like, then I open my heart to understand. Am I surrounding myself with truth, righteousness, the gospel, faith, the Spirit, and the promise of salvation? What would that actually look like? What builds faith and teaches truth and brings the Spirit? I am reminded of the importance of the gospel of Jesus Christ and the opportunities I have to surround myself with those things—church, seminary, scripture reading, temple attendance, prayer, uplifting thoughts and music. Is it possible to surround ourselves with light?

At the end of this chapter, Paul invites us to "put ye on the Lord Jesus Christ" (Romans 13:14). He is the light. Let us enter our battles with Him. —EBF

Reflect and Respond

What is one way you could put on the Lord Jesus Christ today?

Your favorite scripture in Romans 13

ROMANS 14:17

For the kingdom of God is not meat and drink.

There was an unwritten rule on my mission that missionaries didn't drink Coke. At the time, many did not believe it was in line with the Word of Wisdom. There were missionaries, however, who did not interpret the revelation the same way and would drink it. When the Saints in the mission who believed differently would see the missionaries drinking Coke or Pepsi, they would be shocked and offended that these servants of the Lord were living in a way they considered offensive to Him. In some areas, there were arguments about who was right or wrong.

One day, my mission president spoke to our mission and taught us a valuable lesson. He told us he didn't want to talk about the Word of Wisdom, but wanted us to consider this: If it bothered other people when we drank Coke, could we just not do it? Not because of what was right or wrong, but to avoid bothering them. Can our love be stronger than our insistence on being right? Can we give up Coke for a while in order to show love to the people we live near?

I think my mission president learned this lesson from the Apostle Paul. In his day, there was an argument about meat offered to idols and then sold later in marketplaces. Was it right to eat meat that had once been offered to idols? Some thought it was wildly offensive, and others seemed to think it was just meat. No big deal. But the arguments raged, and Paul taught them the same lesson my mission president did. "For the kingdom of God is not meat and drink; but righteousness, and peace, and joy in the Holy Ghost" (Romans 14:17). I think they would both add the kingdom of God is each other. What if instead of passing judgment, we found ways to promote peace and joy? —DB

Reflect and Respond

Is there an area in your life right now where love would be more important than being right?

Your favorite scripture in **Romans 14**

ROMANS 15:1

We then that are strong ought
to bear the infirmities of the weak.

I tend to be a problem solver at heart.

There is something in my clinical makeup that loves to brainstorm and come up with ideas and try to make a situation better. In my earlier years, I wanted to be the fixer. My kids knew that if a toy broke, there was a good chance I could find a way to fix it with duct tape or super glue. Things rarely stayed broken at our house. As I grew older, the problems grew bigger. I realized there are some things that can't be fixed in this lifetime, and that there are a lot of problems I won't ever be able to solve. That knowledge didn't dampen my enthusiasm to help, it just shifted my perspective a little bit. I have learned that Jesus is the ultimate problem solver. He knows how to fix things. He can save us. *There is no other Savior besides Him.* But I also believe He will use each of us to help. When we are strong, we are called upon to help those who are weaker. When we are weak, God will send someone else our way. Maybe we can't solve the problem, but perhaps we could share the burden along the way.

With that knowledge in mind, several years ago I decided to choose a phrase for the year. I know, most people choose a word. This particular year our family was struggling with a lot of heavy things—things that weren't going to be fixed right away. That knowledge can be really depressing for a problem solver. But I knew Christ would know how to help each of my kids with their struggles. I decided that instead of focusing on what would not be resolved right away, I could ask one important question: "How can I help?" I put that quote up in my kitchen window so that I could focus on it each day. A reminder that those "that are strong ought to bear the infirmities of the weak" (Romans 15:1). —EBF

Reflect and Respond

How could you help someone who is feeling weak today?

Your favorite
scripture in
Romans 15

ROMANS 16:13

Salute Rufus chosen in the Lord,
and his mother and mine.

I used to skip Romans 16 when I would read the Bible. I wondered why it was even included. It is just a list of people's names. The book of Romans was written to people who lived in Rome. So, Romans 16, the end of the letter, is a goodbye section with a bunch of shout-outs to people we've never heard of. It's just a really long way to say "Love y'all. Sincerely yours, Paul."

But I was listening to a pastor teach on this chapter once, and he reframed the whole way I read it. He said in his sermon not to call it a list, because it is so much more than just a list. Each name in that chapter has a story. There was a reason that Paul was particular to call out to each of the people that he did. They might not mean very much to us, but they meant something significant to him.

One of my favorites is his callout to Rufus. First of all, I just love the name Rufus. But second, I love that he called him "Rufus chosen in the Lord" (Romans 16:13). That makes me want to meet Rufus so much and hear his story. Why was he chosen in the Lord? What was he like? What did he do to help the kingdom? And help Paul? And then Paul says hello to Rufus's mother, whom he considered to be a mother to him as well. I have other moms like that. Wendy. Nancy. Janeane. Kenna. They don't mean much to you, but there is so much more to these names. Love shared, lessons taught, sacrifices made.

This is what the kingdom is all about—people. —DB

Reflect and Respond

Who would you put on your Romans 16? Who has made a significant impact in your story?

Your favorite scripture in Romans 16

1 CORINTHIANS 1:7

So that ye come behind in no gift.

What is the best gift you have ever been given?

Mine was tied up to a tree in our backyard on Christmas morning. Black wool standing in white snow. A red ribbon tied around her neck. I named my lamb Calypso. I had always wanted a black lamb. That spring she had two babies—one white and one black. I named them Ebony and Ivory. Even now, I still remember how grateful I was for that gift.

Paul begins his epistle to the Saints in Corinth by thanking God in their behalf "for the grace of God which is given you by Jesus Christ" (1 Corinthians 1:4). Perhaps you wonder what grace is. Paul tells us it is what enriches us, both in utterance and in all knowledge; it is what ensures we do not come behind in any gift (see v. 7). Sometimes we think grace is only connected to death and sin. I love how Paul expands our view. He teaches that grace can enrich and strengthen us, it can enable us to become more. It transforms us so that we won't come short in any area. Grace is one of my best gifts.

The Bible Dictionary explains that grace is the "divine means of help or strength, given through the bounteous mercy and love of Jesus Christ." Through grace we are raised to immortality; through grace and belief in Jesus we receive strength beyond our own and also enabling power that will help us reach exaltation (see Bible Dictionary, "Grace").

This grace is a beautiful gift that comes by virtue of the cross through the mercy and love of Jesus Christ. —EBF

Reflect and Respond
What have you learned about grace?

Your favorite
scripture in
1 Corinthians 1

1 CORINTHIANS 2:9

Eye hath not seen, nor ear heard, neither have entered into the heart of man, the things which God hath prepared for them that love him.

I love to travel. I love new places, I love new adventure, I love new food, and I really love meeting new people. I just hung a map up on my office wall where I can put pins in all the places I have been in the world. And even though there aren't very many yet, I have seen and been to some fantastic places. I have seen things that have blown my mind and thrilled my heart. And I have heard things that are similar. My eye has seen, and my ear has heard some remarkable things.

In addition, I have always had a very vivid imagination. As a kid, I lived in entirely different worlds than this one. As an adult, I still visit those worlds. For some reason, that part of my brain is extra active. There have been incredible things that have entered into my heart.

So, when Paul says that eyes have not seen, and ears have not heard, and imaginations and hearts have not even considered the great things that God has in store, I am both intrigued and bubbling with anticipation. I have heard and seen and imagined so much already. And each of these things that I have experienced was already a gift from Him. I am already in His debt and have huge thanks for all He has provided and given. My cup runneth over. There is nothing else I would expect to receive from Him that I haven't already. But Paul said God has more up His sleeve. Things you can't even dream of yet. Wow. Thank you, God. You are fantastic. —DB

Reflect and Respond

What are some of the things you have experienced that you consider great gifts from God?

Your favorite scripture in
1 Corinthians 2

1 CORINTHIANS 3:9

We are labourers together with God.

One year at girls' camp our ward stayed on a lake. One evening, after dinner had been cooked and cleaned up, we walked to the edge of the water. It was twilight—the sun had not yet set. We split the girls up into groups by tent and then handed each of them a picture of a temple. All of the pictures were different. We told the girls they had one hour to build sandcastles resembling their temples. I wish you could have seen them building. Once their structures were complete, they added shells, seaweed, pieces of wood and leaves from nearby trees. Just as the sun was setting, spreading a pink hue across the gentle ripples of the lake, we started taking pictures. It is one of my most favorite twilight memories.

In the third chapter of Corinthians, Paul introduces himself as a "masterbuilder" (v. 10). He had laid the foundation, which is Jesus Christ. He invited every man to build upon that foundation in any way he wanted. He gave them six materials to choose from: gold, silver, precious stones, wood, hay, and stubble (see v. 12). He counseled that every man's work would be made manifest. Consider those materials. If you were going to build a house, which three would you choose?

When we turn the page of this chapter, we are told that every man's work will be tried *with fire* to see what sort it is (see 1 Corinthians 3:13). I consider the list of materials again—gold, silver, precious stones, wood, hay, and stubble. Which of those could withstand fire? I quickly realized some would burn to ashes, while others would become more beautiful. It makes me consider my foundation. Jesus Christ. What is it that I am building upon that foundation? Will it be strong enough to withstand what is ahead? —EBF

Reflect and Respond

How are your building on your foundation? Will your work abide?

Your favorite scripture in
1 Corinthians 3

1 CORINTHIANS 4:10

We are fools for Christ's sake,
but ye are wise in Christ.

I will never forget the lessons that one of my favorite missionary companions taught me. He was not the ideal missionary on paper. He had been serving in Korea for close to a year and a half but still could not speak Korean. But did he ever try! He would study and practice, but just could not get it down. It frustrated him and he felt like it limited what he was able to do. At times, it made him so angry.

When he would speak, it was hard not to giggle a little bit. He was so animated with his hands—one of the only things he could use to communicate. And when he would speak, he spoke with such a strong Southern accent that no one could even understand the Korean words he actually knew or the simple ones in English. He would get closer and closer and talk louder and louder and wave his arms bigger and bigger to the people who couldn't understand him. Some might have said he looked a little foolish.

But do you know what? He was the most loved companion I ever served with. And he did more good than anyone else I served with as well. He had a way of reaching hearts with that Texan-sounding Korean and his big, waving arms. People listened intently to him, and there was power when he bore his witness. Miracles seemed to always be in his wake. He may have looked a little foolish, but like Paul said to the Corinthian Saints, "We are fools for Christ's sake, but ye are wise in Christ" (1 Corinthians 4:10). He knew where his strength came from, and he didn't have anything else to get in the way. —DB

Reflect and Respond

Who do you know that is simple and perhaps considered foolish or weak, but speaks and acts with the power of God?

Your favorite scripture in
1 Corinthians 4

1 CORINTHIANS 5:8

The unleavened bread of sincerity and truth.

One year I learned to bake sourdough bread. It became a fast family favorite. Every Sunday I would bake two loaves. They would be completely gone before dinner was over. I learned something else during that time as well: it is really hard to manage the starter.

Keeping the starter alive requires adding to it every single day. If you forget, it will turn black and rancid, and you must begin again. The best bread comes from a starter that has been tended for a long time. It has a unique taste that anyone who loves sourdough would recognize. Leaven is made from a small amount of starter and is the beginning for a batch of bread.

When Paul talks about the leaven in chapter five, it reminds me of maintaining a sourdough starter. He says, "Know ye not that a little leaven leaveneth the whole lump?" (1 Corinthians 5:6). This is true about sourdough. If the starter has turned black and you still add it to the leaven, it will ruin the entire loaf. Then Paul talks about the unleavened bread of sincerity and truth. For a minute I want to consider that word, *sincerity*. I am reminded of the importance of keeping the start pure, how it requires daily watch-care and keeping. Paul is not talking about sourdough bread here. He is talking about how we worship. The quality of our faith. Is there a process to the daily watch-care and keeping of my faith? Is there a way to make it more pure?

What does it look like to tend faith?

Sometimes it requires purging. Often it requires sacrifice. At the end of the chapter Paul encourages us to strengthen our faith by spending time with those who are strong in faith. That will provide the best leavening. —EBF

Reflect and Respond
What do you do every day to tend your faith?

Your favorite scripture in 1 Corinthians 5

1 CORINTHIANS 6:20

Ye are bought with a price.

My sons are really into baseball cards. It seems like they have millions of them, and usually about 20,000 are somewhere on their bedroom floor. My younger boys collect any card they can find. To them, each one is a treasure. My older boys started to get into collecting special ones. For each card they found that they thought was good, they wanted to know the worth. We found a website that showed the estimated worth of the cards. But I would always tell them it was just an estimate, because the cards were only worth what someone else was willing to pay for them.

That is the definition of worth—what someone is willing to pay for something. That means that worth can change person to person. One person might think a particular baseball card is worth more than someone else does. The first would be willing to pay more for it. The interesting thing here is that the card does not ever get to determine its worth. Only the owner can.

This is what I think of when Paul tells the Corinthian Saints that they are not their own. At first, it sounds like a negative thing to not be their own. To be "owned" by another. Unless you know what he means. He is talking about worth. And worth can only be determined by the owner. Often we try to determine our own worth, but Paul says you can't, because you are not the owner. You were bought with a price, he said. And that price also determines your worth. Because worth is what someone is willing to pay for something—or in this case, someone. Christ Jesus purchased each of us with His precious blood. That is what each of us are worth to Him. —DB

Reflect and Respond

How does it make you feel to know that Christ gave His life for you?

Your favorite scripture in 1 Corinthians 6

1 CORINTHIANS 7:22

A servant, is the Lord's freeman.

My son and his best friend once owned a mowing company. They would go out from early in the morning until late in the afternoon. Their schedule was always full. One afternoon I received a phone call from someone in the ward next to ours. There was a man who had just returned home from the hospital after suffering a significant heart attack. This man was very particular about the maintaining of his yard. He would not let anyone tend to it besides himself. He had been standing by the window for an hour trying to talk his wife into letting him go out to mow the lawn. It was a bad idea. A neighbor next door wanted to know if Josh and his friend could run over and mow the lawn. I immediately called Josh and they went to the man's house to mow in between jobs. After several minutes, the man's wife came outside and stopped Josh. "What are you doing?" she asked him. "Who told you to come?" Josh replied that he wasn't sure who had asked, but he was happy to help. Then she asked, "Well, who are you?" He replied, "I am a Freeman," to which she responded, "*Of course you are.*" Then she turned around and went back in the house.

When he relayed this story to me after mowing, it made my heart so happy. We had a family scripture during my children's teenage years: "For he that is called in the Lord, being a servant, is the Lord's freeman . . . let every man, wherein he is called, therein abide with God" (1 Corinthians 7:22, 24). This experience reminded me of that scripture. Whenever we received the call, we would choose the opportunity to serve with God, knowing it would qualify us to be the Lord's freeman. It was a verse that defined our way of life. —EBF

Reflect and Respond
How might you serve with God today?

Your favorite scripture in
1 Corinthians 7

1 CORINTHIANS 8:12

But when ye sin so against the brethren … ye sin against Christ.

A few months ago, my daughter came home from school and told us about some of the mean things that some of her friends had said and done to her. For the life of me I cannot understand why kids in middle school want to be so mean. It is a new and difficult time of life for all of them, so why not rally together instead of tearing each other down? I don't think I will ever be able to solve the middle school dilemma, but I want to. As our daughter told us what had happened, I could hear the pain in her voice, and I watched it trickle down her cheek. My own heart broke. She is such a tenderhearted, helpful, and sweet girl. And even if she wasn't, I have been there since day one with her, so she is my treasure. We are connected. So, the way people treat her impacts me. And I take it personally.

It is no wonder that Paul tells the Corinthians that when we sin or wound or betray each other, it is as if we are wounding Christ. He has been there since day one for all of us. We are connected. And the way people feel is deeply personal to Him. He mourns with those who mourn. He feels the pain that each of us do, and perhaps it is doubly painful when that pain is inflicted by someone else that He cares deeply about. This life is hard. It is hard for all of us. So perhaps Paul is calling for us to rally together in Christ, instead of tearing each other down.

If Christ takes it personally when we wound others, my thought is He probably takes it personally when we care for others as well. "Inasmuch as ye have done it unto one of the least of these my brethren, ye have done it unto me" (Matthew 25:40). —DB

Reflect and Respond
What can you do today to mend or heal a fight or disagreement you have with another?

Your favorite scripture in
1 Corinthians 8

1 CORINTHIANS 9:20

Unto the Jews I became as a Jew.

I admire Paul as a master teacher. This is a chapter filled with advice about teaching. He had three qualifiers for them that examined him as a teacher. First, a teacher who ministers about holy things must live the things of the temple, and second, those who preach should live of the gospel. Those are good standards to measure ourselves by. The last qualifier is my favorite—a teacher must make himself a servant to all (see 1 Corinthians 9:3, 13, 14, 19).

Paul defines what it looks like to live as a servant to all like this: "And unto the Jews I became as a Jew, that I might gain the Jews; to them that are under the law, as under the law, that I might gain them that are under the law; to them that are without law, as without law, (being not without law to God, but under the law to Christ,) that I might gain them that are without law. To the weak became I as weak, that I might gain the weak: I am made all things to all men, that I might by all means save some" (1 Corinthians 9:20–22).

Paul met people where they were, as they were.

He taught just as Christ did when He was here. To the Jews he became as a Jew, to the weak he became weak. He entered people's stories and he began his teaching there—where they were, as they were. It is a way of teaching that requires the Spirit, empathy, and adaptability. It was what made Paul a master. Perhaps this week you might consider the people you teach. Where are they in their story? How could you see things from their point of view? Have you ever walked in their shoes? Orchestrate your message to meet them there. —EBF

Reflect and Respond

What can you learn from Paul's method of teaching?

Your favorite scripture in 1 Corinthians 9

1 CORINTHIANS 10:13

But will with the temptation also make a way to
escape, that ye may be able to bear it.

When I was teaching seminary, we always started class with a devotional. We would sing a song, pray, and then someone in the class would share a scripture or some sort of devotional thought to get us going. Throughout my years teaching, there were several scriptures that were shared more often than others. Fan favorites. One of those was 1 Corinthians 10:13.

On purpose, I selected the part of the scripture that many people might not recognize in the heading of this page. It is the second part of the scripture. Many people might not recognize it because, in my experience, when I have heard this scripture quoted, I usually only hear the first half. "God is faithful, who will not suffer you to be tempted above that ye are able" (1 Corinthians 10:13). That is the part that has most often been shared when I was around. However, it is not true. Well, I should say that it is not true without the second half of the thought.

There will be things that will be too hard for us to handle. There will be temptations that are too great for us to bear. We are not enough on our own. Each of us has had experiences and temptations that have come that would have crushed us if we had faced them alone. God does not prevent them from coming like the first half of the scripture seems to say, but rather, He gives us the strength to bear it, or provides a way to escape it through His grace.

If we could handle everything that came our way, we would have no need of a Savior. But we do have a Savior. And we need a Savior. And He will give us strength and escape when we need it. There won't be anything we cannot overcome with Him. —DB

Reflect and Respond

What is something you have overcome with the strength and grace of God?

Your favorite
scripture in
1 Corinthians 10

1 CORINTHIANS 11:25

This do ye . . . in remembrance of me.

It is important to me to know that some of the particulars of our worship today were similar in the New Testament Church. The knowledge connects me to them. One of those is the partaking of the sacrament. Paul reminds us how the Lord took bread the same night He was betrayed. "And when he had given thanks, he brake it, and said, Take, eat: this is my body, which is broken for you: this do in remembrance of me. And after the same manner also he took the cup, . . . saying, This cup is the new testament in my blood: this do ye, as oft as ye drink it, in remembrance of me" (1 Corinthians 11:24–25). In our day, it is a weekly reminder of Him.

As a result of the pandemic, we had the unique opportunity to partake of the sacrament in our homes. Every Sunday, members around the world were able to remember and connect to Him. It was a unique opportunity, one that we may never have in that same way again. One of the things I loved most about that experience was the Spirit that entered our home each Sabbath day. Participating in that ordinance in our home sanctified our house. Paul counsels us, "Let a man examine himself, and so let him eat of that bread, and drink of that cup" (1 Corinthians 11:28). It was as if that examination took place every week in our home. We prepared our home for an increase of the Spirit; we dressed ourselves in a way that would allow us to offer our finest to the Lord. We laid out fresh linen on white plates and watched as each piece of bread was broken for us. It became a reverent time for us, as often as we ate that bread. It is a memory I will cherish forever. —EBF

Reflect and Respond
What lessons have you learned from the sacrament?

Your favorite scripture in
1 Corinthians 11

1 CORINTHIANS 12:27

Now ye are the body of Christ,
and members in particular.

Paul calling the membership of Christ's Church a body is one of my favorite analogies. It comes on the heels of (see what I did there) his list of spiritual gifts. It is not a comprehensive list of spiritual gifts, but a good start. As you move through the list, you find gifts of different kinds. The gift to heal, and the gift to be healed. The gift of wisdom, and one of knowledge. The gift of knowing and the gift of believing. Before he listed the gifts, he taught that "there are diversities of gifts, but the same Spirit" (1 Corinthians 12:4). Meaning, they are all different, but they all come from the same source.

Then came the analogy. All of these gifts, and those who possess them, are members of Christ's body. They are all different, but together they make up one whole. The foot cannot say it is not a part of the whole because it is not the hand. And the ear cannot say it is not a part of the body because it is not the eye. The body of Christ is made up of all the different members. And I think Paul is teaching that it is important to remember that each of them is different from each other, but they still need each other.

Everyone in the Church cannot be an eye. They shouldn't be. If we had a church of only eyes, that would be scary. And we don't want a church of only feet. We want a church where all are different, but all are needed by each other. I think this is one of the reasons God scattered the spiritual gifts among us.

So we would come together and need each other. —DB

Reflect and Respond
What spiritual gifts do you see in others that have been a benefit to you?

Your favorite
scripture in
1 Corinthians 12

1 CORINTHIANS 13:8

Charity never faileth.

Paul teaches that charity is the best gift, more excellent than any other. You could speak with tongues, prophesy, understand all mysteries, have all knowledge, remove mountains, but without charity it counts for nothing (see 1 Corinthians 13:1–2). I read what he writes about bestowing goods to the poor, and how it must be done with charity, and I wonder if there is a way to do that without charity. What is the difference between serving and charity? What does the pure love of Christ look like?

Paul gives us a list:

CHARITY

- Suffereth long
- Is kind
- Envieth not
- Vaunteth not itself
- Is not puffed up
- Doth not behave unseemly
- Seeketh not her own
- Is not easily provoked
- Thinketh no evil
- Rejoiceth not in iniquity
- Rejoiceth in truth
- Beareth all things
- Believeth all things
- Hopeth all things
- Endureth all things
  (see 1 Corinthians 13:4–7)

What if you were to cross out the word *charity* above and write Jesus Christ's name there instead? Could you write examples next to each of those descriptions of a story from the ministry of Jesus Christ? What would a study like this teach you? I think you would quickly notice one important truth: Charity never faileth because Christ never fails. —EBF

Reflect and Respond

How might you practice charity today?

Your favorite scripture in
1 Corinthians 13

1 CORINTHIANS 14:26

Let all things be done unto edifying.

For some reason, I have always been particularly interested in and aware of the reasons why we do certain things. In school, I always questioned the schedule, the amount of credits needed, the structure of classes and tests, and almost every other thing. I think my common question was, "Why do we do it like that?" I wasn't trying to be difficult or rock the boat, I just genuinely was interested in the "why."

That interest was not just with school, but with everything I am involved in. Work, family traditions, the kids' sports teams and activities. Sometimes it happens at church. I cannot help but wonder why we do some of the things that we do.

There are some things I have not gotten an answer for, and some of my whys I might need to wait until heaven to figure out, but in this chapter, Paul gave the Corinthian Saints some advice that gives a good "why" for most of the things we do. "Let all things be done unto edifying" (1 Corinthians 14:26). What if that were the standard? And what if it were not just the standard for what we do in church, but what we do in every sphere of our lives? What if we were always asking ourselves—Am I doing this to strengthen and build up others? If not, why am I doing it?

If Paul were in charge, I think he might say that every meeting, song, prayer, talk, interaction, vacation, counsel, and decision should be made with the standard of edification. Will this build up and strengthen others? If the answer to that is yes, then why not? —DB

Reflect and Respond

What are some of the most strengthening and edifying things that you are involved in?

Your favorite scripture in
1 Corinthians 14

1 CORINTHIANS 15:10

By the grace of God I am what I am.

Our son Garett had the opportunity of being invited to the first round of the 2017 NFL draft. I won't forget the memories of that night. How we sat around the table in the green room waiting for the phone to ring, how Garett held his wife's hand for most of the evening. How the phone call came, and the cameras circled in, and they called for Garett to go out on the stage . . . and then that moment when the producer yelled, "Bring the baby, they want him to bring the baby." Garett couldn't have been more proud.

As he walked down those stairs, I couldn't help but think where he had come from— barely graduating, trouble with the law, a broken family life, a learning disability. Honestly, it was simply miraculous that he had gotten there. The fact that he wanted to share that moment with his son made it even more remarkable.

I won't forget when he walked on that stage. He held little Kingston up like Simba, then he wrapped him up in the jersey with the number 1 on the back. The announcer told him it was remarkable that he was on that stage when you thought of where he had come from. He asked him how he did it. His reply was simple. "By the grace of God I am here." I knew it was true. It reminded me of the words of Paul, "But by the grace of God I am what I am: and his grace which was bestowed upon me was not in vain; but I laboured more abundantly than they all: yet not I, but the grace of God which was with me" (1 Corinthians 15:10). —EBF

Reflect and Respond
How has the grace of God made you who you are?

Your favorite scripture in
1 Corinthians 15

1 CORINTHIANS 16:18

For they have refreshed my spirit and yours.

The last few years of my life have been so busy. I have had a full-time job, my hand in a million other projects, a growing family, a Church calling, and a ton of demands on my time. It has been a little overwhelming and kind of heavy to carry. But during these days, I still would often schedule in lunch with friends. I was too busy for it, but my soul needed it. And it wasn't just any friends—I was always very particular who I chose. The friends I spent time with were ones that "refreshed my spirit." Being with them gave me the kind of energy and motivation I needed to conquer the rest of the tasks ahead.

I was so happy to know that Paul had friends like that as well. When finishing his first letter to the Corinthians, he mentioned at the end that he was so glad that Stephanas and Achaicus had come. He said they supplied "that which was lacking" and "refreshed my spirit and yours" (1 Corinthians 16:17–18). Paul was a busier man than I. He was carrying the burdens of a growing Church in a time without any of the conveniences that I have. How thrilling that he had lunch friends who could give him what was lacking. That could fill in the gaps of where he fell short, and, above all, could refresh his spirit and give him the energy and motivation to keep going.

I wonder what kind of conversations they had and what kind of friends they were. It makes me want to be the kind of person who refreshes others when we are together. Who doesn't bring more problems or burdens to a situation, but rather brings light, strength, and encouragement. Who makes others glad when they come. I want to be a refresher. —DB

Reflect and Respond

Who do you have in your life that refreshes your spirit?

Your favorite scripture in
1 Corinthians 16

2 CORINTHIANS 1:11

Ye also helping together by prayer for us.

One summer I participated in an interfaith event with women from all over the United States. As part of that event, there was a prayer wall. As the day went on, each woman had the opportunity to visit that wall. When you arrived, you were given a small piece of paper to write your prayer request and your first name. Then you would place that paper on the wall. Before you left, you were invited to take a paper from the wall home with you so that you could pray for that woman over the next few weeks and months. In the middle of that day, the entire wall was filled with paper prayer requests, but at the end of the event not one paper remained. Imagine how many prayers were offered that night.

In the first chapter of 2 Corinthians, we read about the "Father of mercies, and the God of all comfort" (2 Corinthians 1:3). One of the ways He provides mercy and comfort to us is through each other. A favorite verse from this chapter reads, "Ye also helping together by prayer for us, that for the gift bestowed upon us by the means of many persons thanks may be given by many on our behalf" (v. 11). Often it is by the means of many people gathering in prayer that the gift is bestowed.

There are two other powerful phrases in this chapter. First, "For our rejoicing is this" (2 Corinthians 1:12). How many times have you found reason to rejoice because of prayers offered in your behalf? Second, "We . . . are helpers of your joy" (v. 24). I love the idea of helping someone find joy through offered prayers. Maybe those two ideas will help define what you might pray for today. —EBF

Reflect and Respond
Who needs your prayers today?

Your favorite scripture in 2 Corinthians 1

2 CORINTHIANS 2:8

Wherefore I beseech you that ye would
confirm your love toward him.

President Henry B. Eyring was once telling a story about the time in his life when he would travel with another man on visits to Church members in their area. As they would drive, the man would often say to President Eyring, "Hal, when you meet someone, treat them as if they were in serious trouble, and you will be right more than half the time." In their ministry, they spent a lot of time meeting a lot of people. Over the years, President Eyring said he learned that his friend was not only right, but was also too low in his estimate ("Try, Try, Try" *Ensign*, November 2018).

I am sure anyone reading this would be able to confirm those numbers based on their own experiences. There are so many people who are facing really difficult things in their lives. Tragedies, disappointments, and weakness are the lot of this mortal world. The person in front of you in line, the girl who cut you off driving, the man mowing the lawn across the street. We may never know what burdens they are carrying, but we can probably assume they are carrying a burden.

This is not new to our day and time. Paul spoke with the Corinthians about this same thing. He reminded them that there are many among us who are "swallowed up with overmuch sorrow" (2 Corinthians 2:7). They face enough already. What they need from us is love. And not just an assumed love, but Paul taught the Saints to "confirm your love" toward them (v. 8). They need to hear it. And then they need to hear it again. —DB

Reflect and Respond

Who can you confirm your love to this week?

Your favorite
scripture in
2 Corinthians 2

2 CORINTHIANS 3:3

Be the epistle of Christ.

I often get asked to write letters of recommendation for people. It is my practice to write down a list of qualities, attributes, or characteristics I know about that person before I begin to write. Usually, they are characteristics that would make them a good fit for the job they are applying for.

In chapter 3 of 2 Corinthians, Paul invites us to "be the epistle of Christ" (2 Corinthians 3:3). *Epistle* means letter, and in my mind, I wonder if Paul is inviting us to be a letter of recommendation for Christ. He explains what this letter might look like: "Written not with ink, but with the Spirit of the living God; not in tables of stone, but in fleshy tables of the heart" (v. 3). Not pen and ink on paper, but living spirit on the heart.

I love the thought of this.

Perhaps you might sit down today and write out what your living letter of recommendation looks like. What are the qualities, attributes, or characteristics of Christ that you have taken on?

How are your actions recommending Him to the people you associate with every day? How is the Spirit working on your heart in a way that reflects Him? —EBF

Reflect and Respond

How might you be the epistle of Christ today?

Your favorite scripture in 2 Corinthians 3

2 CORINTHIANS 4:8

We are troubled on every side, yet not distressed;
we are perplexed, but not in despair.

According to my own observations, there is a common misunderstanding that floats around the Christian world. It is an idea that is not true, and is also a little damaging, in my opinion. It is the idea that a Christian should not ever be depressed, disappointed, or down and out. The counter to it is that if they had faith and hope in Jesus Christ, they would know they did not need to be discouraged by whatever they are facing. But I disagree.

If someone with faith in Christ loses their job, I think they should be nervous and a little overwhelmed by it. If a Christian person loses a family member or friend, I think they should weep. If someone with hope in Jesus has a tree fall onto their roof, I think they should be frustrated and upset about the unfortunate accident. These are the normal things of life, and it is ok for a believing person to be upset about them

Paul agrees and taught us all how to balance our hope and faith in Christ with the sorrow we feel during times of tragedy or disappointment. "We are troubled on every side, yet not distressed" (2 Corinthians 4:8). We will have trouble, but we don't have to feel distress. We can be perplexed, but we do not have to dwell in despair. We might be cast down, but it will not destroy us. To me, Paul is teaching and encouraging us that yes, it is ok to feel trouble, confusion, and heaviness, but deep down inside, because of that hope and faith in Christ, we do not have to be totally ruined or completely lost. In the hard times, we can weep, but also sense a sacred security dwelling underneath. —DB

Reflect and Respond

What gives you confidence and hope during tragic or disappointing times?

Your favorite scripture in 2 Corinthians 4

2 CORINTHIANS 5:2

Our house which is from heaven.

C. S. Lewis once described the process of remodeling a house. He taught, "Imagine yourself as a living house. God comes in to rebuild that house. At first, perhaps, you can understand what He is doing. He is getting the drains right and stopping the leaks in the roof and so on; you knew that those jobs needed doing and so you are not surprised. But presently He starts knocking the house about in a way that hurts abominably and does not seem to make any sense. What on earth is He up to? The explanation is that He is building quite a different house from the one you thought of—throwing out a new wing here, putting on an extra floor there, running up towers, making courtyards. You thought you were being made into a decent little cottage: but He is building a palace. He intends to come and live in it Himself" (*Mere Christianity*).

The gospel of Christ is a gospel of improvements. A process of becoming. We often talk of seeds growing, climbing ladders, or building. Paul says, "For we know that if our earthly house of this tabernacle were dissolved, we have a building of God, an house not made with hands, eternal in the heavens. For in this we groan, earnestly desiring to be clothed upon with our house which is from heaven" (2 Corinthians 5:1–2). It sounds so similar to what C. S. Lewis described. Paul understands that it won't be comfortable, this remodeling of a soul, that we will groan, that sometimes the rebuilding will feel like a burden (see v. 4). But he also tells us to be confident and willing as we become a new creature in Christ (see v. 8). —EBF

Reflect and Respond

Which phase of building are you in? Groaning from the burden or confidently willing?

Your favorite scripture in 2 Corinthians 5

2 CORINTHIANS 6:11

Our heart is enlarged.

I cannot read this verse from Paul's second letter to the Corinthians without thinking of Dr. Seuss's *How the Grinch Stole Christmas*. For those of you who are unfamiliar with the story (and if that's you, it is time to fix that!), Dr. Seuss wrote of a whimsical little village called Whoville where everyone loved Christmas. The Grinch, however, who lived in the mountains above the town, did not. The reason, the book said, was perhaps his heart was too small. One year, the Grinch decided he would steal Christmas. He would take away all of the presents and decorations and the feast of roast beast. Then the Whos in Whoville would not be so joyous on Christmas morning—the thing he hated most.

The Grinch carried out his plan, but was caught in a surprise. Christmas morning came. Even though he stole all of their Christmas things, he could not steal their Christmas joy. As the townspeople began to sing, the Grinch's heart grew and grew. He then returned all that he had stolen and enjoyed Christmas together with the Whos.

This story is obviously fiction, but the idea of a heart that can grow is not. Jesus Christ has the ability to increase all of our capacities. That includes our capacity to love and feel with our hearts. Our hearts can be enlarged to take in more people than we thought they could. Our hearts can be changed to love those we may have considered unlovable. Our hearts can be softened and refined to see and believe and love the very way that God does. Like it did for Paul, this seems to happen most and best when we are in His service. —DB

Reflect and Respond

Have you ever felt your heart change or become enlarged?

Your favorite scripture in 2 Corinthians 6

2 CORINTHIANS 7:1

Perfecting holiness.

Is there a process for perfecting holiness? A process of becoming. At times that process might overwhelm us. We live in a world that is vulgar and profane. There are so many distractions meant to limit our ability to hear the Spirit of the Lord. How do we perfect holiness in a world like this? James E. Faust taught, "Holiness is the strength of the soul. It comes by faith and through obedience to God's laws and ordinances. . . . Holiness speaks when there is silence, encouraging that which is good or reproving that which is wrong" ("Standing in Holy Places," *Ensign*, May 2005). Prophets throughout all ages of time have spoken of this process. "In some remarks by President Brigham Young in the Salt Lake Tabernacle, February 16, 1862, he used the expression 'Holiness to the Lord.' He then further explained what 'Holiness to the Lord' meant to him. I quote: 'Thirty years' experience has taught me that every moment of my life must be holiness to the Lord, resulting from equity, justice, mercy and uprightness in all my actions, which is the only course by which I can preserve the Spirit of the Almighty to myself.'"

Paul talks about how overwhelming the process of perfecting holiness can be in a world that is "troubled on every side; without were fightings, within were fears. Nevertheless God, that comforteth those that are cast down, comforted us by the coming of Titus" (2 Corinthians 7:5–6). Sometimes holy places are found in friends or leaders who are sent to strengthen us in a world of distractions and remind us what perfecting holiness truly is. God will send holy people to comfort those in times of trouble. It is why we must grow in holiness. We never know when it will be our turn to be sent. —EBF

Reflect and Respond
Who has God sent to help you perfect your holiness?

Your favorite scripture in 2 Corinthians 7

2 CORINTHIANS 8:11

Perform the doing of it.

I am a man of many ideas. I am a dreamer and a brainstormer and an idea generator. One of my more recent ideas was to get a milk cow for our family. A friend of mine has one, and I am just entranced by the idea of getting fresh milk and cheese and cream from my own milk cow. A cow would not fit in my current backyard, so this idea would require purchasing more land (with money I don't have) and hiring milkers, because I don't necessarily want to actually milk the cow. I just want the milk. And the cheese. And butter.

My sister asked me the other day, "So, what's this about the farm and the cow?" I was surprised she knew, and I asked her how she had found out about it. "Oh, Christian told me. But he also told me, 'It's just another one of Dad's crazy ideas that he will never follow through with.'" And because of that, I am most certainly going to buy the farm and the barn and the cow just to prove to him I can follow through. And I will not be hiring milkers, because Christian will be doing all the milking as a penalty for his disbelief. And for calling me out on what is true.

Perhaps I should follow Paul's advice and "perform the doing of it" (2 Corinthians 8:11) more often. In Paul's letter he was referring to the financial need of other Church members. In addition to financial need, certainly they had needs of other kinds. When help is needed, there is often a lot of sympathy and ideas on how to help, but it is less common to find people willing to actually do something about it. This is what Paul was encouraging.

Be wise. Do what you can.

But be a doer. —DB

Reflect and Respond

What is an idea you have had to help someone in need recently?
How can you perform the doing of it?

Your favorite
scripture in
2 Corinthians 8

2 CORINTHIANS 9:15

Thanks be unto God for his unspeakable gift.

All of my pregnancies were hard, but the fourth one was the hardest of all. I went into early labor and the doctor was unsure if the baby would make it. After several weeks of complete bedrest and constant contractions, my doctor suggested we consider a surgery that would be risky this late in the pregnancy but was our best chance of getting a healthy baby here. The complication was that I wouldn't be able to take the medication that was stopping the contractions for twelve hours before the surgery, and that the surgery could induce hard labor and I would lose the baby immediately. As the anesthesiologist counted down from ten, I remember offering the shortest prayer I had the entire pregnancy, "Lord, Thy will be done."

I remember waking up in the recovery room and seeing the anesthesiologist sitting on a chair near me. I was so groggy I could barely get my lips to move, but I asked him the only thing I cared about. "Did it work? Am I still pregnant?" I remember his short answer, "Yes" and then I drifted off to sleep again. As I closed my eyes I heard the Spirit whisper, *Thanks be unto God for His unspeakable gift.*

That afternoon, I pulled out my scriptures and began searching for the phrase *unspeakable gift.* I stumbled on this verse in 2 Corinthians that has become a favorite of mine, "And by their prayer for you, which long after you for the exceeding grace of God in you. Thanks be unto God for his unspeakable gift" (2 Corinthians 9:14–15). I thought of all of the people who had been praying for me and of the enabling strength I had been given and would continue to receive, and His unspeakable gift.

God is so good. —EBF

Reflect and Respond
When have you received an unspeakable gift from the Lord?

Your favorite scripture in 2 Corinthians 9

2 CORINTHIANS 10:13

A measure to reach even unto you.

I was talking with a good friend of mine once about life. It was a conversation about goals and dreams and ambitions. We were both talking about where we had been and where we would like to go next. As part of the conversation, my friend expressed a little bit of disappointment in himself for who he was and what he was doing with his life. I pressed him on it a little bit. He went on to tell me about how much money everyone else his age was making compared to living paycheck to paycheck the way he was. He told me about the jobs they had and the opportunities they were pursuing. He talked about their relationship statuses and the families they were starting. In all of his observations, he wasn't measuring up.

As we talked, I had him consider what he was measuring his successes and failures off of. What scale was he using, and where did he even come up with it? It was easier to see from my point of view that he was comparing against a measure that wasn't his to use. It was theirs.

Paul counseled others in a similar way, teaching them that we don't boast by measures that are not ours. We should not consider ourselves better or less by using the measures of other people. Instead, we should view our lives "according to the measure of the rule which God" has given us (2 Corinthians 10:13). His standards should be our measure. What are we doing with the life and gifts and direction that He has given to us? We may never live up to the other measures that we compare ourselves to. But God, He has a measure that can "reach even unto you" (v. 13). Wherever you are, and whatever your circumstances are, you can grow and progress in the Lord. —DB

Reflect and Respond

Take some time to look at your life through the measure of the Lord, instead of comparing yourself to others.

Your favorite scripture in 2 Corinthians 10

2 CORINTHIANS 11:23

I am more.

This is a chapter where Paul goes after those who are a counterfeit of Christ. False prophets. Deceivers. I can see why he is frustrated. We live in a day of great influence. Social media abounds with people telling us what to think, eat, and purchase. Philosophies are shared in abundance. All of the noise filters into our society and causes cultural and social unrest. It is hard to know who to listen to and who to mute.

The same must have been true in Paul's day.

There is a moment when he describes what makes them all alike. "Are they Hebrews? so am I. Are they Israelites? so am I. . . . Are they ministers of Christ?" (2 Corinthians 11:22–23). Here is where the separation begins. Paul says, in essence, "*I may be a terrible speaker, but as a minister of Christ I am more*" (see 2 Corinthians 11:23). If we wonder how he is more of a minister of Christ, "I was beaten for Him, shipwrecked for Him, stoned for Him, He is the reason for my frequent journeys, the cause of my perils in the sea, in the wilderness, in my own country, for Him I have been weary, hungry, wounded, cold, and naked, and yet I glory, because God knows my work" (see 2 Corinthians 11:24–31).

I am more.

One year my friends took me to a birthday lunch. It had been a hard year. One of my friends asked me to sum up my year with one word. The word I chose was *more*. I had never cried more, served more, or prayed more, and yet somehow, through it all, I was made more, made enough to overcome it all, through Him. Christ was the difference maker. In Him, I am more. —EBF

....

Reflect and Respond
How has Jesus Christ made you more?

Your favorite scripture in
2 Corinthians 11

2 CORINTHIANS 12:10

For when I am weak, then am I strong.

Sometimes, the words and ways of Jesus are opposite of what we think they would be. For example, once He said, "He that loseth his life for my sake shall find it" (Matthew 10:39). That doesn't make sense at first. How can you find something by losing it? On another occasion He said that those who humble themselves are exalted. In other words, you must go down to go up. My mom always taught me that what goes up must come down. Opposites.

We find another one here in the words of Paul. "For when I am weak, then am I strong" (2 Corinthians 12:10). You see, it just doesn't seem to make sense at first. But maybe it does. Paul explained to the Corinthian Saints that he had a weakness—something he called a "thorn in the flesh" (v. 7). He didn't like it and asked the Lord three times to take it away. But the Lord didn't. Instead, He taught Paul that the weakness was actually a gift. For without weakness, you would never need grace. And grace is strength. It comes alive in places of weakness. So, weakness actually leads to receiving strength. What Paul at first thought was getting him down was actually pushing him down to his knees. And humbly on his knees, he received grace and strength. So, the weakness was a gift. And it led him to say, "When I am weak, then am I strong."

Perhaps after that day, Paul stopped praying for the Lord to take away the weakness. If He did, He also would have been taking away Paul's chance to rely on Him. In doing so, He would have taken away his strength. —DB

Reflect and Respond

What weakness do you have in your life that causes you to trust in God more fully—thus becoming stronger?

Your favorite scripture in 2 Corinthians 12

2 CORINTHIANS 13:5

Examine yourselves.

Several years ago in general conference, President Dieter F. Uchtdorf spoke about ex-amining faith. He said, "It's natural to have questions—the acorn of honest inquiry has often sprouted and matured into a great oak of understanding. There are few members of the Church who, at one time or another, have not wrestled with serious or sensitive questions. One of the purposes of the Church is to nurture and cultivate the seed of faith—even in the sometimes sandy soil of doubt and uncertainty. Faith is to hope for things which are not seen but which are true.

"Therefore, my dear brothers and sisters—my dear friends—please, first doubt your doubts before you doubt your faith" ("Come, Join with Us," *Ensign*, November 2013).

Shortly after that, President Russell M. Nelson counseled, "Stop increasing your doubts by rehearsing them with other doubters." Instead, he suggested, "Take your ques-tions to the Lord and to other faithful sources" ("Christ Is Risen; Faith in Him Will Move Mountains," *Liahona*, May 2021).

This counsel sounds much like the counsel of Paul, "Examine yourselves, whether ye be in the faith; prove your own selves. Know ye not your own selves, how that Jesus Christ is in you?" (2 Corinthians 13:5). He is giving us counsel to continually check the status of our faith, to continue to prove it. To use it. To walk in it. He wants us to reflect on whether or not Jesus Christ is in us. This feels like it might be something to ponder on regularly.

Maybe we could consider making it part of our Sabbath.

A recurring check-in to examine our faith. —EBF

Reflect and Respond
How might you examine your faith today?

Your favorite scripture in 2 Corinthians 13

GALATIANS 1:23

He which persecuted us in times past.

I am a strong believer in second chances. Perhaps it is because I have had the opportunity over the course of my life to witness long and lasting changes in people I love. An alcoholic who has been sober for thirty-seven years. Someone who struggled with a porn addiction and was able to rise above it.

Some things take time.

But they also take people who will cheer you on, support you, believe in you. I will never forget a ward council I participated in many years ago. Our bishop had a list of names of people who were really struggling. He told us he wanted to read through the list and ask one simple question, *is anybody cheering for them?* Then we would discuss as a group who might be the right kind of encourager for their situation. It was one of the most memorable ward councils I have ever attended. It taught me something important. We are all struggling with something, and our success has a greater chance if someone is willing to walk that journey with us and cheer us on along the way. I want to be known as a cheerleader.

There are several places in the New Testament where we read Paul's conversion story. The first chapter in Galatians is one of those. He tells us of his experience with Christ, how he spent time solidifying what had been revealed to him, and then how he finally went up to Jerusalem and stayed with Peter for fifteen days. Then, he began preaching. His story went before him: "They had heard only, That he which persecuted us in times past now preacheth the faith which once he destroyed" (Galatians 1:23). I love that they gave him a chance. —EBF

Reflect and Respond

Who needs you to give them a second chance today? Who are you cheering for?

Your favorite scripture in Galatians 1

GALATIANS 2:20

I live by the faith of the Son of God,
who loved me, and gave himself for me.

When I read this particular verse, I am caught up in the way that it is worded. It might just be a translation thing, but I appreciate the way it comes across. Generally, I hear people use the phrase "faith *in* the Son of God." A phrase that means we trust in Him and live accordingly. Paul says that he lives a life "by the faith *of* the Son of God" (Galatians 2:20; emphasis added). Again, I might be reading too much into it, but I really like the idea of the Son of God having faith in me. That I live my life knowing that He believes in and trusts me. Whether Paul meant this or not, I think it is true. He is a God that is for us. And even if I am reading that first part wrong, I am confident in the second part. Paul lives a life knowing that Jesus loves him and gave Himself for him.

My friend Grace was once on a road trip and did a question-and-answer on her Instagram stories. One of the questions that came in was, "If your students could only take one thing away from seminary, what would you want it to be?" I adore her answer. She said, "A life with God is a life loved." Amen and amen.

One of the thrills of living a life with God is precisely that. You get to live a life with God. You have companionship with Him and encouragement from Him. You get to live each day knowing that He loves you and is looking out for you. What if we all lived loved? I think there would be a lot less contention and comparing. There would be more confidence and compassion. This is the life Paul talked about. This is the life He is calling us all into. —DB

Reflect and Respond

What has been the impact in your life knowing that you are living loved?

Your favorite
scripture in
Galatians 2

GALATIANS 3:29

Heirs according to the promise.

Abraham and Sarah were given a promise from the Lord. That promise included a posterity that would number the stars of heaven. It seemed like a promise that was unreachable, especially because Sarah was barren. Have you ever felt that God's promises were unreachable?

One of my life rules is to never miss a meteor shower. One summer, I grabbed a thick white blanket off the couch and a mug of hot chocolate from the kitchen and went outside to see the display. I had a lot on my mind that night. All of it filled my thoughts as I waited for my eyes to adjust to the darkness. While I waited, I prayed. "Are you here, Lord? Are you aware of this? Are you leading us through what lies ahead?" And then, the first shooting star shot across the night sky, leaving a trail of glitter in its wake. I wonder if Abraham had nights like that. Moments when he wondered if God would remember His promise. If He was able also to perform it (see Romans 4). Did he see God's answer in the small things?

In general conference of October 2020, President Russell M. Nelson said, "As you study your scriptures during the next six months, I encourage you to make a list of all that the Lord has promised He will do for covenant Israel. I think you will be astounded! Ponder these promises. Talk about them with your family and friends. Then live and watch for these promises to be fulfilled in your own life" ("Let God Prevail," *Ensign*, November 2020). Sometimes we have to live and watch, especially when we are feeling barren. We all have the right to God's promise, "And if ye be Christ's, then are ye Abraham's seed, and heirs according to the promise" (Galatians 3:29). —EBF

Reflect and Respond

What is one way you could remind yourself of God's promises today?

Your favorite scripture in Galatians 3

GALATIANS 4:6

And because ye are sons, God hath sent forth the Spirit
of his Son into your hearts, crying, Abba, Father.

I have grown up learning and reading and singing that "I am a child of God." This is a truth I believe, and I believe it literally. I actually think I am a son of heavenly parents. I believe, as Paul said, I am an heir to Them. I think They see me and treat me and think of me as one of Their own. Sometimes, I even think I am a favorite of Theirs.

This verse in Galatians is interesting to me because it seems to describe the moment when someone who knows in their mind that they are a child of God, or has accepted it logically, begins to believe and feel it in their heart as well. This is a different kind of witness. I have always described it as the difference between saying my dad loves me, and then having him pick me up and twirl me around. One of them I hear, and the other I experience and feel.

According to Paul, because we are children, just like Jesus is, we can experience the Spirit of His Son in our own hearts. When Jesus was in the Garden of Gethsemane, and perhaps in other places, He called out to God as "Abba." This is an Aramaic word that has the feeling of tenderness. Similar to someone calling out "Papa" or "Daddy" (see Jeffrey R. Holland, "The Hands of the Fathers," *Ensign*, May 1999).

As His children, we can experience that same type of tenderness and closeness with the Father that we see Jesus had and has with the Father. It is not just an official relationship, but one that we can enjoy the spirit and thrill of.

One where we can feel twirled around. —DB

Reflect and Respond

When have you felt in your heart that you were a loved and adored child of God?

Your favorite
scripture in
Galatians 4

GALATIANS 5:10

I have confidence in you.

"Stand fast . . . and be not entangled" (Galatians 5:1).

"Ye did run well; who did hinder you . . . ?" (Galatians 5:7).

"I have confidence in you . . . that ye will be none otherwise minded" (Galatians 5:10).

Paul was a motivator at his core. He was all about lifting people and making them better. I love that every caution included something positive about the person. I often wonder what made him so good at that. I think the answer might be found in Galatians 5:14, "Thou shalt love thy neighbour as thyself." Paul led with love. It's what he was good at. If you look carefully at what motivates his writings, it is words of love and grace.

Paul had learned how to live and teach with the Spirit. He taught "love, joy, peace, longsuffering, gentleness, goodness, faith, meekness, temperance" (Galatians 5:22–23). Perhaps it was this gift that allowed him to be such an inspiration to people.

I once had a teacher like this. She taught a one-hour class once a week. I never missed it. Partly it was because of what I learned when I was there, but mostly it was because of how I felt when I left. I felt empowered and motivated and like I could accomplish anything. Her teaching style was a gift, and it made me better.

Maybe this week you could consider Paul's teaching style. Look back over the last few chapters and keep the focus as we move forward. What are some characteristics of Paul as a teacher that you might implement in your own teaching? Make a list. Highlight the verses. Our Church classes could use some of Paul's enthusiasm, boldness, and love. —EBF

Reflect and Respond

Consider a teacher that made a great impact on your life. What can you learn from their teaching?

Your favorite scripture in **Galatians 5**

GALATIANS 6:9

And let us not be weary in well doing.

There are a lot of things that we can grow tired of. We can get tired of movies that our kids or younger siblings watch over and over. We get tired of songs that are played on the radio too much. We can get tired of each other when we overstay our welcome. We might get tired of the same dinner our mom makes at least once a week.

It is natural to get tired or bored of certain things. All of us want to quit something every now and then. But Paul says, of anything you may get tired of, please don't get tired of this. "Let us not be weary in well doing" (Galatians 6:9). We can turn off the shows and the radio and we can order DoorDash instead of that same dinner, but please don't quit well doing.

At the end of Matthew chapter 9, a catalog of a day in the life of Jesus, the Lord sees crowds of people who need help and is moved with compassion. He told the disciples with Him that "the harvest truly is plenteous, but the labourers are few" (Matthew 9:37). In other words, there are a lot of people who need help, but not enough helpers. So, He gathered them in prayer to petition the Father to send more helpers.

When I look around me, I see the same thing Jesus saw. Groups of people who are in desperate need of compassion. A whole lot of help needed. I also look around me and see an answer to that 2,000-year-old prayer. I see the helpers. God bless us all to never grow tired of well doing—to never grow tired of helping. —DB

Reflect and Respond
Who do you know that you would describe as someone who never grows weary of well doing?

Your favorite scripture in **Galatians 6**

EPHESIANS 1:9

His will, according to his good pleasure.

I was once sitting on my friend's couch after a particularly hard week. It was one of those weeks where you wonder if the world will ever right itself again. This particular week I was navigating a challenge that wasn't going to right itself in this lifetime, but I had been praying for strength and hope and the best outcome for what we were facing. That afternoon I happened to read a poem that was in a book on her end table.

"Rondel," by George MacDonald

I do not know thy final will,
It is too good for me to know;
Thou willest that I mercy show,
That I take heed and do no ill,
That I the needy warm and fill,
Nor stones at any sinner throw;
But I know not thy final will

It is too good for me to know.
I know thy love unspeakable—
For love's sake able to send woe!
To find thine own thou lost didst go,
And wouldst for men thy blood yet spill!—
How should I know thy final will,
Godwise too good for me to know!

I had never before thought about God's will being good. The hope of that led me to scripture to see if it was true. Paul tells us, "Having made known unto us the mystery of his will, according to his good pleasure which he hath purposed in himself" (Ephesians 1:9). Don't you love that *will* and *good pleasure* are right there in the same sentence? It became a lifelong scripture challenge, to find everywhere in scripture that talks about God's good will. —EBF

Reflect and Respond
What is your favorite scripture that teaches about God's good will?

Your favorite scripture in
Ephesians 1

EPHESIANS 2:19

Now therefore ye are no more strangers and foreigners, but
fellowcitizens with the saints, and of the household of God.

I was in Korea the very first time The Church of Jesus Christ of Latter-day Saints held general conference in the newly built Conference Center. Up until that particular year, general conference had been held in the much smaller Tabernacle on Temple Square. The new Conference Center had the capacity to seat close to 21,000 people, and the room general conference was held in could fit a full 747 jet inside. It was massive, particularly compared to the Tabernacle.

I was watching from a folding chair in the kitchen/Sunday School room of a second-floor rented church space in Seoul. There were four of us in the room. When the conference started, the camera did a sweeping pan across all of the people in the room singing the opening song. Afterward, we bowed our heads and prayed with the Saints all across the world. It was a moving experience for me. I felt what I think Paul was saying to the people of Ephesus.

I imagine they did not have huge gatherings of Saints in Ephesus during the first century. Perhaps they felt isolated, like most of the branches of the Church may have felt. But Paul was teaching them something powerful. He taught them that they were all a part of the household of God. They were each fellowcitizens, wherever they lived, with all of the Saints. When they walked into the homes or worship places of their fellow believers, they were not walking in as strangers or foreigners.

They belonged.

We do too. —DB

Reflect and Respond

When have you felt a sense of citizenship and community with other believers?

Your favorite
scripture in
Ephesians 2

EPHESIANS 3:20

Exceeding abundantly above all that we ask or think.

One of the best scriptures in the New Testament is found in Ephesians 3. As you read through these verses, underline the words that stand out to you about Christ's love:

"That he would grant you, according to the riches of his glory, to be strengthened with might by his Spirit in the inner man; That Christ may dwell in your hearts by faith; that ye, being rooted and grounded in love, may be able to comprehend with all saints what is the breadth, and length, and depth, and height; And to know the love of Christ, which passeth knowledge, that ye might be filled with all the fulness of God. Now unto him that is able to do exceeding abundantly above all that we ask or think, according to the power that worketh in us, unto him be glory . . ." (Ephesians 3:16–21).

Were any of these the words you chose?

- love
- power
- might
- length
- filled
- depth
- height
- rooted
- fulness
- breadth
- abundantly
- strengthened
- worketh in us
- passes knowledge

I have felt the love of Christ many times in my life. Perhaps the same is true for you. I think of moments when He showed up in my story—the middle of the night in my bedroom in Draper, Utah; after a surgery in the recovery room of St. Mark's Hospital; sitting on an orange plastic chair outside the counseling office in Ventura, California. He can show up in the most ordinary places, and His love can reach us anywhere.

A love that passes knowledge. —EBF

Reflect and Respond

What do these verses help you to understand about the love of Christ?

Your favorite scripture in **Ephesians 3**

EPHESIANS 4:11-12

And he gave . . . for the perfecting of the saints . . .
for the edifying of the body of Christ.

God is the giver of all the best gifts, and He is so liberal in His giving. If we wanted to, we could sit down together and begin a list of all of the greatest gifts that God has given to us. I suppose we would start that list and never find a good time to stop. It is a list that is still ongoing. If I were making that list with you, I would begin my section of gifts with people. I think the greatest gift God has given us is each other.

"And he gave some, apostles; and some, prophets; and some, evangelists; and some, pastors and teachers" (Ephesians 4:11). These are all people. And why did He give them? Paul went on to say, "For the perfecting of the saints . . . for the edifying of the body of Christ." He gave them to make our lives better. To build us up and to make us whole. And He will keep doing this until He reaches the end. And according to Paul, the end looks like all of us coming together "in the unity of the faith, and of the knowledge of the Son of God . . . unto the measure of the stature of the fulness of Christ" (Ephesians 4:12–13).

The inclusion and the intention in these verses is breathtaking to me. As I look back on my life, I can see so many people that God has given to me to help bring about these beautiful purposes. Teachers, pastors, prophets, and more. And because I'm not done yet, I expect it is something He will continue to do. —DB

Reflect and Respond
Who has God given to you to help you become more whole?

Your favorite
scripture in
Ephesians 4

EPHESIANS 5:19

Speaking to yourselves in . . . spiritual songs.

A friend once asked me what I do when life feels dark. He wondered if I had a go-to list of things that brought the light back in. I actually do. There are several things I do on dark days. Simple things like eating chocolate chip cookies at 3:00 in the afternoon for a pick-me-up. Going for a walk outside. Calling a good friend to talk things through.

One of my best go-tos is a playlist of songs that fill me with hope and light. I add to that playlist all of the time, anytime I find a song that lifts my heart. If I ever wake up feeling down, I just hit play and turn up the speaker really loud. Paul did the same thing. You might not believe me, but it's true.

"Speaking to yourselves is psalms and hymns and spiritual songs, singing and making melody in your heart to the Lord; giving thanks always for all things unto God and the Father in the name of our Lord Jesus Christ" (Ephesians 5:19–20). What are your psalms and hymns and spiritual songs? What is the music that lifts your heart? Do you have a playlist that brings light in the darkness?

I love the second piece of counsel Paul gives here as well, to give thanks. Sometimes the only thing that can lift a heart on the darkest days is to find something to be thankful for. There are many nights I have climbed in bed after a hard day and found it hard to fall asleep. On those nights I always do the same thing . . . I start listing what I am thankful for. It brings peace. It quiets a troubled soul. It reminds me I haven't been forgotten.

Maybe you could start a playlist filled with light this week. Perhaps you will make a list of things you are grateful for. Here's hoping your week is filled with light and joy! —EBF

Reflect and Respond

If you were to add one song to your playlist of happy songs, what would it be?

Your favorite scripture in Ephesians 5

EPHESIANS 6:11

Put on the whole armour of God, that ye may be able
to stand against the wiles of the devil.

When I was younger, I went to a camp that had an archery field. I loved Robin Hood and Hawkeye and Legolas, so I knew that was where I wanted to spend most of my time. The first day I went, the instructor took us through all the dos and don'ts of shooting a bow and arrow and then had us select our weapon of choice and begin our training.

I was standing in my spot, sliding the arrow onto the string, when one of the helpers came to me and said, "You are probably going to want to put on an arm guard." I didn't really think I needed one, so I told him thanks and continued to ready myself for shooting. My first arrow was a moderate success. Perhaps I was an archery protégé. But when I shot the second arrow, the string came whipping forward right into my forearm. Ouch! That's why I wanted an arm guard.

The thing about the arm guard is it was available and ready.

I just didn't put it on.

I was thinking about that experience while reading Paul's teachings about the armor of God. "Put on" the armor, he tells the Ephesian Saints. I hear him saying something like, "It is there, you just have to put it on. It will protect you. You will need it. Without it, you will get hurt."

The battle rages around us. The consequences of this battle seem more severe than a welt on the forearm. "We wrestle not against flesh and blood, but against principalities, against powers, against the rulers of the darkness" (Ephesians 6:12). No matter how scary the description of the enemy may be, there is a promise, "You will be able to stand." No matter the circumstance you are in, the outcome is certain—if we just put it on. —DB

Reflect and Respond

When have you felt protected or encouraged or strengthened in your battles?

Your favorite
scripture in
Ephesians 6

PHILIPPIANS 1:6

He which hath begun a good work in you will perform it.

In February of 2019, Elder Ronald A. Rasband spoke to seminary and institute teachers around the world. One thing he told them was the importance of helping their students find a protection scripture. "Help students identify a 'protection scripture,' one they can call to mind when they are in a perilous situation or need the strength" ("Jesus Christ Is the Answer," Evening with a General Authority, February 2019). I was teaching seminary at the time, and I remember spending an entire class period where each student found his or her protection scripture. At the end of class, we passed around a piece of paper for everyone to write the reference of their protection scripture. No one picked the same scripture—isn't that amazing? I copied that list and gave one to every student to keep in the back of their scriptures in case they ever needed strength.

Over my life I have had the practice of gathering scriptures that bring me strength. In almost every chapter of scripture I will have marked a favorite verse. I have leaned on some of those verses enough that I have them memorized. One of those is in this chapter. It reads, be "confident of this very thing, that he which hath begun a good work in you will perform it" (Philippians 1:6). In the moments when I am up against a hard thing, if there is a task I don't think I am qualified to perform, if I ever get nervous or uncertain about my abilities, I say this scripture to myself, *be confident of this very thing, that he which hath begun a good work in you will perform it.* Just the reciting of it over and over again gives me courage and strength. I have confidence in Him because He has helped me perform those good things before. —EBF

Reflect and Respond
What good thing has He helped you to perform?

Your favorite scripture in Philippians 1

PHILIPPIANS 2:10

That at the name of Jesus every knee should bow.

A few years ago, I went on a trip to China with a friend. At one point we were sitting in a hotel lobby with several new Chinese friends chatting. As we talked, the topic of religion came up. They asked us about our faith. We, in turn, asked them about theirs. I was surprised to learn that of all of our new friends who were there, none of them believed in God. I couldn't get over it. Most of the people I know have some sort of belief in God. As I walked the streets of the city that day, I passed by what seemed like hundreds of thousands of people. As I walked, I thought about my conversation in the hotel lobby, and I wondered how many of the people I was passing also didn't believe in God.

It made me sad to think of so many people living their lives not knowing about their Father in Heaven. Not knowing they have an all-powerful and all-compassionate set of parents watching over what they see, think, feel, and do. They have access to empathy, and strength, and love unbounded—and they don't know.

Paul says there will come a day when every knee will bow at the name of Jesus.

That scripture gives me such great hope. I have so many reasons to bow my knee before Jesus. He has done so much for me and the people I love. He has been there for me in my hardest hours. He has forgiven me on countless occasions and encourages me to try and try again. He has loved me better than anyone else. It thrills me to know that one day, everyone will get to know Him in this way. One day, everyone will have their own reasons to bow before Him. —DB

Reflect and Respond

What reason do you have to bow your knee before Jesus today?

Your favorite scripture in **Philippians 2**

PHILIPPIANS 3:13

Reaching forth.

I took marine biology my senior year of high school. When you go on field trips in marine biology you don't take a bus, you take a boat. On this particular day we were going to tour the Channel Islands. On our way to the islands, we saw a blue whale, some flying fish, and several dolphins who played in the wake of the boat. Just before the island we saw a shark. When we finally arrived at the island we were going to tour, I was surprised. I hadn't realized that to get to the island we would have to climb up a cliff. I don't remember all the details, but I do remember a ladder that had been drilled into the face of the cliff, and I remember having to reach up and grab the ladder when the tide rose high enough.

I'm not going to lie; I was so nervous about the reaching that I almost stayed in the boat, but then I remembered the shark. I can remember in detail the boat rising, the reaching, the moment my hands grasped hold, and the climbing. I don't remember anything else about the entire field trip. I think sometimes we underestimate the power of reaching moments in our lives. They are also some of the most powerful moments in scripture. Consider the woman reaching for Christ's robe, and Peter reaching for the Lord when he was drowning. Consider how the Savior was right there with them in those reaching moments.

Paul experienced reaching moments too. I love what he teaches about them: "This one thing I do, forgetting those things which are behind, and reaching forth unto those things which are before, I press toward the mark for the prize of the high calling of God in Christ Jesus. Let us therefore . . . be thus minded" (Philippians 3:13–15). Forget what is behind you. Reach. —EBF

Reflect and Respond
What have you learned from the reaching moments in your life?

Your favorite scripture in
Philippians 3

PHILIPPIANS 4:13

I can do all things through Christ which strengtheneth me.

Philippians 4:13 must be one of the most oft-quoted scriptures of all time. It is surely in the scripture Hall of Fame. I have seen it on T-shirts, hats, Instagram accounts, necklaces, bracelets, and on the sides of shoes. It is a verse that strikes a chord with so many people. It is encouraging, hopeful, and simple.

The book of Philippians is believed by many to have been written from prison. Paul spent a lot of time behind bars for his faith in Christ. During one of these prison sentences, Paul wrote this prison sentence. He wrote this letter as a way to encourage the Saints in Philippi. I don't know if it encouraged them, although I would guess it did, but it has certainly encouraged whole crowds of people since then. I wonder if Paul had any idea his words would have such an impact on the world.

Especially words that he scratched out in a prison cell.

His prison sentence.

I think that is what I love most about it. This is a lesson he learned in prison. I am sure the conditions behind bars were not good. At the very least, his freedom and privileges were limited in some capacity, if not entirely. He was being treated unfairly and unjustly. These were certainly hard days for Paul. But like they are for so many of us, the hard days were what taught him this lesson. It was his prison sentence. In those days he seems to have become acquainted with Jesus. And he seems to have received His strength. Even in his prison, Paul still believed that he could do all things through Christ, which strengthened him. —DB

Reflect and Respond

What is your prison sentence? What is a powerful truth you have learned in a hard time?

Your favorite scripture in **Philippians 4**

COLOSSIANS 1:23

Continue in the faith grounded and settled, and be not moved.

I love to visit the ocean. I have a few rituals that I do every time I go. My first rule as soon as I get to the beach is to take off my shoes. There is something about the sand squishing between my toes that soothes me. Second, I go down to say hello to the ocean. Once I have set out all of my beach things I will go and stand in the water up to my ankles and watch the tide roll in and out and in and out again.

This past year I took my grandchildren with me to the beach. They saw me standing near the water and came to join me. I grabbed their hands and showed them how to dig their feet firmly into the sand, and then they watched their feet become more firmly planted and buried as the tide washed in and out. If you stay in that place long enough, you will find it hard to move. Even if a strong wave comes, the force of the sand around your feet will help you to stay upright. My grandkids loved watching the process of settling take place.

I think of that experience when I read this scripture: He will "present you holy . . . if ye continue in the faith grounded and settled, and be not moved away from the hope of the gospel" (Colossians 1:22–23). Reflect for a minute on those words—continue, grounded, settled, not moved. It is the word *continue* that captures my thoughts first. It is like standing next to the water and letting the tide roll in and out. Continuing is a process. To continue in the faith will take time and repetition, just like sinking your feet into the sand. It doesn't happen when you first plant your feet; it requires the repetition of the tide. Through time and repetition, we become grounded and settled. It is through the process that we become immovable. —EBF

Reflect and Respond

What are the rhythms and repetitions that would help you continue in the faith right now?

Your favorite scripture in Colossians 1

COLOSSIANS 2:14

Blotting out the handwriting of ordinances that was against us
… and took it out of the way, nailing it to his cross.

I once had to go to the emergency room in the middle of the night when Jenny and I were first married. I cannot remember what was wrong, I just remember being in so much pain. We stayed there through the night, and they treated whatever the problem was, and we were able to go home the next day—pain free. That is, until the bill came.

Unknowingly, we went to an emergency room that was not covered by our insurance policy. When I opened the envelope and read the bill I almost fainted. We were newly-wed college students with part-time jobs and not very many pennies to our name. We were barely affording the rent and the macaroni and cheese we were living off of. There was no way we could pay that bill. Yet, there it was, with my name on it. A debt I owed.

It isn't the only debt I owe. Paul says that each of us is indebted because of our sins. Someone could essentially write up the bill of all of our wrongs and send it to us in the mail. Our name would be on it. It would be our debt. But in describing the work and gift of Jesus, Paul said that "the handwriting of our ordinances," or in other words, our bill of debt, was blotted out by Jesus (Colossians 2:14). The bill was nailed to His cross. In Roman times, the soldiers would often nail a piece of paper describing the crimes of the criminal to the cross. Paul seems to be referencing this, explaining that Jesus took our crimes and debts and nailed them to His own cross as if they were His own crimes. In doing so, we were set free through His love. —DB

Reflect and Respond

Have you felt set free from a debt? How does Paul's analogy about Jesus make you feel?

Your favorite scripture in **Colossians 2**

COLOSSIANS 3:23

Whatsoever ye do, do it heartily.

Most of my kids have Bible names. I wanted them to look up to someone in scripture as they lived out their lives. I wanted to name Megan *Magdalene*, but my husband Greg thought it was weird . . . so she is Megan Belle on her birth certificate and Magdalene Belle on my phone. If I could rename Garett, I would choose Hezekiah, but since he is way too old for a renaming, I had to settle for naming him that in my phone as well. Perhaps you wonder why I would choose Hezekiah. The Old Testament describes Hezekiah like this: "And in every work that he began . . . he did it with all his heart, and prospered" (2 Chronicles 31:21).

Out of all my kids, Garett has the biggest heart. If you spend time with him, it doesn't take you long to realize that. He is one of the most forgiving and loving people I have ever met, sometimes to a fault. And yet, his life has been prospered because of that. He is 6' 5" and 305 pounds, and nothing he does is small, including how he loves. He loves big, with his whole heart. Every year at Christmas, Garett's family does a sub for Santa through his work, and every year he asks for the family with the most need. His family takes special care to make sure the presents they choose for each of the children are just what they would give if those children were theirs. I love watching his eyes and his smile as he prepares the packages. It is as if his heart might overflow.

Paul counsels, "Whatsoever ye do, do it heartily, as to the Lord" (Colossians 3:23). Go big. Give everything you have. Put your whole heart into it. What if we lived our whole lives like that? Heartily. Should we try? —EBF

Reflect and Respond
What could you do with your whole heart today?

Your favorite scripture in **Colossians 3**

COLOSSIANS 4:6

Let your speech be alway with grace, seasoned with salt.

When I left home for college, one of the things my family gave me as a going-away gift was a big container of salt. I love salt. I think I love all seasonings, but salt is one of my favorites. I don't think I ate any meal my mom made without adding at least a little extra salt. There are some things I even refuse to eat if there isn't any salt to put on them. It just makes everything taste better.

According to Paul, a little bit of salt makes conversations better as well. These days, the word "salty" means something a little different than it did in Paul's day. Today salty conversations might be described as sassy or having a little bit of bitterness or anger. In Paul's day, when the Saints heard salt, they may have thought of Jesus's commission to His followers to be the salt of the earth. To bring flavor to things. To make them better. Anyone can say and do bland things, but Jesus was calling His disciples to live and speak differently. To be deliberate about adding in something savory to the places we go and the people we are with.

"Let your speech be alway with grace, seasoned with salt" (Colossians 4:6). In our time, let all of your conversations—whether they are in the elevator, at the doctor's office, in line at the DMV, or perhaps most importantly, online—be filled with grace and sprinkled with salt.

Hopefully our presence leaves the conversation and situation a little better.

Just like salt, it doesn't take much to enhance what would otherwise be bland. Our simple kindness and graciousness can leave people with a taste of Jesus. —DB

Reflect and Respond

What little things can you do this week to add grace and Jesus to your conversations?

Your favorite scripture in
Colossians 4

1 THESSALONIANS 1:9

And how ye turned to God.

Sometimes when I read the word *repentance* in scripture, I replace it with "turn again" toward God. It helps me remember the purpose of the word *repentance*. I think of it like a continuum. A process of continually *turning away* and *turning again* as we go through the day.

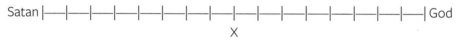

Satan |——|——|——|——|——|——|——|——|——|——|——|——|——| God
X

Paul describes it like this: "For from you sounded out the word of the Lord . . . in every place your faith to God-ward is spread abroad. . . . For they themselves shew of us what manner of entering in we had unto you, and how ye turned to God from idols to serve the living and true God; and to wait for his Son" (1 Thessalonians 1:8–10).

It's the word *God-ward* that I am in love with. It could also be translated as toward God. But I love the thought of *God-ward*. It's like forward and upward mixed together. Heaven bent. Which way are you facing? God-ward. Turning *to* God, *from* something else. It's the entering in. Placing your faith in Him. If you wonder how it is done, Paul gives us a hint. It happens as we *sound out the word* of the Lord. I wonder if you have ever taught a child to read. If you have gone through the process of sounding out words. Paul suggests that is what is going to help us to continue to turn again toward God, sounding out the word. Practicing. Repeating. Turning again and again and one more time. Until we are proficient.

Here's the beauty.

We have a lifetime to get it right. —EBF

Reflect and Respond

What helps you to stay facing God-ward?

Your favorite scripture in
1 Thessalonians 1

1 THESSALONIANS 2:4

We were allowed of God to be put in trust with the gospel.

Whenever I read the Christmas story, I always wonder how the angel who came with the message for the shepherds was chosen. This was one of the greatest nights and most important messages of all time. That angel got to announce the birth of Christ! "Fear not: for, behold, I bring you good tidings of great joy, which shall be to all people. For unto you is born this day in the city of David a Saviour, which is Christ the Lord" (Luke 2:10–11). I cannot get tired of those words. And someone got to be the messenger who would tell the shepherds the good news and ignite the chorus of angels in the sky. How did God choose that angel? What was the criteria to be trusted with such an important message on such an important night? I would have loved that job.

All angels, not just the Christmas one, are sent by God with a message. Each of them is entrusted to carry the mind and word and will of the Lord to whomever they are sent. I have learned that each of them has just as important of a job as the Christmas angel did, for each of God's children are just as important to Him as the next. I think Paul felt that importance when he said, "We were allowed of God to be put in trust with the gospel" (1 Thessalonians 2:4). The people Paul brought the good news to were VIPs. They were the children and heirs of God, Himself. It was an act of great trust to send such an important message to such important people.

So it is with everyone who shares the good news. With everyone sent by God with such glad tidings. How amazing that He would trust any of us with such an assignment. —DB

Reflect and Respond

Who has God entrusted you with to share the glad tidings of great joy?

Your favorite scripture in
1 Thessalonians 2

1 THESSALONIANS 3:2

To establish you, and to comfort you concerning your faith.

Have you ever had a trial of faith so big you weren't sure you were going to make it through? Perhaps it was an illness. Maybe it had to do with emotional health. It could have been a job, or a relationship, or an unanswered promise from the Lord. Trials of faith can leave us feeling fearful and forgotten. I have had several of those.

During one particularly hard trial in our life, we had been promised a resolution that would come through my faith. The thought of that was daunting. As the trial wore on with no end in sight, my faith started to falter. I can remember standing in our bedroom and sobbing to Greg that I didn't have enough faith. I was scared to admit it, but it was true. And the worst of it was that I was certain in saying it out loud, our promise would never be realized. Greg's response was so quick in that moment of devastation. He replied, "If you don't have enough faith tonight, that's fine, I will have enough faith for both of us." His response was so sure and so quick it brought me immediate peace, and I let him be in charge of the faith that night.

Paul talks about something similar. "Wherefore when we could no longer forbear, we . . . sent Timotheus, our brother, and minister of God, and our fellowlabourer in the gospel of Christ, to establish you, and to comfort you concerning your faith: that no man should be moved by these afflictions" (1 Thessalonians 3:1–3).

Perhaps that is why God places us in faith communities, so that when one is weak, the others can establish us in faith and help us to stand fast in the Lord (see 1 Thessalonians 3:8). —EBF

Reflect and Respond
Who has been sent to you in a time of trial to strengthen your faith?

Your favorite scripture in
1 Thessalonians 3

1 THESSALONIANS 4:18

Wherefore comfort one another with these words.

When my parents and some friends were flying from Tokyo, Japan, to Seoul, Korea, their plane was struck by lightning. They said that all of a sudden there was a loud, crashing boom, the whole plane shook, everyone screamed, and the lights flickered. In a flash it was over, but the people riding the plane were still terrified. Soon after, the flight attendant got on the loudspeaker and spoke for a long time in Korean. Finally, when she was done, she spoke in English and said these seven words, "Ladies and gentlemen, everything will be ok." That was not wildly comforting to the English-speaking passengers, considering she had spoken so long in Korean first. Also, how did she know? Was she the god of thunder? Was she in control of the weather?

A lot of times, when someone is in distress or worry or in the middle of a problem, a friend will come to them with the same words. "Everything is going to be ok." And just like with my parents on the plane, those words don't have much weight or promise to them. They are nice to hear, but they are hard to believe. What power does the friend have to bring them about?

This is why I love what Paul teaches to the Thessalonians. "Wherefore comfort one another with these words." Which words? If you look a few verses back, you find Paul talking about the hope that each of us can feel when someone we love dies. The hope that they will rise again. And this hope, Paul said, comes from "the word of the Lord" (1 Thessalonians 4:15). For "the Lord himself shall descend from heaven with a shout" (v. 16). The words of comfort that we can share are powerful because they are His words.

They are His promises. —DB

Reflect and Respond
What promises and words of Jesus can you share to comfort someone else today?

Your favorite scripture in
1 Thessalonians 4

1 THESSALONIANS 5:23

And the very God of peace sanctify you wholly.

Chapter 5 of Thessalonians contains a list of ways to increase the Spirit in your life. As you read through this list, consider which ones you might need to work on right now. You might consider underlining or circling them. Maybe you will copy them down in a place where you will see them and reflect on them daily:

- put on the breastplate of faith and love
- comfort the feebleminded
- support the weak
- be patient toward all men
- ever follow that which is good
- rejoice evermore
- pray without ceasing
- in every thing give thanks
- quench not the Spirit
- despise not prophesyings
- prove all things
- hold fast that which is good
- abstain from all appearance of evil (see 1 Thessalonians 5:8, 14–22)

These are just some of the admonitions Paul gives. Advice to sanctify us wholly. Which ones stand out to you? Did you find any others in this chapter that you could add to this list? —EBF

Reflect and Respond

Which of these suggestions from Paul could you work on today?

Your favorite scripture in
1 Thessalonians 5

2 THESSALONIANS 1:3

And the charity of every one of you.

There are a few times in my life when I have seen charity abound. One of those moments happened many years ago. A good friend of ours had a son who spent all of the money he had saved for his mission on a puppy. The hope was that he would be able to raise this puppy and then breed her and sell those pups to raise enough money for his mission. It was a good plan until his mother backed out of the garage and ran over that little pup.

It was devastating. First, because of the loss of that little creature they had come to love. But second, because it was all the money that boy had, and the family did not have enough money to compensate for the loss. My friend and I thought something must be done. Immediately, we reached out to the man who had sold the first puppy to see if there were any left from the litter. There happened to be one, but my friend and I did not have enough money to cover the cost. So, we reached out to our friends, and they reached out to their friends, and within a couple of days charity abounded from people who had never even met this boy, and the new puppy was purchased. I wish you could have been there on the day we walked into the classroom of the boy. We had called his parents to meet us there. They didn't know why. But when that little brown puppy ran into the room with a large yellow bow tied around its neck, they knew. There were so many tears. I think that's a result of so much charity.

"We are bound to thank God always for you . . . as it is meet, because that your faith groweth exceedingly, and the charity of every one of you all toward each other aboundeth" (2 Thessalonians 1:3). —EBF

Reflect and Respond
Where could you help charity abound today?

Your favorite
scripture in
2 Thessalonians 1

2 THESSALONIANS 2:16

Now our Lord Jesus Christ himself, and God, even our Father . . .
hath given us everlasting consolation and good hope.

When I first read this verse, I was so intrigued with the phrase "good hope" (2 Thessalonians 2:16). It made me wonder if there was bad hope out there. I mean, there are good and bad oranges and good and bad days—is there good and bad hope? I am not sure what Paul meant by that phrase, but I like it.

Hope is a word that can be used in so many different contexts. I could hear someone say, "I hope it doesn't rain tomorrow." Or, "I hope the Astros win tonight." Or, "I hope her flight isn't delayed." This kind of hoping doesn't seem any different than wishful thinking. It is based off of luck. So many factors determine the outcome of situations like this. But Christian hope, the kind that Paul is teaching about, the good hope, seems to be something more.

One Sunday in church, the speaker said that "hope is waiting based on promise." I believe that. The good hope is based on a promise, not on a maybe. It might not be fulfilled yet, but we wait in hope because of who actually promised it. Hope in Christ is not a wishing for something, but rather a trusting in Someone.

Paul said, "Now our Lord Jesus Christ himself, and God, even our Father, which hath loved us" are the ones who are making the promises (2 Thessalonians 2:16). They are the source of the "everlasting consolation" and the "good hope." They have fulfilled promises before, and it is not in Their nature to break them now. As we wait for those promises, we can wait in good hope. And instead of merely positive thinking, we can do some trust placing—in Them. —DB

Reflect and Respond

What do you have good hope for? What promises are you confidently waiting on?

Your favorite
scripture in
2 Thessalonians 2

2 THESSALONIANS 3:11

But are busybodies.

Sometimes I get the biggest kick out of Paul. He just said things how they were. He didn't hold back. This was an occasion like that. "For we hear that there are some which walk among you disorderly, working not at all, but are busybodies" (2 Thessalonians 3:11). Who knew they had busybodies clear back then? I loved Paul's solution for those in this condition. "Now them that are such we command and exhort by our Lord Jesus Christ, that with quietness they work, and eat their own bread" (2 Thessalonians 3:12).

I have a son who believes in this advice. He works at a high-stress job. Sometimes his workplace is emotionally charged. The culture isn't always the best. When people get heated, he will call me and say, "I'm going in silent mode." It always makes me smile. But it works for him. Sometimes the answer for people who meddle or stir the pot is to just go silent for a time.

But that wasn't the end of Paul's advice. The next piece of counsel was to "be not weary in well doing" (2 Thessalonians 3:13). Sometimes quietness has its place, and other times serving has its place. I love the thought of practicing both.

We will all face situations where someone is stirring the pot, meddling, acting disorderly, or causing trouble. Our first response could be irritation, anger, or contention. But what if we were to take a lesson from Paul? What if our first response was to go quiet and serve? To be not weary in well doing, and to go about our business without recognition? I wonder what difference it would make in our homes, in our workplaces, in our faith communities? Should we give it a try? —EBF

Reflect and Respond

How could you be not weary in well doing today?

Your favorite scripture in
2 Thessalonians 3

1 TIMOTHY 1:5

Of whom I am chief.

The first epistle of Paul to Timothy actually comprises all the first four chapters. The letter was a call to arms, and because Timothy was so young, it contained a lot of counsel for the youth. Knowing that he is speaking to someone young, I love the hidden lesson we find in verse 15, "This is a faithful saying, and worthy of all acceptation, that Christ Jesus came into the world to save sinners; of whom I am chief" (1 Timothy 1:15). I love Paul's vulnerability here. How he has nothing to hide. I love that he teaches that the gospel of Jesus Christ is for people who sin, and there is no one there who has sinned more than him. I want to know more about that kind of gospel, especially from that kind of man.

Have you ever met someone who shares the story of their life and their struggles and it is their vulnerability that wins your heart? And you think to yourself, *if Christ could do that for them, I wonder what He could do with me?* Those teachers have the gift of bringing hope through Christ. It is a powerful gift.

Sometimes as parents or teachers we are worried about sharing our mistakes with others. We hide behind a mask of perfection. We never let people see how Christ worked with our weakness because we are ashamed that we are weak. We forget Christ actually does His best work with imperfect people. He creates miracles from the mess. He once healed a man with dirt. Perhaps we might all be a little bit more like Paul. Maybe we could share the vulnerable parts of our stories with the hope that someone will see Christ's best work in us and be led to turn to Him. —EBF

Reflect and Respond

How might you help someone feel worthy of Christ's acceptance through your example?

Your favorite scripture in
1 Timothy 1

1 TIMOTHY 2:10

But ... with good works.

Whenever the scriptures talk about clothing or jewelry or expensive apparel, I always perk up. I need to, because I am the kind of person that genuinely loves clothes. And jewelry. And shoes are my weakness. I could spend all of my dollars on shoes if someone let me. So, I need Paul and others to counsel me on these kinds of things—to keep me and my priorities in check.

In these particular verses, Paul was making a comment about the way people were dressing. He said that people ought not dress themselves with fancy hair, "or gold, or pearls, or costly array" but rather with "good works" (1 Timothy 2:9–10). I don't think Paul has a problem with combing your hair, or with gold or pearls or clothes, but rather he is helping people think more about something else. Instead of focusing all your energy on what you look like, perhaps, he seems to be saying, you could focus on the way you treat other people. Sure, clothe yourself with a new coat, but also clothe yourself with charity. And if you have to pick one or the other, pick the second.

I saw a quote on my Instagram stories the other day that said, "If you're pretty, you're pretty. But the only way to be beautiful is to be loving. Otherwise, it's just 'congratulations about your face.'"

That Instagram post's words or Paul's are not going to make me go clean out my closet—although I probably should—but rather they are going to make me think more about how I treat people than how I look.

To try on virtues more often than shoes. —DB

Reflect and Respond
What characteristics and virtues of Jesus can you wear today?

Your favorite scripture in 1 Timothy 2

1 TIMOTHY 3:2

A bishop then must be . . .

I will never forget one particular Sunday that I was missing church because I was home on bedrest. Greg had gotten up and dressed, gotten our other three kids dressed and ready, and then left for church. I watched our red van pull out of the driveway and sobbed. I was so tired of sitting home alone, of missing out on everything, of not seeing friends or singing hymns or being able to gather. I was just so lonely. And forgotten.

It wasn't long before I heard a car pull up in the driveway. I heard a door slam shut and I glanced up to see who would be coming in. It was my bishop. Right in the middle of church. "What are you doing here?!" I asked, flabbergasted. "Aren't you supposed to be at church?" I know, it was a random thing to ask—*of course* he should have been at church. He was the bishop.

"The Spirit told me to come check on you," the bishop replied simply, "so I came."

I remember thinking that my need wasn't *that* dire. It would have been fine for him to wait until after church was over. But the fact that he left church in the middle of the service to check on one of his ward members taught me a really important lesson—I hadn't been forgotten. The Lord knew about my situation, and so did my bishop.

Over my lifetime it has been my opportunity to have been blessed by many kind and caring bishops. Some have had a greater influence on my life than others, but my life has been blessed by each. Paul describes that service like this: "A bishop then must be . . . vigilant, sober, of good behaviour, given to hospitality, apt to teach" (1 Timothy 3:2–6). I am so grateful for the calling of bishop. —EBF

Reflect and Respond
Could you send a letter of gratitude to your bishop this week?

Your favorite scripture in
1 Timothy 3

1 TIMOTHY 4:15

Meditate upon these things;
give thyself wholly to them.

There is a church I visited in Germany one summer that I will never forget and want to visit again and again. It was not any grander or more beautiful than any other church we visited while in Europe, but the thing that made it stand apart from the rest was the path leading up to it. The church was built on the rolling hills just outside the city. You couldn't access it by car. The only way to the church was a walking path that was about a mile long. This was done on purpose. It was done with the intention that people would slow down before they came to the house of worship. That they would take time to think and meditate before they got there.

We live in a world that is so busy. We are overscheduled and overstimulated. Our minds are constantly being presented with new images, sounds, and ideas. We are suffering from what some call "hurried sickness." Go, go go. More, more, more. Our bodies and spirits were not created to run at this breakneck speed. We need time to think. We need time to meditate. We need time to give ourselves wholly to the Lord and His causes.

In another letter to the Thessalonanians, Paul counseled them to "study to be quiet" (1 Thessalonians 4:11). I appreciate the fact that even in earlier (and what I imagine were simpler) times, the practice of quiet was something that didn't come naturally. It had to be studied. It had to be deliberate. Perhaps that is why the church in Germany was built the way it was—to give people that chance to "meditate upon . . . things," to live out what Paul had counseled. —DB

Reflect and Respond

Where could you go or what could you do to implement the practice of meditating into your worship?

Your favorite scripture in 1 Timothy 4

1 TIMOTHY 5:10

If she have lodged strangers.

Every so often we find beautiful descriptions of women in the scriptures. I try to mark every one. I love the description of what it looked like to be a woman of Christ in the New Testament Church: "If she have brought up children, if she have lodged strangers, if she have washed the saints' feet, if she have relieved the afflicted, if she have diligently followed every good work" (1 Timothy 5:10). The New Testament culture surrounding women doesn't always make sense, but the descriptions often give hints of insight that inspires me, reminding me of images of faithful women in my own time who have left an impression on my own life. One of those was a woman by the name of Jeanne Kesler. I love how she raised her children—diving into the learning with them, providing picnics for our pet rabbits and pool parties with strawberries. I remember how her front door was always open. She was a mother who wanted to spend time with us, listen to us. She believed in us.

In March of 2021, I wrote her a thank-you letter for the impression she left on my life. She responded a couple of weeks later. I pulled the envelope out of my mailbox on a Wednesday, and she died unexpectedly a few days later. That letter has become a keepsake. She wrote, "I have wonderful memories of your growing up. I can remember standing in my study with you listening to your ideas. You were about twelve years old with the talents and ideas of an adult. You are a dear friend also! I am so proud of you!" I want to be the kind of woman that stands in the study listening to the ideas of a twelve-year-old and feels pride. An encourager. A cheerleader. —EBF

....

Reflect and Respond
Who has been this kind of woman for you?

Your favorite scripture in
1 Timothy 5

1 TIMOTHY 6:7

For we brought nothing into this world,
and it is certain we can carry nothing out.

I have a genuine love/hate relationship with funerals. The hating part comes with an obvious explanation. No one likes the fact that someone is now gone—even if it was expected and timely. It is hard to say goodbye. As sad as funerals are, I also think they have been my most uplifting and spiritually refreshing meetings that I have ever been to. I am always encouraged and motivated to be a better husband, father, neighbor, and friend. It lets me remember again what life is really about.

President Russell M. Nelson, who spent his professional career as a surgeon, once told a story about a man he operated on. The man was extremely wealthy and thought his money could buy his way back into health. Unfortunately, it was not the case, and the man passed away. President Nelson recounted that "Someone asked, 'How much wealth did he leave?' The answer, of course was, 'All of it!'" ("Now Is the Time to Prepare," *Ensign*, May 2005).

This seems to be the same thing Paul was teaching when writing to Timothy. Timothy must have had association with people who were wealthier. Paul knew that their money and wealth could be a great blessing to the growing kingdom, but he also knew that it was something that could distract someone from what really mattered. Each of us, Paul taught, "brought nothing into this world," and just like President Nelson emphasized, when we leave, "we can carry nothing out" (1 Timothy 6:7).

Perhaps this truth did and will motivate a wise investment strategy. —DB

Reflect and Respond

How would you describe a healthy relationship with money as a person of faith?

Your favorite
scripture in
1 Timothy 6

2 TIMOTHY 1:6

Stir up the gift of God, which is in thee.

There is a moment in Timothy's story when Paul encourages him, "Neglect not the gift that is in thee" (1 Timothy 4:14). We learn more about that gift in 2 Timothy, "When I call to remembrance the unfeigned faith that is in thee, which dwelt first in thy grandmother Lois, and thy mother Eunice; and I am persuaded that in thee also. Wherefore I put thee in remembrance that thou stir up the gift of God, which is in thee by the putting on of my hands" (2 Timothy 1:5–6). Timothy had the gift of faith. It was a gift that was found in his grandmother Lois, and also in his mother, Eunice. A gift that was passed down from generation to generation. I wonder if your family has a gift like that.

People often tell me I have too much energy. I regularly get asked if I ever sleep. Once a bishop told me I needed to work on simplifying. I tried really hard for a full year. It just isn't in me. Sometimes I feel bad about that characteristic. There were many years the guilt of being an achiever hovered over me. Until my daughter Megan received her patriarchal blessing. During the blessing the patriarch blessed her with the vigor and energy that is characteristic of our family. Immediately a sense of relief overcame me. My vigor and energy *is* a characteristic of my family. My mom has it, and both of my grandmothers. Now I feel like it is a privilege and a gift.

One that I don't want to neglect.

Perhaps there is a gift like that in your family line—a spiritual gift that has been handed down through generations. Maybe you are good at serving, or teaching, or the welcoming in. —EBF

Reflect and Respond

Is there a gift your mother has that you see in your grandmother or grandfather? What is it?

Your favorite scripture in **2 Timothy 1**

2 TIMOTHY 2:3

Thou therefore endure hardness, as
a good soldier of Jesus Christ.

There is absolutely no chance that I could ever serve as a member of one of the armed forces. I was not built or made to be a soldier. I know this about myself. I adore this country I live in with all my heart. I would defend the freedoms of my family and others at all costs. But I would not voluntarily choose to be a soldier. The thought of boot camp alone scares me out of it. Further, I don't like lines and orders and commands and drill sergeants. I have never been in the military, so the only thing I know about them is based on movies, so my assumptions could be way off, but the whole idea of military and war just intimidates and scares me.

Having said that, the people I admire the most are soldiers. I am thinking of one in particular—my friend Dale. I have never met a man with more honor. I have never found someone so bound to duty. It is a duty that is rooted in love and good causes. He is a man who, alongside and with his family, has sacrificed again and again for the welfare of other people. Jesus said that "greater love hath no man than this, that a man lay down his life for his friends" (John 15:13). Dale and his family have done this their whole lives, one day at a time.

I think of Dale and my other military friends when I read Paul's commendation to Timothy: "Thou therefore endure hardness as a good soldier of Jesus Christ" (2 Timothy 2:3).

Battle for Him the way others battle for freedom. Lay down your own life in love of others. Stay true, and don't quit, even when it is boot camp hard. Be a good soldier for Jesus. —DB

Reflect and Respond

How can you practice the same kind of principles soldiers live by in your faith journey?

Your favorite
scripture in
2 Timothy 2

2 TIMOTHY 3:1

In the last days perilous times shall come.

The first few verses of this chapter describe what the world will look like in the last days. A time when people will be focused on self. Their own authenticity and needs. An unthankful people. Unholy. It will be a culture without love, who easily break covenants and promises, people without self-control. A culture without need of goodness, church, God. Sufficient on their own. A people laden with sin, with lust. Fascinated with learning at their fingertips, but none of it truth (see 2 Timothy 3:2–7).

There is an answer for those living in a world like that. Paul says, "Continue thou in the things which thou hast learned and hast been assured of, knowing of whom thou hast learned them; and that from a child thou hast known the holy scriptures, which are able to make these wise unto salvation through faith which is in Christ Jesus. . . . Scripture is given by inspiration of God . . . for doctrine, for reproof, for correction, for instruction in righteousness" (2 Timothy 3:14–16).

Our safety will be found in the word of God. It will instruct us in the right ways when perilous times come. Elder Jeffrey R. Holland taught, "In moments of fear or doubt or troubling times, hold the ground you have already won, even if that ground is limited . . . *hold fast to what you already know and stand strong until additional knowledge comes. . . .* I am not asking you to pretend to faith you do not have. I *am* asking you to be true to the faith you *do* have. . . . Furthermore, you have more faith than you think you do" ("Lord, I Believe," *Ensign*, May 2013). One of the ways we can hold fast to what we already know is to immerse ourselves in the word of God, to continue in the things we have already been assured of. —EBF

Reflect and Respond

How have the scriptures strengthened your faith in times that are perilous?

Your favorite scripture in
2 Timothy 3

2 TIMOTHY 4:7

I have fought a good fight,
I have finished my course, I have kept the faith.

My wife Jenny loves to run, and when we first got married, she always wanted me to go with her. I, on the other hand, do not love running as much as Jenny does, so it was always a struggle to convince me to come. One day, she told me that if I ran a full 26.2-mile marathon, she would never make me run again. I took her up on it and began training. When the day before the big race came, I got some advice from Jenny's grandpa that I have thought about often since then. He told me, "Just keep putting one foot in front of the other." It was so simple, and so obvious, but wildly motivating.

When I was tired on mile 12 and 16 and 21, I would hear Grandpa's voice, "Just keep putting one foot in front of the other." And so, I did. And foot by foot, I finished the race, and Jenny has never made me run again.

Sometimes I wish living as a disciple of Jesus Christ were more like a sprint instead of a marathon. But it isn't. It is a lifetime pursuit. One that Paul knew well. And when he got to the last legs of his race, he looked back and said, "I have fought a good fight, I have finished my course, I have kept the faith" (2 Timothy 4:7). In most races, you wear a number pinned to your shirt while you run. There is a practice among some runners that when the race is over, you trade your number or jersey with another runner that you admire. If I ever get the chance, I would want to trade mine with Paul. Not only for everything he taught, and everything he sacrificed, but for showing me how to run the race well—one foot in front of the other, all the way to the end. —DB

Reflect and Respond

Do you know someone like Paul? Someone who has fought a good fight and finished the course? What do you admire about them?

Your favorite scripture in 2 Timothy 4

TITUS 1:5

Set in order the things that are wanting.

There are two times a year that I feel inclined to set in order my life. January and August. The beginning of the year and the beginning of the school year seem to cue my soul for a reset. It is a time of renewing and refreshing and refocusing. A time for determining what is most important. The call from Paul to "set in order the things that are wanting" reminds me of this pursuit (Titus 1:5). He talks about two important things in this chapter.

The first encourages us to be "a lover of hospitality" (Titus 1:8). Many years ago, I did a study on the word *hospitality* in scripture. It became one of my most favorite words. I didn't realize that there is a hospitality code, a way of living that was given clear back in the time of Moses. A way of welcoming in, of entertaining strangers, of taking care of God's children. It is a study you might enjoy. Just search for the word *hospitality* and see what you learn.

Another verse counsels that we hold fast "the faithful word as he hath been taught, that he may be able by sound doctrine both to exhort and to convince" (Titus 1:9). Understanding and holding fast to the word is also an important way to encourage and strengthen the belief of those we serve. This verse reminds me of the call President Nelson gave for women "who express their beliefs with confidence and charity" ("A Plea to My Sisters," *Ensign*, November 2015). I want to be one of those. —EBF

Reflect and Respond

How might you set in order the things that are wanting as you consider this chapter?

Your favorite scripture in
Titus 1

TITUS 2:3

Teachers of good things.

I have been a teacher for most of my adult life. I left as a full-time missionary when I was nineteen years old and taught people for two years. When I came home, I worked as a teacher at the MTC in Provo, Utah, and taught newly called missionaries there for a few years after that. During my last semester teaching at the MTC, I was hired as a part-time seminary teacher at a junior high in Spanish Fork, Utah. Soon, I was offered a job teaching seminary full time, and I took it. Since then, I have been teaching high school and college-age students full time for more than fifteen years. And when I go home at night and on weekends, I teach my kids, teach on YouTube, and teach in my Church callings. I have lived my life as a teacher.

One of the challenges in teaching is trying to decide what to teach. The scriptures are so long and have so many words in them. Every day, teachers, parents, and friends have to decide which of the words they are going to share or teach. When deciding, it might be helpful to take Paul's words to Titus as a guide and be "teachers of good things" (Titus 2:3). That's what I want to be. A teacher of good things.

Recently, I ran into one of my students out and about. While we were talking, someone else I knew came up and joined the conversation. He asked, "How do you two know each other?" My past student quickly replied, "David introduced me to Jesus." It is the best compliment I have ever received. It made me think what an honor and privilege it has been to be a teacher of good things. —DB

Reflect and Respond

What are some of the good things teachers have taught you over the years?

Your favorite scripture in
Titus 2

TITUS 3:8

These things I will that thou affirm constantly.

"This is a faithful saying," Paul says, "and these things I will that thou affirm constantly, that they which have believed in God might be careful to maintain good works" (Titus 3:8). At the beginning of this chapter Paul encourages us to "be ready to every good work" (v. 1). It reminds me of the covenant we made at baptism, to mourn with those that mourn, comfort those that stand in need of comfort, and to bear one another's burdens. In other words, to stand as a witness of Jesus Christ.

One year I set a goal to leave time open every day to serve. I didn't schedule service opportunities, I just left myself open for them. I prayed in the morning that I would know the one thing the Lord needed me to do that day. Then I tried to live in a way where I might be more observant to the needs of those around me. I listened more carefully in conversations; I watched for opportunities to serve as I went about my ordinary tasks in my community. After a year, that goal became part of who I was. Now it is common for me to offer help or to ask how I might be of service to someone when I see a need. I think it is because I have such a desire to be *ready to every good work*. I want to be more like the Savior in that regard.

It is what I love most about the story of Ephraim Hanks. In the moment when Brigham Young stood at the pulpit and called for volunteers to go and help the people on the plains, Ephraim recounts, "Some of the brethren responded by explaining that they could get ready to start in a few days, I spoke at once saying, 'I am ready now!' The next day I was wending my way eastward over the mountains with a light wagon all alone." It's something I want to be good at also—careful to maintain good works. —EBF

Reflect and Respond
What could you do to be more ready for every good work?

Your favorite scripture in
Titus 3

PHILEMON 1:21

Having confidence in thy obedience . . .
knowing that thou wilt also do more than I say.

This book of scripture is a letter from Paul to his friend and brother Philemon. The person delivering the letter is a man named Onesimus, who at one time was a servant of Philemon. When you read the letter, it seems as if Onesimus wronged Philemon in some way in the past. Now, after having spent some time with Paul, Onesimus is returning to Philemon—perhaps to make amends or resolve whatever the past issue was.

When Onesimus comes to Philemon's house, he comes with this letter from Paul. I wonder what feelings Philemon had toward Onesimus. Was there a grudge? Did his heart stir with anger when he opened the door and saw him there? Did he want some sort of payback or revenge? We aren't sure. But as much as I wonder how Philemon felt when he saw Onesimus, I wonder more about how he felt after he read the letter. Paul, his friend, made a request to Philemon on Onesimus's behalf. A hard one.

He asked him to "receive him for ever; not now as a servant, but above a servant, a brother beloved . . . receive him as myself. If he hath wronged thee, or oweth thee ought, put that on mine account" (Philemon 1:15–18). And then Paul, knowing the heart of Philemon, wrote that he was sure he would do all of this anyway—even without the request—and probably more than asked.

Every time I read this letter, I wonder how I would feel, particularly if the letter didn't come from Paul, but from Jesus.

What if He asked the same of me on behalf of someone else? —DB

Reflect and Respond

How would you feel if Jesus asked you to forgive and do good to someone who had wronged you?

Your favorite scripture in **Philemon**

HEBREWS 1:9

God . . . hath anointed thee with
the oil of gladness above thy fellows.

The book of Hebrews is a call to faith. Knowing this, I love that the first chapter is all about Jesus Christ. One of my favorite verses about the Savior is contained in this chapter. It reads, "Thou hast loved righteousness, and hated iniquity; therefore God, even thy God, hath anointed thee with the oil of gladness above thy fellows" (Hebrews 1:9).

I often turn to Isaiah when I read this verse. "The Spirit of the Lord God is upon me; because the Lord hath anointed me to preach good tidings unto the meek; he hath sent me to bind up the brokenhearted . . . to comfort all that mourn; . . . to appoint unto them that mourn in Zion, to give unto them beauty for ashes, the oil of joy for mourning, the garment of praise for the spirit of heaviness" (Isaiah 61:1–3). It is an anointing of exultation, of gladness, of joy. Do you love that it comes when we are brokenhearted, mourning, heavy?

In New Testament times, oil was used for many different reasons. It was a sign of hospitality. It was used for healing the sick or the maimed in the same way we use medicine today, but it was also used as part of the sacred procedure for healing the sick in the same way we use consecrated oil today.

We speak of Jesus as our Messiah, which means anointed one, because we believe He is anointed of the Father to be His personal representative in all things pertaining to mankind's salvation (see Bible Dictionary, "Anoint," "Anointed One").

From these descriptions of healing and hospitality, it is clear why Jesus was given the title of Anointed One, the One who would bring the oil of gladness. He is the healer. He is the welcoming in. —EBF

Reflect and Respond
Where have you experienced the oil of gladness?

Your favorite
scripture in
Hebrews 1

HEBREWS 2:10

The captain of their salvation.

When I was in high school, my family was lucky enough to go on a vacation together on a cruise ship. These ships are massive! They are legitimately floating hotels. They have lobbies, and elevators, and grand staircases. Some of them have waterslides and pools on the deck and levels and levels of rooms. Oh, and the restaurants. Several of them—with all-you-can-eat food! You could easily forget you were on a boat, unless you are out on the upper deck overlooking the water or feel the occasional sway of the boat at dinner. It is amazing how big they are, and even more amazing that they float.

One morning on the cruise, I woke up to the sound of the captain's voice over the loudspeakers telling us he was going to attempt to dock one more time. Other members of my family were already awake, and they told me it was his third attempt. The water was super choppy, and the lane to put the boat in wasn't much wider than the boat itself. I was so glad I was not the captain. I don't even like parallel parking. I cannot imagine the pressure and the skill set needed to dock a gigantic floating hotel with hundreds of people on board!

It makes me even happier to not be the captain of my salvation. That is a title that Paul gave to Jesus. He is driving this ship. As overwhelmed and incapable as I would be to dock a cruise ship, I am infinitely more unable to bring about my own salvation. It is a task, especially considering who He has to work with, that could not be put into anyone else's hands except for His, our captain.

The Captain of Our Salvation. —DB

Reflect and Respond

How does it make you feel knowing that Jesus is the Captain of Our Salvation? We are in His hands!

Your favorite scripture in Hebrews 2

HEBREWS

HEBREWS 3:13

Exhort one another daily, while it is called To day.

One of the things the world needs a lot more of is encouragers.

Our culture is so filled with people who find fault, who cause shame, who thrive on division and contention. I am weary of it. Life is hard enough on its own. What we don't need is more people calling us out, bringing us down. Sometimes I wonder if people realize that most people are just doing the best they can with what they have.

I can remember one particularly crazy day. I was running one million errands. It was the year we had four weddings in seven months . . . that should explain how crazy the day was. On this particular day I was returning several bridesmaids' dresses for one wedding and then running to pick up bridesmaids' dresses for another. I kept checking my phone for other errand requests that were coming in constantly. As I waited for the clerk to finish my return, a mother and her young daughter got in line behind me. The darling mom turned to her daughter and said, "We are doing so good!" I couldn't help it, I blurted out, "I need someone to tell me that right now," and we all laughed. Then that cute mother put both of her hands on my shoulders, looked me in the eye, and said, "You are doing so good," with all of the sincerity in the world. I nearly started crying, it was the kindest thing. And you know what? It helped. It made me feel like I really was doing good. My best. Exactly what I was capable of on that day.

I think the world needs more people like that young mom. People who aren't afraid to look around and find someone who needs some encouragement, and then be brave enough and sincere enough to actually share it.

You are doing so good right now. —EBF

Reflect and Respond
Who could you encourage today?

Your favorite scripture in **Hebrews 3**

HEBREWS 4:16

Let us therefore come boldly unto the throne of grace.

I didn't even want to get out of the car. A few hours before, Jenny and I had gotten into a silly argument about something insignificant, and I had lost my temper. I stormed out of the house barefoot, hopped in my car, and just drove away. Soon I realized how irrational I had been acting and knew that I needed to turn around, go back home, and apologize for how I'd responded. I drove back into the garage and just sat there in my car. I was so embarrassed. I didn't want to face anyone. It had taken me long enough to get the courage to drive back home, and now it was going to take even longer to get the courage to go inside. I was afraid of what everyone was going to think of me. How disappointed the look in their eyes would be when they saw me. I was tempted to not even walk in at all, but the garage was cold.

We all do things we are ashamed of. We all have words and actions we wish we could take back. Sometimes we may imagine ourselves walking into the presence of God and being tempted to keep our heads down. To drag our feet and delay walking in in the first place—afraid of what He might think of us, more afraid of seeing that look of disappointment in His eyes. But Paul painted us a new approach. He told us of Jesus, who knew what temptation and mortality were like, and who was filled with compassion, mercy, and grace. Considering that is who we will see, Paul said to "therefore come boldly unto the throne of grace" (Hebrews 4:16). To keep your chin up. I believe when we approach Him closely and look into His eyes, there won't be a hint of disappointment in them. —DB

Reflect and Respond

What about the character of Jesus and the Father will motivate you to walk into Their presence with more confidence?

Your favorite scripture in Hebrews 4

HEBREWS 5:8

Yet learned he obedience.

Obedience is a word that fascinates me. Some in the Church have talked about "exact obedience." People often ask me what I think that means. It is an interesting coupling of words. I can think of two examples of this phrase in the New Testament. One would be the Pharisees. They were exactly obedient to the law. The right number of steps on the Sabbath, the lighting of the candles, the rules of the Torah. Did you know they counted 613? The other example would be Jesus. Isn't it interesting that they were nothing alike?

In order to truly understand exact obedience, we must first come to a sincere understanding of the word *obedience*. The Greek translation of the word *obedience* is the word *hupakoe*, which means attentive hearkening, or submission. The Pharisees attentively hearkened and submitted to lists of rules and routines. The Savior attentively hearkened and submitted to the will of His Father. One was routine, the other was relationship.

In a scripture that could have defined Jesus or Melchizedek we read, "Who in the days of his flesh, when he had offered up prayers and supplications with strong crying and tears unto him that was able to save him from death, and was heard in that he feared; though he were a Son, yet learned he obedience by the things which he suffered; and being made perfect, he became the author of eternal salvation unto all them that obey him" (Hebrews 5:7–11). Consider what we learn here about obedience—sometimes it is hard, it might cause us to cry strong tears or even feel fear, it will require sacrifice, and it will perfect us. Those are important truths. Obedience is attentive hearkening and submission to the will of the Father. It is all about relationship. Over time it will perfect us. We will become like Him. —EBF

Reflect and Respond

What does obedience look like for you?

Your favorite scripture in Hebrews 5

HEBREWS 6:15

And so, after he had patiently endured,
he obtained the promise.

I have met people who are very serious about pinky promises. They are big deal in my circles, but some people take them to the next level. I remember asking someone to do something for me and then after they agreed, I extended my pinky to make a pinky promise. They froze in hesitation. "I can't." I persisted and they persisted back even harder. "I just can't. What if I forget or something comes up? I can't break a pinky promise, so I don't even want to make it." I thought it was a little overboard, but I appreciated their commitment level to promises. Paul explained a commitment level infinitely more sure than that one. "For when God made promise to Abraham, because he could swear by no greater, he sware by himself" (Hebrews 6:13). God is a promise-keeping God. His promises are as secure as His name. He will fulfill them at any cost.

Abraham, like so many of us, believed the promises, but had to wait to see their fulfillment. He did not see the fulfillment of his promises begin to take shape until he was over one hundred years old. That is a lot of waiting. But even though he needed to be patient and wait, the promises eventually were obtained. Sometimes when I think about God's unfulfilled promises in my life, I begin to get anxious and wonder if they will ever come to pass. I have started remembering Abraham in moments like this and have created a life rule—I cannot complain about waiting on God's promises until I am at least a hundred years old. Perhaps even better than that would be to remember who God is, and how sure I am that He will keep His word. —DB

Reflect and Respond

What do you know about God that makes you believe He will keep His promises no matter what?

Your favorite scripture in **Hebrews 6**

HEBREWS 7:1

Priest of the most high God.

There are times when stories from the Old Testament will help us better understand messages in other scripture. In the first verse of this chapter we are introduced to Melchizedek, the King of Salem. This chapter refers to an event that took place in the book of Genesis.

After Abraham rescued Lot and his goods and the women and the people, two kings went out to meet him. One was the King of Salem, the other was the King of Sodom. Melchizedek, the King of Salem, "brought forth bread and wine: and he was the priest of the most high God. And he blessed him, and said, Blessed be Abram of the most high God, possessor of heaven and earth" (Genesis 14:18–20). Then Abraham gave the King of Salem tithes of all. Important to this story is the underlying symbolism—the sacrament, the tithes, the office of a priest. We recognize the hint of priesthood promise given to Abraham. When the King of Sodom approached Abraham, he offered him all the goods he had reclaimed, but Abraham declined, saying, "I will not take from a thread even to a shoelatchet" (Genesis 14:23). The King of Sodom represented everything worldly, the King of Salem represented everything godly. Abraham wanted to give all the glory to God.

Paul talks of this Melchizedek, the "king of Salem, priest of the most high God, who met Abraham returning from the slaughter of the kings, and blessed him; to whom also Abraham gave a tenth part of all; first being by interpretation King of righteousness, and after that also King of Salem, which is, King of peace . . . but made like unto the Son of God; abideth a priest continually" (Hebrews 7:1–3). This chapter is a reminder of the important promise of priesthood given to Abraham, and through him to each one of us. —EBF

Reflect and Respond

How has the priesthood or the paying of tithes blessed your life?

Your favorite scripture in **Hebrews 7**

HEBREWS 8:10

I will be to them a God, and they shall be to me a people.

Hebrews 8 is a chapter that is filled with covenant language. It is something the Hebrews were familiar with. The name *Hebrews* was the name given to the children of Israel in the days of the Old Testament. They were a people who were also familiar with covenants, for they were the covenant people of the Lord. He made promises with them and commissioned them to take those promises and through them bless every nation and family in the world. Here in the book of Hebrews, that idea of covenants and promises was taught and refreshed in the minds and hearts of the people of Paul's day.

In our day, the apostles and prophets have done a similar thing. They have reminded us and encouraged us to study the covenant promises that God made with ancient Israel. President Nelson challenged us "to make a list of all that the Lord has promised He will do for covenant Israel. I think you will be astounded! Ponder these promises. Talk about them with your family and friends. Then live and watch for these promises to be fulfilled in your own life" ("Let God Prevail," *Ensign*, November 2020).

One of the promises to covenant Israel, and one that seems to summarize all of them, is a teaching that Paul quoted when he said, "I will be to them a God, and they shall be to me a people" (Hebrews 8:10). This is covenant language. It is an intimate and binding type of language. It is also a type of language that signifies a claim. He claims us as His people, and we claim Him as our God. We live and face all of our mortal days in this type of relationship with Him. —DB

Reflect and Respond

What does your covenant relationship with God mean to you?

Your favorite scripture in **Hebrews 8**

HEBREWS 9:11

An high priest of good things to come.

Every time I read this verse, three quotes from a general conference talk given by Elder Jeffrey R. Holland in 1999 come to mind. My daughter had been born two weeks before, after six months of bedrest. I believed every word of this talk because I had just lived it. I wonder if you have a favorite conference talk like that. One that spoke to you directly. As I sat on the couch that day holding my little Grace, these quotes were emblazoned on my heart:

"On those days when we have special need of heaven's help, we would do well to remember one of the titles given to the Savior in the epistle to the Hebrews. Speaking of Jesus' 'more excellent ministry' and why He is 'the mediator of a better covenant' filled with 'better promises,' this author—presumably the Apostle Paul—tells us that through His mediation and Atonement, Christ became 'an high priest of good things to come.'"

"To any who may be struggling to see that light and find that hope, I say: Hold on. Keep trying. God loves you. Things will improve. Christ comes to you in His 'more excellent ministry' with a future of 'better promises.' He is your 'high priest of good things to come.'"

"Some blessings come soon, some come late, and some don't come until heaven; but for those who embrace the gospel of Jesus Christ, *they come*" ("An High Priest of Good Things to Come," *Ensign*, November 1999).

It was Elder Holland's testimony of Christ, the high priest of good things to come, but his was a witness that matched my own. —EBF

Reflect and Respond
Where have you experienced Christ as the high priest of good things to come?

Your favorite scripture in
Hebrews 9

HEBREWS 10:39

We are not of them who draw back...
but of them that believe.

Recently, three of my friends started an Instagram account and movement called "Why We Stay." It started with a conversation about living during a time when everyone seemed to be sharing and giving reasons why they wanted to leave their church or their faith. There was a lot of discussion happening about what is wrong with faith and religion and believing. None of these three necessarily think it is wrong to push back against things they wish to see changed or made better, but it didn't seem like that was the kind of talk they were seeing. So, they decided to begin sharing the reasons they stay. Instead of sharing what was wrong with faith and religion and believing, they started sharing what was right and good and thrilling about it. I am so proud of them. They are gathering people together to consider what a life of faith can be and mean and why it would be worth working through some of the hardships or questions that come with a journey of faith.

While reading the book of Hebrews, I found a verse that describes them and the people they are gathering. "We are not of them who draw back . . . but of them that believe" (Hebrews 10:39). I want to be numbered in that same kind of group. A group of people who see faith under attack and do not draw back, but rather share the reasons that they believe.

To share why they stay with faith, religion, and ultimately with Jesus.

I want to be like that. —DB

Reflect and Respond

What does it look like to you to be one of those that does not draw back, but rather believes?

Your favorite scripture in **Hebrews 10**

HEBREWS 11:1

The evidence of things not seen.

Chapter 11 is a list of heroes. Perhaps you might call it a Hall of Faith. It is a list of some of God's finest, and how they responded with faith. By faith Enoch was translated. Noah, moved with fear, prepared a refuge to protect his family. Abraham obeyed. Sara received strength. Isaac blessed Jacob. Jacob worshipped. Joseph gave commandment. Moses suffered affliction, forsook Egypt, kept the Passover, and passed through the Red Sea on dry land. All by faith. By faith the walls of Jericho came down. Rahab perished not. Faith filled up the stories of Gideon, and Barak, and Samson, and David and Samuel. Through faith they "subdued kingdoms, wrought righteousness, obtained promises, stopped the mouths of lions, quenched the violence of fire, escaped the edge of the sword, out of weakness were made strong, waxed valiant in fight, turned to flight the armies of the [strangers]" (Hebrews 11:33–34).

Sometimes when I read this chapter I wonder if these are what made up the bedtime stories of the children living in New Testament times. It makes me want to go back and recount every one of those stories. The heroes. The faith.

My favorite verse in chapter 11 is actually found in chapter 12. It is the very first verse, "Wherefore seeing we also are compassed about with so great a cloud of witnesses, let us lay aside every weight . . . and let us run with patience the race that is set before us" (Hebrews 12:1). That cloud of witnesses? It is everyone listed in chapter 11. People whose stories will motivate us to lay aside every weight, to run our own race . . . with the courage they did. With the faith they did. Does your faith need to be strengthened? Just choose one of these stories from the Hall of Faith. What do you learn? —EBF

Reflect and Respond

Which story from chapter 11 would you like to learn more about today?

Your favorite scripture in Hebrews 11

HEBREWS 12:2

Looking unto Jesus . . . who for the joy that was
set before him endured the cross.

Hebrews chapter 11 is such a beautiful summary of so many people who endured and overcame through faith in Jesus Christ. A list like that gives us hope that we can do the same. In my scriptures, I crossed out the heading for Hebrews 12 because I don't want to stop on the last verse of Hebrews 11 without finishing Paul's thought. After giving his great list of faith heroes, he tells us to look at the "cloud of witnesses" that surround us. To gain strength and encouragement from people like Sarah and Abraham and David and Moses and Rahab to lay aside our sins and things of this world and run the race the way they did. And then Paul told us how they did it. They were not the heroes. Christ is.

"Looking unto Jesus the author and finisher of our faith" (Hebrews 12:2). I love this line. It is Jesus who gave us our faith, and it is Jesus who will make us whole in our faith one day. He is the beginning and the end. He started this and He will finish it. And He will not give up. He has already proved that to us. And just as we look to Him for the strength to endure, Paul teaches us that He looked to us for the strength to endure as well.

"For the joy that was set before him endured the cross" (Hebrews 12:2). How did He make it? Paul seems to say that one of the things that helped Him endure the cross was looking to the joy that was set before Him. Looking to the reason for why He was there. You. Me. Almost as if He saw us as He endured the Crucifixion. Knowing what joy would come, and what joy He already had in us, He finished the work. —DB

Reflect and Respond

Who is someone in addition to Jesus that you look to for inspiration to endure your own trials and life?

Your favorite
scripture in
Hebrews 12

HEBREWS 13:2

Be not forgetful to entertain strangers.

I have three verses marked in my scriptures that teach about the hospitality code that began clear back in the days of Moses.

The first scripture is in Exodus 23:9, "Also thou shalt not oppress a stranger: for ye know the heart of a stranger, seeing ye were strangers in the land of Egypt."

The second is found in Matthew 25:35, "For I was an hungred, and ye gave me meat: I was thirsty, and ye gave me drink: I was a stranger, and ye took me in."

The last is here in Hebrews 13:1–2, "Let brotherly love continue. Be not forgetful to entertain strangers: for thereby some have entertained angels unawares."

It is a code of welcoming in, of loving well, of taking care. We see it when Abraham and Sarah entertain the three holy men who promise Sarah will have a son. It is the reason the woman at the well would have given Jesus a drink. It is the message behind the story of the Good Samaritan. It was a way of living that was expected and honored in early times.

I wonder how well we live it today.

This chapter ends with a plea, "Make you perfect in every good work to do his will, working in you that which is wellpleasing in his sight, through Jesus Christ" (Hebrews 13:21). These good works, this hospitality, saving a seat at the table, making room on the bench, reminding people that they belong, that is the good work of Christ. Wellpleasing in His sight. It is how we stand as witnesses of Him. —EBF

Reflect and Respond

How might you practice the art of hospitality today?

Your favorite scripture in Hebrews 13

JAMES 1:5

If any of you lack wisdom.

Have you ever noticed that this is a chapter that begins by talking about trials? And not just a few trials—the Joseph Smith Translation tells us "many afflictions" would be a better word choice (see James 1:2). Whenever we turn to James 1, we seem to always start at verse 5, but what if you were to start at verse 1? James tells us that when we fall into many afflictions, we should know this, "that the trying of your faith worketh patience. But let patience have her perfect work, that ye may be perfect and entire, wanting nothing" (James 1:3–4).

I see four lessons here:

1. We are all going to experience affliction.
2. The trying of our faith will teach us patience.
3. There is work that takes place in times of patience.
4. In the end we will be whole, wanting nothing.

It is this process that leads us into the scripture that became the motivation for Joseph's trek into the grove on that spring day, "If any of you lack wisdom, let him ask of God, that giveth to all men liberally, and upbraideth not; and it shall be given him. But let him ask in faith, nothing wavering" (James 1:5–6).

When I read this chapter from the beginning, I begin to realize that perhaps what led Joseph into the grove was many afflictions. A trying of his faith. Maybe because he wanted something so desperately that verse 5 became a clarion call, "If any of you lack . . ."

The invitation is open to all of us, and a promise. If we ask, nothing wavering, the process will leave us with nothing wanting. —EBF

Reflect and Respond

What do you lack wisdom for today?

Your favorite scripture in **James 1**

JAMES 2:8

*If ye fulfill the royal law ... Thou shalt love
thy neighbour as thyself, ye do well.*

I adore that James called the second great commandment "the royal law" (James 2:8). To me, loving your neighbor is the highest and holiest way of living out our faith. It is what matters most. In the chapter right before this, James described pure religion as taking care of people (see James 1:27). There are many ways someone might describe religion. They might describe it as patterns or habits of worship like prayer and study of scripture. Those are all wonderful, but it seems as if James is saying that those should fuel something more wonderful—loving our neighbor. The royal law.

I was talking to my friend Nish once about religion. She is of another Christian faith, and we were talking about how Nish has a different theological belief about the nature of God and the Godhead than I do. At the end of the conversation, we had two conclusions. The first was that we believed infinitely more similarly about the Godhead than we did differently. The second was this—some may define our doctrinal discussion itself as religion. They may say that the list of what someone believes is religion. But James taught us that what we say we believe is not as important as what we actually do.

I won't ever forget what Nish taught me that day. She said that if we spent all of our time discussing and even arguing with others about what we believe—about who is right and who is wrong—and pass by people who are hurting and broken and lonely while we are doing so, we are missing the whole point. We would be missing true religion. We would be missing the royal law. —DB

Reflect and Respond
In what ways will you live the royal law this week?

Your favorite
scripture in
James 2

JAMES 3:5

How great a matter a little fire kindleth.

Oscar Kirkham was one of the great men of the Church and among the Church's most respected Scouters. He served in the First Council of the Seventy and was a significant presence wherever he went. Often in meetings he would rise to a "point of personal privilege" and then, when recognized, would proceed to say something good about someone. Near the end of his life, he spoke briefly at Brigham Young University on the theme "say the good word." On the morning that Elder Kirkham died, Elder Marion D. Hanks was invited to the Kirkham family home. There he was handed a small, inexpensive notebook in which Elder Kirkham had kept his notes. The last two entries were: "Say the good word" and "Your name is safe in our home" (see Marion D. Hanks, foreword to *Say the Good Word*, by Oscar A. Kirkham [1958], 4).

I was twenty-nine years old when I heard this in a conference talk. It was at a time when our telephones were still kept in a central location in our homes. I hung this quote next to my phone to encourage me to be kind when I spoke about others. James teaches, "The tongue is a little member, and boasteth great things. Behold, how great a matter a little fire kindleth!" (James 3:5). It is true, what we say can have great power for good or for evil. What if we always chose to say the good word? "Who is a wise man and endued with knowledge among you? let him shew out of a good conversation his works with meekness of wisdom" (James 3:13). What if our goal with our good conversation was to make sure every name we spoke was safe in our house? —EBF

....

Reflect and Respond
How might you work on keeping names safe in your home?

Your favorite scripture in **James 3**

JAMES 4:7

Submit yourselves therefore to God.

One of the classes I taught in institute was a class on world religions. As we studied the faith of Islam, I became fascinated by the meaning and translation of the name *Islam*—it is "submission." One of the most important tenets of the Islam faith is to learn to submit to God. In doing so, they believe you will find peace. So do I.

Submission is something I have always had a hard time with. I don't like authority or people telling me what to do. If there is a rule, at the very least I question it, and usually I am wondering who came up with it in the first place. That is what makes submission to God easier for me. I know who is asking.

When Moses went to Pharaoh to speak God's command to him to let His people go free, Pharaoh replied with a legitimate question. "Who is the Lord, that I should obey his voice" (Exodus 5:2). I relate. Pharaoh did not know who the Lord was, so why should he listen to what He was saying to do? Submission is difficult, but it is meaningful and easier when we are submitting to someone that we know and someone that has our best interests in mind.

There is a line in the hymn "Come Thou Fount of Every Blessing" that says, "Here's my heart, Lord, take and seal it." There are not many people I would hand my whole heart over to. It even makes me hesitate when I sing that line in the song. But then I remember who it is that I am handing my heart to. I am putting it in hands that are marked with love. I know He will keep it safe. I know He will make it better. I know Him. And so, I submit. —DB

Reflect and Respond

What is something you know about the Lord that makes it easier to submit to Him?

Your favorite scripture in
James 4

JAMES 5:16

The effectual fervent prayer of a righteous man availeth much.

After a particularly difficult and draining experience in my life, I ran into a friend of mine walking down the streets of our neighborhood. It was the first time we had seen each other since the problem I was dealing with. He asked how I was doing and got an update on the situation. As a part of that conversation, he told me that he and his family had been praying for me. I normally don't respond like this, but when he said it, it triggered a question back from me. "Were you really?" I was surprised I even asked it, but later on I figured out why. You see, I had used that same line when talking to other people in the past. When they were sick or hurting from something, it sounded like a nice thing to say to them—"You were in our thoughts and prayers." Sometimes they really were, but other times I was just being polite.

But something happened during that hard time for me. I genuinely felt the power of people's prayers. It was tangible. It was meaningful. I survived on it. It was the first time in my life when I experienced firsthand what James taught, "The effectual fervent prayer of a righteous [person] availeth much" (James 5:16). It's true. The prayers that were offered on my behalf mattered. They availed much. They made a difference in my story.

I believe that about prayer. I believe that God responds when we petition for others. I believe a change can happen and be made by simply asking for it. Sometimes I hear people say, "Well there is not much to do for them other than prayer." That is spoken as if prayer is at the bottom of the list of things you could do for someone, but my experiences have put it at the top. —DB

Reflect and Respond

When have you seen the influence of others' prayers? Is there someone you could be praying for right now?

Your favorite scripture in **James 5**

1 PETER 1:7

The trial of your faith, being much more precious than of gold.

I had the opportunity to go to a jewelry store with several friends. Each of us chose to make a different piece of jewelry. I chose to make a ring. Through the process I learned much more than how to make a piece of jewelry. I discovered Him. How He can take a bunch of scraps and see the beauty within. How He knows how much heat is needed as He allows the fire to purify and strengthen and make solid. How He knows just when the purifying and cool waters should be used in the process.

On my own, I would never have known. I would have melted the piece beyond repair. There is a balance between the fire and the water. *He knows.* And He knows about the dipping in black acid and coming out white, the polishing, the scrubbing.

Through the process the teacher reminded me, "Do not touch the stone to the metal while you are working." So, it sat off to the side, waiting. Until after the fire and the water. After everything had been strengthened and polished and brushed clean. At the very end, the precious stone was carefully laid into the work, and there was beauty there.

Better than I could have ever imagined.

And when I placed it on my finger, my hands still bore the mark of the refining. And why did that make the piece more beautiful still?

"That the trial of your faith, being much more precious than of gold that perisheth, though it be tried with fire, might be found unto praise and honour and glory at the appearing of Jesus Christ: whom having not seen, ye love" (1 Peter 1:7–8). —EBF

Reflect and Respond

What are you learning about the refining process?

Your favorite scripture in
1 Peter 1

1 PETER 2:5

Ye also, as lively stones, are built up a spiritual house.

There was a little rhyme that I learned as a kid that you may be familiar with. As you would say it, you would clasp your hands together, interlocking the fingers, and then say, "This is the church, here is the steeple, open the doors, see all the people." Your fingers would be interlocked on the inside of your hand so that when you "opened the door" you would see all of the fingers as people wiggling around. The second half of the rhyme went like this, "Close the doors, hear them pray, open the doors, they all run away." And then you would separate your hands, wiggling your fingers as if the people were all running away. Cute, right?

However, recently I have wanted to rewrite the rhyme. I like it, and it is fine, but it teaches something that I want to change. When you say the rhyme, you create a church building and steeple with your hands and call it the church. Then, when you open it, you show your fingers and call them the people. However, I want to emphasize that the Church is not a building, but the Church in fact is the people. They make up the Church. The organization and buildings are not the Church. The heartbeat is found within the people.

Peter said to the Saints, "Ye also, as lively stones, are built up a spiritual house" (1 Peter 2:5). He used an analogy of a building to talk about the Church, but in his analogy, the stones are the people. Together, they create the Church. They create a safe place for people to come. They create a haven for connection with God.

It isn't the building—we, the people, are the Church. —DB

Reflect and Respond

You and I are the Church. When people see us, what is their opinion and feeling about church?

Your favorite
scripture in
1 Peter 2

1 PETER 3:10

He that will love life, and see good days.

Often, I will look on the bottom of a receipt and see a familiar phrase there, "Have a good day." But what if it isn't? What should you do then? How do we find a perspective that will get us through the bad days?

There is a scripture found in 1 Peter that says, "For he that will love life, and see good days . . . happy are ye" (1 Peter 3:10, 14). Peter's suggestion is simple but profound: love life, and see good days. It's so interesting that the scripture does not say, *love life, and have good days.* Sometimes I wish Peter would have written that. I need more good days. Instead, the counsel is clear—see good days.

How different would our outlook be if that became our motto? What if we trained ourselves to *see* good days? Stephen L. Richards, a former member of the First Presidency, taught this about the spirit of discernment, "This gift . . . when highly developed arises largely out of an acute sensitivity to impressions—spiritual impressions, if you will—to read under the surface as it were, to detect hidden evil, and more importantly to find the good that may be concealed. The highest type of discernment is that which perceives in others and uncovers for them their better natures, the good inherent within them" (in Conference Report, April 1950).

I wonder if this could be true about a day also. Would the spirit of discernment help us to find the good that may be concealed in our days? The good inherent within?

I love the idea of approaching our days with this perspective. Maybe someone should tell the grocery stores. I want to find a store that prints that message on the bottom of their receipts. SEE a good day! —EBF

Reflect and Respond

What will you do to love life and see good today?

Your favorite scripture in 1 Peter 3

1 PETER 4:14

If ye be reproached for the name of Christ, happy are ye.

Living as a Christian in the first and second centuries was difficult and at times disastrous. All throughout the epistles we read encouragement and hope for those who are persecuted. From the records, it seems like that was the common lot of anyone who claimed to be a believer in Jesus Christ. Peter even said in his epistle that if hard times come, do not think of them as a strange thing or out of the ordinary—it is to be expected. And not only should the Saints expect it, but they should rejoice when it happens.

I can think of a lot of reasons I would want to rejoice. My birthday is something I get excited about. When my teams win, I rejoice. When I get a tax return, it is a happy day! The list of reasons to rejoice could fill pages and pages of this book. However, nowhere on the list would I include suffering or fiery trials. But Peter would. "If ye be reproached for the name of Christ, happy are ye" (1 Peter 4:14).

There are also a lot of reasons why people may be reproached. You could commit a crime, do some sort of evil, or get involved in people's business (see 1 Peter 4:15). If you are retaliated against for any of these, I suppose you deserve it. But if you are persecuted because of your faith in Christ, then you have reason to rejoice. For so was He persecuted. It was evidence He was doing good. Perhaps yours is too. At the very least, your persecution connects you with Him.

You become companions in the trial, and perhaps that is worth rejoicing over. —DB

Reflect and Respond

What other reasons can you think of for why Peter would say persecution is a reason to rejoice?

Your favorite scripture in 1 Peter 4

1 PETER 5:7

Casting all your care upon him; for he careth for you.

One of my biggest hesitations in life is asking other people for help. I know I am not alone in this. It makes me wonder what it is about asking for help that is so difficult to do. Perhaps when we ask others for help, we are admitting that we need help, and we don't like that. Maybe it makes us feel weak or insufficient or not good enough. I know that I, personally, like to be self-sufficient, and perhaps it is too humbling for me to admit that I am not.

I think another reason it is hard for me to ask for help is simply because I don't want to bother other people. Everyone I know is really busy with life. They have their own schedules to manage and burdens to carry. I just don't want to add to everything they are already dealing with. I chalk this up as kindness to other people when it really might be a different face of pride, but whatever the reason or motivation for not sharing my burdens with other people is, it does not need to be the same reason I hold my burdens back from the Lord as well.

He is never too busy for us. And He never has too much on His plate—even though He has the whole world in His hands. He is both willing and able to carry us through the seasons of life we need carrying through. He is willing and able to carry us through any and every season of life. His invitation through Peter is clear: "[Cast] all your care upon him" (1 Peter 5:7). Not some of it—all of it. Whatever it is, we can cast it upon Him, because He cares about it. He cares about what is happening and He cares to help. It is one thing we never need to hesitate on. —DB

Reflect and Respond
What cares do you have to cast upon Him today?

Your favorite scripture in 1 Peter 5

2 PETER 1:8

They make you.

One of my favorite sentences in the Gospel of Mark is when the Lord tells the Apostles, "I will make you to become . . ." (Mark 1:17). Then we watch the becoming happen in their lives over the course of the Gospels. Watching the Lord work in them gives me faith He can work within me. There is something empowering about knowing that the Lord is working within us.

Perhaps Peter was thinking about that early invitation when he taught the Saints how to achieve a divine nature. Exaltation would require a process of becoming. In the first chapter of 2 Peter, he laid out a plan, "giving all diligence, add to your faith virtue; and to virtue knowledge; and to knowledge temperance; and to temperance patience; and to patience godliness; and to godliness brotherly kindness; and to brotherly kindness charity. For if these things be in you, and abound, they *make you* that ye shall neither be barren nor unfruitful in the knowledge of our Lord Jesus Christ" (2 Peter 1:5–8; emphasis added). It was almost as if acquiring those characteristics would help you stand firm in your knowledge of Christ. I am compelled to learn more about each of those words. What if you were to write a definition of each one?

diligence_____   knowledge_____   godliness_____
faith_____   temperance_____   brotherly kindness_____
virtue_____   patience_____   charity_____

At first glance, I wonder if there is a progression taking place there. What might you discover? —EBF

Reflect and Respond
Which of those characteristics would you like to learn more about?

Your favorite scripture in 2 Peter 1

2 PETER 2:1

But there were false prophets also among the people.

We live in a time when our culture has an extra sensitivity toward authority. People, in general, do not want to be told what to do. We also hear so many stories of corruption within organizations and leadership that it becomes difficult to trust anyone associated with either of these. This seems to be one of the underlying concerns that people have with prophets. There are some who claim that they don't want prophets. They don't want someone telling them how to run their life. They want to be in control.

There is, however, something that Peter taught the Saints of the early Christian Church that is extremely relevant to us today. Peter wrote that "there were false prophets also among the people" (2 Peter 2:1). In addition to the true prophets that the people had access to, they also had access to false prophets. This is true today also. Everyone has prophets. Even those who claim they don't want anyone having authority or influence over their decisions. Each of us is constantly influenced, and we are religiously looking to others to get or confirm our ideas and ways of living. We are all obedient, in some sense, to someone or something.

If that is the case, then the decision is no longer about whether or not we want to have "prophets," but rather which ones we are going to choose. And when choosing, perhaps we should consider what the promises and intentions of either side might be. —DB

Reflect and Respond

Who are some of the people you look to for influence and decision-making? Why do you choose them?

Your favorite scripture in 2 Peter 2

2 PETER 3:9

The Lord is not slack concerning his promise.

One morning I was driving behind a truck with a bed full of wooden shipping pallets. They were stacked at least ten high. The back of the bed was open and from what I could see, there was only one strap holding all of them in. I wasn't super happy about driving behind this truck, but the one thing that gave me a little piece of mind was how securely that single strap was tightened around the pallets. There wasn't any slack.

Sometimes you want there to be a little slack in things. You want some flexibility or freedom. But other times, you don't—particularly when you are being held by a rope or line. A slack in a hammock means you smack your back or rear as you swing. Too much slack in a bungee jumping cord is never desirable. And a slack in a truck full of wooden pallets is out, too.

I love Peter's teaching at the end of his letter when he reminded the Saints that the "Lord is not slack concerning his promise" (2 Peter 3:9). He is tight and firm on His commitments. He is also not overbearing, because Peter taught in the same verse that He is "longsuffering to us-ward." He has patience, and He gives us slack when we need it, but He is never slack on His word or promises to us. You can trust Him with the full weight of your choices and life. You can swing or jump or ride in confidence when His word is holding you up.

He will never let you down. —DB

Reflect and Respond

What is one promise you are confident the Lord will not be slack on with you?

Your favorite scripture in 2 Peter 3

1 JOHN 1:5

God is light, and in him is no darkness at all.

One evening I called my grandson on the phone, and he asked if I wanted to see his trains, and I told him I did, so he started walking me on the phone up the stairs to his room. About halfway up the stairs, he said into the phone, "It's dark up there," so he ran back downstairs, got his flashlight, and we started walking up the stairs again. As soon as we got to the door of the room he whispered again, "It's dark in there," and then he took off running down the hall and all the way down the stairs. Finally, he got down next to his mom, and he said, "Mom, it's dark up there. Can you come with me?" I guess I wasn't a very good companion, being so far away on the phone. So, his mom came, and we all went back up the stairs, me on the phone, and we got close to his bedroom, and we stopped right outside his room, and again he said, "It's dark in there," and then we started tiptoeing into the room with his flashlight and his mom. And then, his mom, who is the biggest prankster in the world, screamed as loud as she could, and then we all screamed, even me on the phone, and then we started laughing so hard. Except for Luka. And I told her, "He is never going to sleep alone in this room again." She immediately turned the light on, and we saw it was all safe, and we pulled out the trains, and we played.

I am a lot like Luka. I don't really love darkness. I leave the lights turned on all over the house. Perhaps God is the same way. John says that "God is light, and in him is no darkness at all" (1 John 1:5). I love knowing that ours is a Father of light. He will bring courage to the dark places through His light and through the light of His Son. A companion we can look to in the darkest moments of our life. —EBF

Reflect and Respond

How has God brought light into your dark places?

Your favorite scripture in
1 John 1

1 JOHN 2:20

But ye have an unction from the Holy One.

When I first read this chapter, I was so interested in this phrase. I was so happy to "have an unction from the Holy One" but wasn't entirely sure what it meant. If you look in other translations of the Bible, like the ESV, for example, you see the word "unction" translated as a "holy anointing." When I looked the original Greek word up in Strong's Concordance (my go-to reference companion for understanding the ancient Biblical languages), it was defined also as a "special gift or endowment of the Holy Spirit." Now I was extra interested.

John seems to have been confirming and reminding the Saints that they were gifted with an anointing or special endowment from the Holy Spirit. They were gifts and abilities beyond their own.

This morning, Jenny and I were talking about a friend of ours who runs an orphanage in Mexico. He, his wife, and their children have made great sacrifices in order to help this small group of orphans. As we talked about it, I thought to myself, "Why and how is he able to do this?" He doesn't make money doing it, and it is an extremely difficult job. How has he not quit by now? Then I thought about this verse. I think he has an "unction from the Holy One" (1 John 2:20). I think he was gifted with a special measure of grace—one that enables him to love and endure through the hardships that come with his job. This special gift allows him to take care of the children. It made me wonder what unctions were given to each of us in order to do the great work of loving and taking care of God's children. —DB

Reflect and Respond

What special gift or endowment do you feel like God has given you to assist in His work?

Your favorite scripture in
1 John 2

1 JOHN 3:17

And seeth his brother have need.

Many years ago, I sat in a ward council meeting. We were discussing a family in our ward who was struggling. The bishop felt prompted to ask every member of the council to take one person in the family to watch over. By the time the circle got around to me, there was only one person in the family left. I had heard of this boy. He caused a lot of trouble in the neighborhood, vandalizing homes, riding his four-wheeler through yards that had been prepared for sod, keeping people up into the late hours of the night. He was big, and loud, and impulsive. I agreed to the challenge.

For the next four years, our family, along with two other families in our ward, tutored that boy. We fed him dinner. We took him in when things were hard at home. He often slept over. Over time his life turned around. Time in jail was replaced with time on a mission. Now he spends a lot of his free afternoons and evenings talking to troubled youth like him. He tells them there is hope, that they will be able to live their dreams. That boy who used to be my neighbor now calls me mom.

I think of him every time I read the scripture in 1 John, "But whoso hath this world's good, and seeth his brother have need, and shutteth up his bowels of compassion from him, how dwelleth the love of God in him? . . . And this is his commandment, That we should believe on the name of his Son Jesus Christ, and love one another" (1 John 3:17, 23).

Loving that boy changed our life and our family. It taught us about compassion, but more importantly, it led us to Christ. —EBF

Reflect and Respond
How could you love and show compassion today?

Your favorite scripture in 1 John 3

1 JOHN 4:19

We love him, because he first loved us.

I lost track of how many times 1 John 4 says the word *love*. It is easily the most mentioned word in the entire chapter. It feels like a chapter you would want to read on Valentine's Day. For John, it seems like the very essence of the gospel of Jesus Christ is wrapped up in love. Simple, powerful love.

He teaches about the love of God toward us, particularly and most impressively in sending His Son, Jesus Christ, to the world to save us from our sins. This is the greatest manifestation of love the world has ever known. We may run into trouble and trial or have times in our lives when we feel like our prayers aren't being heard. We might feel distant from God at times for one reason or another. All of these things could tempt us to believe that God no longer loves us. John would point us to Jesus and the cross. That act of the Father sending His Son, and the Son willing to die, will always be the best evidence we have that God loves us. No matter what our lives may look like, we can look to that moment as our reassurance.

That moment not only reassures Their love for us, but it also fuels our love for Them and for others. John said, "We love him, because he first loved us" (1 John 4:19). I love that God took the first step. Before we ever had a chance to show Him our love, He proved His love to us. In doing so, it gave us one million more reasons to love Him even more. And a person who lives their life filled with that kind of love, knowing that they are accepted and adored by the Father and the Son, cannot help but love other people as well. It comes naturally. —DB

Reflect and Respond

Who do you see that could use a little more love right now?
How will you show it?

Your favorite scripture in 1 John 4

1 JOHN 5:14

This is the confidence that we have in him.

John says this, "These things have I written unto you that believe on the name of the Son of God . . ." (1 John 5:13). Then he lists all the reasons why he believes in God. "This is the confidence that we have in him, that, if we ask any thing according to his will, he heareth us: and if we know that he hear us, whatsoever we ask, we know that we have the petitions that we desired of him" (vv. 14–15). I have that confidence in God because I too have had prayers answered. Reflecting on those answered prayers strengthens my belief.

Then John lists a couple other important things he knows:

"We know that we are of God" (1 John 5:19).

"We know that the Son of God is come" (1 John 5:20).

This pattern John sets out is an important one for strengthening faith—take the time to write down what you know, share it with others, let it reinforce belief.

President Henry B. Eyring talked about a similar prompting he received. He said, "I was supposed to record for my children to read . . . how I had seen the hand of God blessing our family. . . . Before I would write, I would ponder this question: 'Have I seen the hand of God reaching out to touch us or our children or our family today?' As I kept at it, something began to happen. As I would cast my mind over the day, I would see evidence of what God had done for one of us. . . . As that happened, and it happened often, I realized that trying to remember had allowed God to show me what He had done" ("O Remember, Remember," *Ensign*, November 2007). If you were to write down what you know, where would you start? —EBF

Reflect and Respond

If you were to write a list of what you know, what would you include on that list?

Your favorite scripture in
1 John 5

2 JOHN 1:1

Unto the elect lady and her children.

I want to believe this chapter from John was written to a woman, because you know I am inclined to look for women all throughout the scriptures, but most scholars think John was talking about a congregation. The Lord's bride. He was talking to the Church. His call to the Church is that they would love one another, to walk after His commandments. There are many deceivers, he warned; be careful of them. "Look to yourselves," he said, "that we lose not those things which we have wrought" (2 John 1:5–8). I imagine that he is talking about people, how he doesn't want to lose any of them. I particularly love how the chapter ends, "The children of thy elect sister greet thee" (2 John 1:13). He's talking about another Church congregation. A sister church. It makes me consider the importance of faith communities. How needed they are as a gathering place for those who want to remain firm in Christ. A place of safety from deceivers. A place for the keeping of people. But also, how important it is to recognize and learn from our sister churches, those who are also trying to provide places of safety and refuge.

Many years ago, my friend and I traveled to Jonesboro, Arkansas. A local Baptist church was having a fish fry at 6:00 p.m. on a Thursday night. There was a Christian band singing "Great Are You Lord" as we walked in, and on the back wall one word had been written in huge white letters on a black background: REFUGE. Volunteers wore matching shirts with "servant" written across the back. I took pictures. I wanted to learn from them. I thought how amazing it would be to do something like that in my own faith congregation. Good ideas from a sister church intent on providing their people with a place of safety. A refuge. —EBF

Reflect and Respond

What have you learned from another congregation that was able to strengthen yours?

Your favorite scripture in 2 John

3 JOHN 1:14

Greet the friends by name.

It is such an interesting phenomenon to me that I can be in a room crowded with people, with multiple conversations going on at the same time—including the one that I am in—and not notice or pay attention to anything anyone is saying unless they say my name. It does not matter what crowd or conversation I am in, but my mind perks right up if I hear my name. I think a lot of people are like this. We just notice the sound of our name. It must alert our brain in a noticeable way or something.

Maybe there is something more to it. Our name is connected to who we are. And as people, I think we like to be known and recognized. So, when someone uses our name, it makes us feel both of those things. This is also true when someone remembers my name.

One day I was at my son's soccer game, and I ran into a past neighbor. We were not super close, and it had been years since I had seen her, but when we walked up to the sidelines to sit down, she noticed us and immediately called out, "Hey, David!" It was so simple, but it meant so much to me. This is what made John's last line in his letter stand out to me. He gave instructions to Gaius, the friend he was writing to, to greet their friends—but when he did so, he should greet them by name. To make them feel known. To make them feel seen.

Every time I read this request, I can't help but think about how God does the same—greets me by name. He and His angels have done so throughout time. They greet people by their name. It seems like it is important to Him—perhaps because it is important to the ones He calls. —DB

Reflect and Respond
When have you felt like God knew your name?

Your favorite scripture in
3 John

JUDE 1:22

And of some have compassion, making a difference.

One of the saddest and loneliest times of my life so far was spent in a hospital room. I was in a lot of physical pain and had to be there for several days. To make things worse, I was in a foreign country, couldn't understand the doctors very well, and was sharing a hospital room with others. Plus, I was missing my trip that I had been anticipating for such a long time. All of this added up together put me in an emotionally and spiritually tough place. It makes me tear up even when I think about it.

But all the tears are not bitter, sad ones. Some of them are thankful. Luckily, I was on this particular trip with my mom. There were several nights when I would wake up and see her there sitting in a chair next to my bed. The wife of the gentleman in the bed next to me brought me a fresh fruit smoothie every morning. It made me sick to drink it, but it made my heart happy. The family of the man in the bed on the other side of the room came and visited me every day. They tried hard to cheer me up in English. The mother of that family would come over and wipe my forehead with a wet towel and give me a kiss on the head every morning.

When I think about this experience, I think about Jude's counsel in his epistle. "And of some have compassion, making a difference" (Jude 1:22). How right he was. The little things I described to you that people did for me in the hospital were in fact little. But they were acts of compassion. And each of the acts of compassion brought as much healing to me as the medicines the doctors were giving. They all made a difference. —DB

Reflect and Respond

You can make a difference with compassion. When have you seen this be true? How will you pass it on?

Your favorite scripture in
Jude

REVELATION 1:10

I was in the Spirit on the Lord's day.

The book of Revelation can feel overwhelming for so many reasons. First of all, the symbolism; second, the thematic nature; and last, the prophecies. But if you read between the lines, you discover some basic and important truths that are relevant no matter what age of the world you live in. One of my favorite examples of this can be found in the very first chapter. John's book is made up of 22 chapters that describe one revelation. It was a revelation so powerful that it is actually called The Revelation of St. John the Divine. *The* Revelation. Can you imagine being so proficient at receiving and recording your personal revelations that people might actually name a book after your revelation? It makes me wonder what made John so good at receiving and writing down the revelations that came from the Lord, particularly this one. We find part of that answer here in chapter 1. After a brief introduction, John begins to write. He tells us he is in Patmos, and then there is a really important statement, "I was in the Spirit on the Lord's day" (Revelation 1:10). It was then that revelation began.

What important truths do you learn from those nine words?

It was the Sabbath. John had chosen to live that day in such a way that the Spirit could be with him. It was the preparation that occurred before the revelation came. Could the same thing work for each of us? I'm not suggesting that we would receive a revelation meant for all of the children of the Lord. But what about personal revelation? Are there things you are seeking for greater understanding on in your life? Questions that you need some personal revelation for? What if you kept this Sabbath holy? What if you invited the Spirit to be present in your life on that day? —EBF

Reflect and Respond

What could you prepare so that you might invite the Spirit to be with you this Sabbath day?

Your favorite scripture in **Revelation 1**

REVELATION 2:7

To him that overcometh will I give to eat of the tree of life,
which is in the midst of the paradise of God.

The book of Revelation was written in a letter that was addressed to seven branches of the early Christian churches. In the opening sections of the letter, the Lord addressed each of the cities individually. He calls them by name and tells them what He sees that is good, gives counsel on what could be changed, and makes a promise for overcoming and enduring to the end.

The first branch he addressed was Ephesus. He saw their good works, their labor, and their faithful patience. He counseled them about priorities and warned them about the danger of wanting to be called Christians but still living after the ways of the world. And then came the promise. "To him that overcometh will I give to eat of the tree of life, which is in the midst of the paradise of God" (Revelation 2:7).

I am sort of a foodie. I like trying new places. It is one of my favorite things about going to a new city. Wherever I go, I look on Yelp, an app that gives restaurant ratings for a given area. I want to go to the places people rave about. Eat the food that is tried and true. If there is a line or a wait, I know it will be good. Throughout scripture, the fruit of the tree of life is one that multiple prophets and dreamers have spoken of and described. Nothing else seems to compare to it. Nothing on the earth could satisfy the soul the way it can. It is the very taste of eternal life and love. And it doesn't just grow anywhere. If you are eating from its branches, it means you are standing in the paradise of God. In a new Eden, where everything has been made right and beautiful again. That is the promise to those in Ephesus or anywhere else who overcome. —DB

Reflect and Respond

What is one thing you look forward to about the future paradise of God?

Your favorite
scripture in
Revelation 2

REVELATION 3:15

Thou art neither cold nor hot.

There are a few common things that occur as we read about the seven churches. The Lord knew their works, but He also knew their challenges. He was invested in helping them progress. Sometimes I read through these chapters and ask myself how I am doing in each of those areas.

One of the verses that always causes me to pause is Revelation 3:15. "I know thy works, that thou art neither cold nor hot: I would thou wert cold or hot." It's an interesting way of describing apathy. When I try to think about what this example might look like in real life, I think of chocolate milk. Good cold. Delicious hot with a spray of whipping cream on top. But so disgusting to drink chocolate milk that has been left out on the counter for several hours on a summer afternoon. Who would drink that? It makes sense that you would spew it out of your mouth . . . at least I would.

What does it mean spiritually?

Perhaps the Lord is suggesting that remaining stagnant isn't healthy. That apathy, or lack of desire, feeling, or interest, is not good. It's hard to move in any direction if you are apathetic. One of the Lord's solutions for this condition is for us to anoint our eyes that we might see. I love His suggestion for a new perspective, a new direction, a focus on Him. Instead of apathy, He suggests valor and offers an invitation to His table.

Will you accept? —EBF

Reflect and Respond
What is the difference between apathy and valor?

Your favorite scripture in
Revelation 3

REVELATION 4:8

Holy, holy, holy, Lord God Almighty, which was, and is, and is to come.

Revelation 4 is a chapter that describes a vision of the throne room of God. I don't think we have enough colors, sounds, or descriptive words to capture what the full essence of that place will actually be. But in language clothed in bright and enchanting symbolism, John described what he saw.

There was a throne that was sparkling with the colors of jasper and sardine stones with a rainbow of emerald surrounding it. God was sitting upon it. There were others in the room as well. Twenty-four elders who had once faced the troubles of mortality were now dressed in white robes with crowns upon their heads. Each of them was sitting on a throne as well. The throne room seemed to be floating upon a sea of glass that was like a crystal, and there in the middle of the throne room were animal-like creatures that had multiple wings.

It is difficult to know for sure with symbolic language, but with the earth as glass, and the people with crowns, and animals of every kind, it seems like John was seeing a picture of all of creation exalted before the throne of God. The final scene. The final hope for creation. And every creature in the room was compelled to worship. The elders and beasts all fell down and cried out their praises. "Holy, holy, holy, Lord God Almighty" (Revelation 4:8). They praised Him for who He was, who He is, and who He will continue to be.

My soul longs to praise. I think it anticipates a future day like this, when together with all of creation, we can praise God for how wonderfully good He was, is, and will be. —DB

Reflect and Respond
What is something you have to praise God loudly for today?

Your favorite scripture in
Revelation 4

REVELATION 5:5

Weep not . . . the Lion of the tribe of Juda . . . hath prevailed.

Sometimes the world can feel broken and the days filled with despair. Even though the book of Revelation promises that good will conquer evil, that light will overcome the darkness, perhaps you wonder—how? Maybe, like me, you long for the day when the earth will be made new again, the day when Jesus will return.

For some reason, that reality feels so out of reach. Especially on the dark days when it feels the world is groaning from the weight of the wickedness here. On those days, we hope and maybe even pray for the Second Coming of the Lord. It is a way of reminding ourselves that He will triumph in the end. Like John, perhaps we have days when we long for the opening of the seventh seal.

Who is worthy? John asks.

Who can break the seal and open the scroll?

John weeps because he fears there is no one. Then one of the elders answers. "Weep not," he says, "behold, the Lion of the tribe of Juda . . . hath prevailed" (Revelation 5:5).

There is One who will prevail.

I have a playlist of songs that I listen to when the world feels broken. One of my favorite songs is titled "Is He Worthy?," by Chris Tomlin. It hints toward this chapter in Revelation. I love when he asks this one question, "Is He worthy of this?" And the simple answer.

He is. —EBF

Reflect and Respond
Why does this verse bring you hope?

Your favorite scripture in
Revelation 5

REVELATION 6:11

And white robes were given unto every one of them;
and it was said unto them that they should rest.

The scroll with seals that was introduced in the chapter before this one seems to symbolize, at least in part, a history of the Lord's creation. As the Lamb opened up each of the seals on the scroll, a different scene unfolded. In one there was famine, in another death, in a third there was sorrow, and in yet another there was sickness and persecution. Some have read these different scrolls as the different periods of time in the history of the earth—each of them marked by some kind of sorrow.

It is true that this world has known a lot of sorrow. The children of God have faced awful things throughout the history of creation. As Saints from any age read this chapter of scripture, they might find themselves in any one of these seals of time. These are not just conditions that were unique to their particular time period, but rather the range of the depravities that all of us experience during mortality.

As I read through them, something stands out to me. It is how aware the Lamb of God was about each of the experiences that were happening. He was opening each of the seals. He saw what was happening and was involved. He has been watching over His good earth since the very beginning, and this book testifies that He will see it through all the way to the end. That is true of my own life as well—from beginning to end He is there. He gave to each and every one of the martyrs their own white robe. He saw all of their lives. Each one at a time. —DB

Reflect and Respond

When have you been sure God was aware of your own personal world?

Your favorite
scripture in
Revelation 6

REVELATION 7:4

... an hundred and forty and four thousand ...

I spent a few minutes one afternoon talking with a man who was a Jehovah's Witness. I love talking about the Bible with people. We stood on my front porch for almost a half hour and talked. As it often does, the conversation moved to the 144,000 number found in Revelation 7:4. He and I talked about that for a long time. I told him I believed in a God who has more seats at His table than 144,000. He laughed. But it got me thinking. What did God mean by that number?

You may know that most numbers in the book of Revelation are symbolic. Many years ago, I memorized the symbolic meaning of the first twelve numbers in Hebrew. I don't remember all of them anymore, but the symbolic meaning of the number 12 is one I have never forgotten. It is symbolic of priesthood. If it is in multiples, it means more. You might also be interested to know that 1,000 means completion or fullness. If it is ever paired with another number, it magnifies the symbolism of the other number. With that in mind, if you think of 144,000, it is 12 x 12 x 1,000. Priesthood times priesthood times a fullness.

That's a really big table.

Every time I read the number 144,000, that's what I think of. Room for everyone. Many years ago, we went on a trip to the Bible Belt. I saw a woman there wearing a shirt with *Genesis 31:49* written on it. I asked her what it meant, and she told me it was their family scripture. *Who wants a family scripture?* It says, "The Lord watch between me and thee, when we are absent one from another." I think that might be God's family scripture. If so, we have work to do.

We have an entire table to fill. —EBF

Reflect and Respond
How could you be better at making room for everyone at Christ's table?

Your favorite scripture in **Revelation 7**

REVELATION 8:4

And the smoke of the incense, which came with the
prayers of the saints, ascended up before God.

My parents taught me starting at a young age to pray. It is something that has always been a part of my life. Prayer has always been a lifeline to me. It is my most sincere and meaningful way of connecting with God. Usually, the more famous, rich, or powerful a person becomes, the harder they are to reach. Some of them become virtually inaccessible. But it is the opposite with God. He is the most powerful, rich, and all-knowing being in the universe, and yet He is also the most accessible. He is only a whisper or heartbeat away.

Some of the chapters of the book of Revelation almost seem to be out of control. So much is going on. There are thunderings and earthquakes and fire and lightning and trumpets blasting. Yet, in this chapter, for just a moment, there is a brief pause. There is silence in the heavens for half an hour. During that silence, John sees an angel standing before the altar of incense. As the smoke rises, it rises with the prayers of all the Saints. I love this imagery. I love how sweet and silent it is in the middle of commotion. Such it is with prayer.

I love that the prayers are wisping up into heaven, reaching the throne of God. They will rise no matter what; nothing can interfere with them. No matter how chaotic or commotion-filled our lives may be, we can always pray. That time of prayer could be like that half hour of silence. A pause. A sweet, sacred moment. And like the vision shows, every one of the prayers made it before God.

So it is too, with ours. —DB

Reflect and Respond

*What is your prayer life like? Are you taking advantage of the
sweet, silent, sacred moments?*

Your favorite
scripture in
Revelation 8

REVELATION 9:20

Which neither can see, nor hear, nor walk.

One of the qualifiers that sets the wicked apart from the righteous in the book of Revelation is what they worship. One group worships the True and Living God; the other group worships idols, "which neither can see, nor hear, nor walk" (Revelation 9:20).

I find it so interesting that we are introduced to these idols that can't see, hear, or walk in the very beginning pages of the Bible, and here at the very end of the Bible, man's struggle is still the very same. It seems like such a simple thing to become confused about.

I want a God that sees me. A Father who is aware of my story. I want Him to see my tears, and my troubles, and the discouraging things. I need to believe that He sees ahead of where I am right now. That He knows there are better days ahead because He sees them. I need Him to give me hope. I need Him to help me see others as He sees them.

I need a God who sees.

I want a God who hears me. I want Him to hear my cries for help, my pleading, the worries of my heart. I want Him to hear my dreams and my ideas and the imaginations of my heart. I want Him to hear what I need for my children, for my work, for my day-to-day struggles.

I need a God who hears.

I want a God who will walk with me. The same as He did with Adam, and Enoch, and Noah. I want to know I'm never alone. I want to share His yoke when I am weary and heavy laden.

I need a God who will walk with me.

I believe in a God who sees, hears, and walks. —EBF

Reflect and Respond

Why do you need a God who can see, hear, and walk with you?

Your favorite scripture in
Revelation 9

REVELATION 10:9

Take it, and eat it up; and it shall make thy belly bitter,
but it shall be in thy mouth sweet as honey.

For most of the experience that John was writing about, he seems to take the role of an observer. He sees and then writes, sees and then writes. But there is this moment in the book when an angel turns to John and involves him as a participant in the story. John saw that an angel held a small book in his hand. He then heard a voice from heaven that told him to go and take the book and then to eat it. There are several ways to interpret this scripture, but my favorite way is symbolic. The Lord had a mission for John to fulfill. Perhaps eating the book would be a visionary way of showing someone accepting and fully taking in what they were called to do. Before John eats the book, the angel warns him that it will be bitter in his belly, but also as sweet as honey. When John eats the book, it was exactly as the angel said—both bitter and sweet (see Revelation 10:9–10).

Each of us is called by God to represent Him and to be a participant in His holy work He is doing on the earth. Just as John's role would bring him both bitterness and sweetness, so will ours. As I look back on the times when I was doing the Lord's work, I can see both of these. My time as a missionary was so wildly bitter to the belly on some days, and yet as I read my journals, they seem to drip with honey. Being a parent has been the hardest thing I have ever done. I go to bed some nights with a pit in my stomach. Other nights I fall asleep thanking God for how sweet it is. Friendship, leadership, mentorship, and relationship all have these two elements. The work of God will always be this way—bitter at times, and oh, so sweet. —DB

Reflect and Respond

When have you experienced both the bitter and the sweet of doing the work of God?

Your favorite scripture in
Revelation 10

REVELATION 11:3

My two witnesses.

It's hard to tell if the details in this chapter are figurative or literal. We probably won't know for sure until Jesus really comes again. But there is a symbolic lesson here that comes from the Old Testament. The footnote for the two witnesses (see verse 3) leads us to Zechariah 4:11–14. In order to understand that reference, we need to know what is happening in the book of Zechariah.

In chapter three, we read of Joshua the high priest, and in chapter four, we are introduced to Zerubbabel. It is important to understand the role of these two men. Joshua is the high priest; he was in charge of restoring and gathering. Zerubbabel had been tasked by Haggai to rebuild the temple starting with the foundation; he was in charge of rebuilding and dedication. With those two things in mind, we turn to Zechariah 4:11–14, "Then answered I, and said unto him, What are these . . . ? And he answered me and said, Knowest thou not what these be? And I said, No, my lord. Then said he, These are the two anointed ones, that stand by the Lord of the whole earth."

Many Bible scholars believe these candlesticks in Zechariah represent Joshua and Zerubbabel. I can't help but consider their great mission of restoration, gathering, building, and dedication. It was important in the rebuilding of Jerusalem in the Old Testament Church; it is also important to the Church today. Perhaps that is why the two candlesticks are mentioned again in Revelation. Consider our prophets and apostles who have a similar responsibility and the promise that they will be able to finish their testimony (see Revelation 11:7). We don't know the details of what will happen when their testimony is finished, but we do know the importance of their role in the last days. —EBF

Reflect and Respond

Why would restoration, gathering, building, and dedication be so important in the last days?

Your favorite scripture in **Revelation 11**

REVELATION 12:11

And they overcame him by the blood of the Lamb,
and by the word of their testimony.

In the very beginning book of the Bible, Genesis, the devil is portrayed as a conniving serpent. In this last book of the Bible, Revelation, he comes as a dragon. And not just any dragon, but a huge red one, with seven heads and ten horns and crowns upon each of those heads. He is chasing a pregnant woman, seeking to devour her newborn baby. His tail whips a third of the stars of the heavens down from their place to the earth. He is wild and powerful and making war against all that is good and anyone who stands for it.

The description of the war with the dragon that happens in this chapter seems to move time periods. One of the time periods it seems to describe is the time before anyone was born to this earth. The dragon fought against God and failed and was cast down to the earth. Here on the earth, he continues to fight. Same battle, new battlefield. His fight is more intense, though. As John said, the devil fights with "great wrath, because he knoweth that he hath but a short time" (Revelation 12:12). He seems scary and powerful, but the chapter gives hope, because he was defeated once before. In the battle before we were born, John saw that people overcame him "by the blood of the Lamb, and by the word of their testimony" (Revelation 12:11). This is the same way he will be defeated again. Just as it was in ancient Egypt during the Passover, those who are marked with the blood of the Lamb will be passed over by the destroyer. They will be protected and safe. Our trust in Jesus will always lead us to victory. —DB

Reflect and Respond

What are you doing to overcome the devil with the blood of the Lamb and the word of your testimony?

Your favorite
scripture in
Revelation 12

REVELATION 13:10

Here is the patience and the faith of the saints.

There are two words that stand out in this chapter—*patience* and *faith*.

Patience, translated in Greek, is *hupomone*, meaning endurance, constancy, patient continuance. Faith, translated in Greek, is *pistis*, meaning reliance upon Christ, assurance, belief, fidelity. This chapter of Revelation suggests these are the qualities the Saints will need to make it through the very last days. Take a moment to consider both of those definitions and how they might bring strength in times of darkness and doubt:

PATIENCE	FAITH
hupomone	*pistis*
endurance, constancy, patient continuance	reliance upon Christ, assurance, belief, fidelity

In a time of failing earthly kingdoms where evil dictators rise up, a time when Satan seems to be in his prime, making war with the Saints and overcoming some, a time when it almost feels that darkness might win, we are told to have patience and faith. Right will prevail. "He that leadeth into captivity shall go into captivity" (Revelation 13:10).

There will be an end.

Until then, we must endure with patient continuance and stay loyal to our belief and reliance upon Christ. All will be made right in the end. —EBF

Reflect and Respond

How have you learned to practice patience and faith?

Your favorite scripture in **Revelation 13**

REVELATION 14:3

And they sung as it were a new song.

We were all together as a family, just hanging out, and my brother-in-law started to play a song he liked from his phone. It was only a few seconds into the song when there was a collective groan from everyone else in the room. "No! Turn it off! Not this one!" The first time any of us heard it, we actually liked it, but then it seemed to be on every radio station, playing in everyone's car, grocery store, and playlist. Soon, everyone was sick of the song. We all wanted a new one.

I am so intrigued by this idea in Revelation 14 of a new song that will be sung. If there is a new song, there must be an old one. Perhaps the old one is the song of mortality. The same old tune we have been listening to for all of these years. It is the tune of selfishness, hurt, and despair. The same notes we have heard through every dispensation of death, sickness, and sin. The fallen world has been playing a song, and everyone is tired of it.

When Jesus comes again, there will be a new one. A new song for His new, redeemed world. All things will be made new. Perhaps the first lines of the new song will be what John said later on in the same chapter: "Babylon is fallen, is fallen" (Revelation 14:8). Wickedness, which is symbolized in the book of Revelation as Babylon, has had its reign. There has been a lot of hurt and heartache caused by it. But one day it will be gone. All of this evil that has caused so much pain will be no more. Babylon had its chance to play its song, but it will fall, and we will be singing a new song. —DB

Reflect and Respond
What are you looking forward to when Babylon falls?

Your favorite scripture in Revelation 14

REVELATION 15:3

They sing the song of Moses . . . and the song of the Lamb.

The book of Revelation is filled with dark days and prophecies that might seem over-whelming. But every so often, carefully placed between all of the chapters with the evil fighting against the light, there are interludes of hope—chapter breaks that remind us that light will prevail against the darkness.

Chapter 15 is one of these interludes of hope.

A reminder that good will win.

Just before the seven plagues are poured out, John saw a sea of glass mingled with fire, "and them that had gotten the victory over the beast, and over his image, and over his mark, and over the number of his name, stand on the sea of glass, having the harps of God. And they sing the song of Moses" (Revelation 15:2–3).

If you were to ask people the greatest deliverance story ever told, I think most people would tell you the story of Moses. It is a story of miraculous rescue in which God prevailed when all of the odds suggested otherwise. Perhaps the same will be true in the very last days.

God will pull off another deliverance.

John says there will be a great victory with great works, and all of the nations will worship Jesus Christ. The interlude might be short—it is only four verses of chapter 15—but it is filled with power and promise and hope. It makes me think that is how the last days will be. Darkness and despair with interludes of power, promise, and hope. And then, victory will come. A great deliverance.

Perhaps the greatest deliverance ever told. —EBF

Reflect and Respond

What is the lesson of having interludes of hope sprinkled through the book of Revelation?

Your favorite scripture in **Revelation 15**

REVELATION 16:7

Even so, Lord God Almighty,
true and righteous are thy judgments.

In an earlier chapter of Revelation, there was a symbolic telling of plagues and judgments being poured out upon the earth. Similar plagues and judgments are repeated again in this chapter. The difference in the first telling is the destruction only causes a third part of everything to be destroyed. Perhaps it was teaching us that God will protect and set bounds on any of the destruction that happens in this world. In this particular chapter, everything is destroyed by the plagues and judgments. Perhaps it is teaching us a different nuance of judgments—that every bit of evil and wickedness will be destroyed.

Whatever the lessons are with plagues and judgments, they don't seem very pleasant. Even though it seems symbolic, it makes me uncomfortable to read about God's angels coming with vials that cause the waters to turn to blood and the forests to burn with great heat. In the middle of all of this destruction description there is a line that seems out of place. "Even so, Lord God Almighty, true and righteous are thy judgments" (Revelation 16:7).

I like that line, because the judgments and plagues could make us think that God is out of control or losing His temper. But that is not what He is like. He will not allow wickedness to rule and reign in His good earth. And for that we thank Him. But any of the judgments or plagues He sends or allows has the purpose of healing and restoration, not destruction. For that we thank Him too. —DB

Reflect and Respond

When have you seen consequence or hardship become something healing for you?

Your favorite scripture in
Revelation 16

REVELATION 17:10

A short space.

I love these words in the book of Revelation. You probably wonder why. By now we have met the fierce beasts, the mother of harlots, and the dragon. Chapter 17 will define how widespread the wickedness is. The world will be drunk with it. But there are two short phrases meant to bring hope, "a short space" (Revelation 17:10) and "one hour" (Revelation 17:12).

Have you ever been on a long road trip with children? I can't help but think of the two most common questions, "Are we almost there?" and "How much longer?" It makes me so happy when the answer is less than an hour, or it's so short. For some reason it gives everyone in the car a little extra patience. We feel the anticipation of arrival. You know you are going to make it.

I just imagine our Heavenly Father doing something similar here. It's as if we are asking the same question, "Are we almost there? How much longer?" He gives us two clues: *a short space*, and *one hour*. Once we get to the signs of this chapter we are almost done.

We can begin to look forward to the Savior's arrival.

We will know we are going to make it. —EBF

Reflect and Respond
Why might those two phrases bring you hope?

Your favorite scripture in **Revelation 17**

REVELATION 18:19

For in one hour is she made desolate.

Several years ago, I had to stop watching or looking at any news websites. I wanted to live in innocence. I know it is not the way of a disciple to ignore what is happening in the world around me, but I needed a break from all of the awful things I was seeing or reading about. It seemed like everywhere you looked, there was something horrible happening. Hatred seemed to fill every nightly news broadcast. Racism was rampant on social media. Violence, drugs, and crime were commonplace in so many areas. From the looks and sounds of things, evil was certainly having a great day of power, and it still is right now.

Babylon, an ancient city known for wickedness, is the symbolic representation of evil in the book of Revelation. It is described as a place where you can buy anything. Everything is for sale, including and especially heartbreakingly, the "souls of men" (Revelation 18:13). We are all witnesses of that. We are losing people we love to Babylon. And Babylon is in every alley, corner, nook, and cranny of this world. It has infiltrated so many homes. It is organized from the top to the bottom with strongholds that seem immovable.

But not for God. For Babylon, He says, will fall in one day. As strong and pervasive and undefeatable as it may seem, it will not and cannot last. In just one hour, every bit of the wickedness will be wiped clean, no matter how enduring or influential it may seem. I love knowing that it won't be chipped away bit by bit, but rather gone in an afternoon. I look forward to the day when Babylon will be "found no more at all" (Revelation 18:21). —DB

Reflect and Respond

Babylon will be defeated in an hour. In the meantime, what can you do to avoid its influences?

Your favorite scripture in
Revelation 18

REVELATION 19:10

The testimony of Jesus is the spirit of prophecy.

In the book of Judges, we read of a woman named Deborah who dwelt under the palm tree. We are given a description of Deborah in Judges 4:4, "And Deborah, a prophetess, the wife of Lapidoth, she judged Israel at that time." In the margins of my scriptures, I have two important notes. First, "wife of Lapidoth" could have also been translated as *woman with a torchlike spirit.* I don't know about you, but if I had been on the translation committee, I would have chosen that one for sure! Think about it, *Deborah, a prophetess, the woman with a torchlike spirit.*

Don't you want to go sit under her palm tree?

The other important characteristic is that she was a prophetess. As we read her story, we find that she is a woman of great inspiration, an encourager, and led by God. For many years I wondered what the title of prophetess would have meant in her time. Then I read the nineteenth chapter of Revelation. It didn't answer my question completely, but it gave me some insight. "I am thy fellowservant, and of thy brethren that have the testimony of Jesus: worship God: *for the testimony of Jesus is the spirit of prophecy*" (Revelation 19:10; emphasis added). We don't know exactly what *prophetess* means, but when I read this verse, I like to think she was a woman with a strong testimony of Jesus Christ.

Deborah, a woman with a testimony of Jesus and a torchlike spirit.

I want to be known as a woman like that. —EBF

Reflect and Respond
Do you know a woman with a testimony of Jesus and a torchlike spirit? Write and let her know.

Your favorite scripture in **Revelation 19**

REVELATION 20:3

And cast him into the bottomless pit,
and shut him up, and set a seal upon him.

I have looked forward to the Millennium since I was really young. For some reason it is something that has always fascinated me. I can remember lying in my bed as a kid just thinking about how amazing it was going to be. I couldn't wait to own a white tiger, skateboard without getting hurt, and fly. I don't want anyone to tell me that these aren't a possibility, because you don't know, but since then, I have begun to anticipate even more.

As amazing as riding my white tiger may be, the thing I am looking forward to most about the Millennium is Satan being bound. For one thousand years, he will have no influence on this earth. For one thousand years he will not be able to tempt or inspire any of the nasty things he has been behind for so long. For one thousand years he will be gone, and Christ will rule and reign. I can't wait.

John wrote that an angel will "cast him into the bottomless pit, and shut him up" (Revelation 20:3). I know this is probably not what the scripture means, but when I read those words, I get excited for someone to shut him up. To quiet his voice. For too long he has spoken lies into our ears about ourselves, about others, and about God. He has told us we are not good enough and can never be accepted. He has told us that others are worthless and that God is someone we should be afraid of. During the Millennium, he will not be able to speak into our stories anymore. We do not have to listen to or hear his voice any longer. I would take that over a white tiger any day. —DB

Reflect and Respond

What are some of the lies that the devil is telling you about yourself, others, and God? What is the truth?

Your favorite
scripture in
Revelation 20

REVELATION 21:4

God shall wipe away all tears from their eyes.

I was texting with a friend one day. She commented on how busy I'd been lately, and she wanted to know what I had been working on. I thought through my past several weeks. Life had been hard lately. A lot of heavy things. Work. Family. "It feels like we've been carrying a lot," I replied. "You need a rest," she said. My immediate answer was, "If Jesus would just come my life would be a lot quieter. A whole lot quieter haha!" "Yep," she said, "you need a nice long millennial break."

Doesn't that sound nice?

A break from the heaviness of mortality?

I am guessing there are things you could use a break from. Mortality is full of those kinds of things—illness, addictions, relationship problems, death of loved ones, mental illness, those who have stepped away from religion. There are some nights when tears cover my pillowcase. I am sure you have nights like that as well.

One day it will end.

"And God shall wipe away all tears from their eyes; and there shall be no more death, neither sorrow, nor crying, neither shall there be any more pain: for the former things are passed away. . . . Behold, I make all things new. . . . I am Alpha and Omega, the beginning and the end. I will give unto him that is athirst of the fountain of the water of life freely" (Revelation 12:4–6).

I can't wait for that day. A day of no more tears and no more sorrow. It sounds so nice.

Come, Lord Jesus, come. —EBF

Reflect and Respond
What part of the millennial promises are you most looking forward to?

Your favorite scripture in **Revelation 21**

REVELATION 22:20

Surely I come quickly. Amen. Even so, come, Lord Jesus.

On one of the first pages of the Bible, Adam and Eve heard the voice of God coming into the garden, and they ran and hid from Him. This breaks my heart every time I read it—especially as a dad. I cannot imagine what it would feel like to have my kids run and hide from me in fear. Who did Adam and Eve think He was? What did they think He was going to say, think, or do to them that would make them want to run and hide from Him?

The last chapter of the Bible describes a new Eden. The earth was made whole and glorified as promised. Sometimes I read the chapter just to fill my heart with hopeful anticipation. In that new Eden, there will be a river of life-giving water, clear as crystal. On either side of the river will be the tree of life, which will give fruit during every month of the year. Twelve different kinds. And it will have leaves for the healing of all the people of all the nations of the world.

There also will be no night in this place. There will be no candles or sun, because the light of the presence of God will shine forth always. Every curse of mortality will be lifted, and God will personally wipe all tears away from everyone's eyes. The same God who calls out to everyone, "Come. And let him that is athirst come. And whosoever will, let him take the water of life freely" (Revelation 22:17). This is not a God we would run from. And once we come to understand that, we might share with John's excitement when the Lord says, "I come quickly" (Revelation 22:20). And we might call back as he did, "Even so, come, Lord" (Revelation 22:20). —DB

Reflect and Respond
What reason do you have for the Lord to come quickly?

Your favorite scripture in **Revelation 22**

ABOUT THE AUTHORS

EMILY BELLE FREEMAN is a best-selling author and popular inspirational speaker. She has a deep love of the scriptures, which comes from a desire to find their application in everyday life. She is the author of numerous books, including *Grace to Become, Grace Where You Are; Creating a Christ-Centered Home; Closer to Christ;* and *And These Words: An Emily Belle Freeman Scripture Study Journal.* She is a favorite speaker at Time Out for Women and a cohost with David Butler of *Don't Miss This*, a *Come, Follow Me* study channel on YouTube. Her greatest joy comes from spending time with her family. Read more at emilybellefreeman .com and follow Emily on Instagram and Facebook @emilybellefreeman.

DAVID BUTLER'S greatest love is people. His favorite people are his wife, Jenny, and their six darling children. Some of his other loves include good food, spontaneous adventures, Christmas morning, and the sea. David cohosts the popular YouTube scripture study channel *Don't Miss This* with Emily Belle Freeman and is the author of many religious books, including *Ites: An Illustrated Guide to the People in the Book of Mormon; The Peter Potential;* and *Almighty: How the Most Powerful Being in the Universe Is Also Your Loving Father.* Follow him on Instagram @mrdavebutler.